M000023167

"Shuster and Sale have joined forces to bring to the LDS audience and other readers an impressive presentation of Mormonism, drawing solely on the Bible for its evidence and support. This, of course, is not a new phenomenon. The early Saints used the Bible extensively and, in some cases, exclusively, to understand the doctrines of the Restoration. The authors have happily brought us back to that time when biblical support for Mormon doctrine was widely understood and appreciated. This is a book worth owning and savoring."

Jeffrey Needle, Association for Mormon Letters

"I wish this book had been available twenty-four years ago when I was making my decision to become a Latter-day Saint. It makes Mormon doctrine perfectly clear and answers key questions about the Bible and Mormon beliefs. The scripture references leave no room for doubt. This book is a page-turner for anyone interested in religion in general and a unique missionary tool for Latter-day Saints."

J. Adams, author of The Journey and Tears of Heaven

"*The Biblical Roots of Mormonism* is unique. In contrast with Shuster's earlier work, *Catholic Roots, Mormon Harvest*, which relied on Catholic and LDS publications and discussions on doctrine to support its comparisons, *Biblical Roots* incorporates very little literature beyond the text of the King James Version of the Old and New Testaments.

Biblical Roots is well organized and well written. Though it is interesting to read through as a complete work, the detailed table of contents creates a user-friendly reference book organized by topic.

Shuster and Sale write that *Biblical Roots* is intended for a three-fold audience: those looking for a religion, those who are already members of the Church of Jesus Christ of Latter-day Saints, and those who are skeptical or critical of the LDS church, its origins, and/or its truthfulness. . . .

Seeing the way the authors brought out important pieces of doctrine helped me to see that I have at times taken the Bible for granted. . . . With the help of *Biblical Roots*, I read the Bible more closely and found that it is written with a framework and assumed understanding of the same principles put forward in modern scripture. . . . To the great benefit of their readers, Shuster and Sale have carefully illustrated how repeated themes throughout the Bible coincide directly with the primary tenets of the Mormon faith."

Jennifer Lords, Lords of the Manor—Writes and Reads

"With careful research and attention to detail, Shuster and Sale present a compelling look at Mormonism from its earliest foundations, those found in the Bible. After reading this book, you will have a clear understanding of how this precious work of scripture did indeed point to the Restoration of the gospel of Jesus Christ as practiced by the Latter-day Saints. A faith-building, thought-provoking read—I highly recommend it."

Tristi Pinkston, media reviewer and author of Secret Sisters

"Time after time during my mission, I wished for a resource that would enable me to point without hesitation to specific biblical support for the doctrines I was teaching. I had to memorize or cite over 600 Bible passages. If *The Biblical Roots of Mormonism* had been in my hands those many years ago, it would have been much easier to show, point-by-point, how the doctrines of the Church were evident in the Bible, the scripture I had in common with the people I was teaching.

The format of *The Biblical Roots of Mormonism*—presenting 'biblical teaching' side-by-side with 'Mormon understanding'—is truly inspired. The book helps me to have friendly and informative discussions with people who are not members of my faith, but who share my devotion to the Bible. I can help them to understand my beliefs from the common ground of the Bible. I am then better able to introduce The Book of Mormon as another testament of Jesus Christ.

The Biblical Roots of Mormonism is a perfect gift for missionaries, Church members interested in the specifics of their biblical foundations, and other Christians interested in knowing what Mormons believe. This book has the power to renew interest in Christianity. The authors have created a powerful resource for anyone interested in studying the gospel of Jesus Christ."

Collin Smith, Arvada, Colorado

"Latter-day Saint readers [will gain] a deeper understanding of the Bible and how it supports their beliefs. Non-Mormon readers will discover how and why Latter-day Saints revere the Bible as the word of God."

John Webster, LDS Resources

"I do not concur theologically with the authors. . . . However, I welcome this book as a platform for friendly engagement between Latter-day Saints and those not of the LDS faith. . . . I would hope that this volume would encourage many conversations between evangelicals and Latter-day Saints about what is and what is not biblical theology."

Reverend Gregory C.V. Johnson, Baptist minister,
co-author with Dr. Robert Millet of Bridging the Divide

THE
BIBLICAL
ROOTS OF
MORMONISM

THE
BIBLICAL
ROOTS OF
MORMONISM

ERIC SHUSTER
CHARLES SALE

CFI
Springville, Utah

© 2010 Eric Shuster & Charles Sale

All rights reserved.

No part of this book may be reproduced in any form whatsoever, whether by graphic, visual, electronic, film, microfilm, tape recording, or any other means, without prior written permission of the publisher, except in the case of brief passages embodied in critical reviews and articles.

This is not an official publication of The Church of Jesus Christ of Latter-day Saints. The opinions and views expressed herein belong solely to the author and do not necessarily represent the opinions or views of Cedar Fort, Inc. Permission for the use of sources, graphics, and photos is also solely the responsibility of the author.

ISBN 13: 978-1-59955-406-8

Published by CFI, an imprint of Cedar Fort, Inc., 2373 W. 700 S., Springville, UT 84663
Distributed by Cedar Fort, Inc., www.cedarfort.com

LIBRARY OF CONGRESS CATALOGING-IN-PUBLICATION DATA

Shuster, Eric, 1962-
  The biblical roots of Mormonism / Eric C. Shuster and Charles A. Sale.
    p. cm.
  ISBN 978-1-59955-406-8
  1. Church of Jesus Christ of Latter-day Saints--Doctrines. 2. Mormon
Church--Doctrines. 3. Bible--Theology. I. Sale, Charles A. II. Title.

  BX8635.3S575 2010
  230'.93--dc22

2010010208

Cover design by Danie Daly
Cover design © 2010 by Lyle Mortimer
Edited and typeset by Melissa J. Caldwell

Printed in the United States of America

10 9 8 7 6 5 4 3 2 1

Printed on acid-free paper

. . . to the brave souls who search, we dedicate this tiny piece of the map.

CONTENTS

PREFACE

*D*o Mormons believe in the Bible?
Are Mormons biblical Christians?

Does Mormonism have any biblical foundation?

These are serious questions, and they deserve serious answers.

The biographies of Joseph Smith, Brigham Young, and other well-known Church leaders are interesting and sometimes controversial. The coming forth of the Book of Mormon is interesting and controversial. The history of The Church of Jesus Christ of Latter-day Saints from the early nineteenth century to the present is interesting and controversial.

Indeed, so interesting and controversial are these subjects that a certain fascination—for some a fixation—has grown up around them. This fascination often blocks a comprehensive view of Mormonism and causes many to deny it a place among the world's Christian religions.

In writing this book, we set out to discover the biblical history of The Church of Jesus Christ of Latter-day Saints and the biblical foundations of Mormonism. What we found may surprise some Latter-day Saints. It will also surprise some Christians who are not members of the Church. We hope surprise leads to interest, and interest to inquiry, for it is good to know the truth.

We were not born into the Church, nor have we ever been part of the Utah Mormon culture. We are not graduates of Brigham Young University, nor did we participate in the admirable system of religious education the Church provides. We did not enjoy these privileges because we were members of other Christian churches and other Christian families.

We were mature adults when we came into the Church, and to make entry, we had to reconcile our past religious experiences and commitments. It was not easy.

We have sometimes thought of our late conversion to Mormonism as a disadvantage. We have asked ourselves and each other how our lives might have been if we had enjoyed the benefits of growing up in the Church, serving a two-year mission, and so forth.

But in the process of writing this book, our seeming disadvantage proved to be an advantage, an opportunity to make a unique contribution. We found we had the ability to look from the outside in. We had been elsewhere for most of our lives, so we could compare and contrast in ways that are not available to men and women who grew up in the Church.

The Bible is common ground for all Christians. Therefore, we sought to discover whether the Bible, standing alone, could sustain Mormon theology and practice. We found that it does. We wrote this book to show how.

We hope our work will deepen the appreciation of Latter-day Saints for their biblical heritage. We also hope it will strengthen ties between Latter-day Saints and other Christians.

—*Eric Shuster and Charles Sale*

ACKNOWLEDGMENTS

Eric Shuster

To the Lord, who sustains me, inspires me to do his will, and chastises me when I turn off course.

To the many men and women not of my faith who challenged me with their questions, especially to my sister-in-law Therese Bullock. It is they who led me to study, ponder, pray relentlessly—and then write. Without them, this book would never have been.

To my family, who loves and puts up with me, even when I fall asleep on Friday night watching a movie because of too many early mornings during the week.

To our beloved Church leaders, who provide such inspired encouragement to the entire world, not knowing they so often are speaking directly to me.

To my editors and friends at Cedar Fort, especially the Mortimer family, Sheralyn Pratt, Jennifer Fielding, and Melissa Caldwell. You made this possible.

To my wife, Marilyn, and my friend Andrew Shumway, who provided their invaluable edits and inputs on the original manuscript. And to my son, Ryan Shuster, who painstakingly ensured that each Bible quotation was correct.

And to Chuck, my co-author and friend, who needs no thanks—just as my right hand needs no thanks from my left. I love you, brother.

what does this mean?
⌐ Biblical basis?

Charles Sale

Teri Sale read the manuscript, corrected my errors, and made countless improvements. She is my toughest critic and most devoted fan, my wife and eternal companion, and she is in every page of this book.

My children—Michael, Elizabeth, Teresa, Katherine, and Christine—and their mother, Jane, deserve special thanks. They are not Latter-day Saints. Their doubts, concerns, and thoughtful questions helped guide me in this work.

My Latter-day Saint friends and mentors provided much of the inspiration for this book. Bob Taylor, Steve Francom, Dave Jeffrey, Peter Snow, Cliff Potter, Mark McConkie, Keith Handy, Kevin Fink, Kurt Kofford, Ben Porter, Gary Christensen, Mark Kimball, Don Vincent, and so many others contributed in ways too various to describe. Bob Taylor and his wife, Rosemary, read the manuscript and gave vital criticism and suggestions.

Adam Brown, my cousin (who became my elder brother at the times when I most needed one), has my eternal gratitude. He worked on me from my childhood. He never gave up. Finally, when I could no longer resist, he baptized me into the light. Nothing has been the same since he pulled me up out of the waters of baptism.

Most important, I thank Eric Shuster, my co-author. Eric hired me to edit his first book, *Catholic Roots, Mormon Harvest*. In this collaboration, we discovered a rare thing—synchronicity. I knew his thoughts and he knew mine, and we both liked what we saw. Successful writing partnerships are exceedingly rare. Among those partnerships are a few that produce joy in the work. This book is the product of joy.

INTRODUCTION

To hold the pearl of great price, one must not close the fist too tightly around it: The hand will tire quickly and the pearl will be lost. Neither should the fist be held too loosely, for the pearl will fall away between the openings.

This book is the result of a two-year effort to discover Mormonism—root and branch—as it is revealed in the Bible. Latter-day Saints want to know the biblical ground they stand on. Others want to know what Mormons believe, and they want to know how those beliefs conform to biblical teachings.

READERS: LATTER-DAY SAINTS, SEEKERS, SKEPTICS

Latter-day Saints

You are a Latter-day Saint. You have studied the Bible—but never far from the light of modern revelation. The Book of Mormon, the Pearl of Great Price, the Doctrine and Covenants, and the Bible—all these are scripture to you, so why separate yourself from any of them?

Yet some nagging questions may arise, usually posed by your non-Mormon friends: Can your Mormon faith stand upright on the platform of the Bible alone? Would your Mormonism fracture and topple over if you did not prop it up with modern scripture and modern revelation?

In this book you will discover how the Bible, standing alone, supports your beliefs. Reading this book, organized as it is, you will attain fresh insights about the Bible and how to learn and teach from

How do you know your documents are scripture + revelation?

1

it. Your testimony will be strengthened as you discover how deep your biblical roots go.

This book is an excellent reference for talks and discussions centering on the Bible. You may want to give a copy of this book to your friends and associates, Mormon and non-Mormon alike, so they might see the restored gospel of Jesus Christ as it is recorded in the Old and New Testaments.

Gal. 1:8-9

What's wrong w/ the original gospel?

The biblical foundations of Mormonism are there, in plain sight.

Seekers

You are not a Mormon. You have heard or seen things about The Church of Jesus Christ of Latter-day Saints that made an impression on you. Someone you know or something you read has caused you to be curious about Mormonism. Or perhaps you are searching for a church to join, and you want to know more about this unique faith that creates such a stir in the Christian world.

This book will explain the core doctrines of The Church of Jesus Christ of Latter-day Saints and help you relate those doctrines to the scripture with which you are probably already familiar—the Bible.

The biblical foundations of Mormonism are there, in plain sight.

I've read the Bible many times & never felt it pointed to Mormonism.

Skeptics

You are not a Mormon and do not intend to become one. You know about Mormonism. What you know comes from personal study, from explanations of your priest or pastor, or from Mormons or ex-Mormons themselves. What you have learned has led you to believe that Mormonism is a false religion. You may feel that The Church of Jesus Christ of Latter-day Saints fits the definition of a cult. You may sincerely believe that Mormons are not Christians. You may even believe that Mormonism is of the devil and that it is your Christian duty to save as many people from it as possible—particularly the good Mormon people you know. You do not believe that the Mormon religion is biblically based, and you intend to read this book to prove to yourself and to others that it is not.

"Why do you call me good?"

Perhaps you are an atheist, Christians an agnostic, a Buddhist, a Hindu, a secular humanist, or a follower of some other cultural, religious, or philosophical tradition—or no tradition at all.

This book will expand your knowledge of the Bible and the

relationship of Mormons to this important literature of the Jews and Christians.

And it may do much more.

THE BIBLE: TWO TESTAMENTS

The Bible consists of two testaments, the Old Testament and the New Testament.

The New Testament builds upon the Old Testament; it does not replace it.

Jesus quoted the Old Testament throughout his public ministry. He highlighted its importance in his fulfillment of the Mosaic law. Indeed, the Old Testament was his messianic context, his history.

The authors made full use of both testaments in uncovering the foundations of Mormonism.

TRANSLATION

This book uses the King James Version (KJV) of the Bible exclusively. This is the KJV known to all Christians. It is not a "Mormon version" of the KJV; there is no such thing.

INTERPRETATION

Differences   *what are the differences?*

There are over 33,000 Christian denominations throughout the world today.[1] The Gordon-Conwell Theological Seminary reportedly estimates the number to be as high as 38,000. These denominations differ in their beliefs and interpretations of the Bible.

Roman Catholics have their own version of the Bible, and they interpret it in their own way. Protestants turn to various other versions of the Bible and interpret them in their own ways. Methodists, Evangelicals, Baptists, Pentecostals, and other Protestants agree on some things, but not on others. Like other Christians, the Latter-day Saints reach their understanding of the Bible through their beliefs. However, unlike other Christians, Latter-day Saints also rely on modern revelation and living prophets to increase their understanding of God's will.

Christianity is not static, nor, perhaps, should it be. The search for truth is—and must be so in this life—a search. This book is offered as but a small piece of the map.

Interpreters

Most Christian denominations place heavy emphasis on education and scholarly study to produce reliable biblical interpretation. Biblical scholars often attend theological seminaries and spend many years in academic study to become recognized for their interpretations of the Bible.

Who considers it a Christian denomination?

The Church of Jesus Christ of Latter-day Saints is one of the largest Christian denominations in the world. It conducts some of the world's most respected theological study programs, including those at Brigham Young University, which has campuses in Utah, Hawaii, Idaho, and Jerusalem. The Church has more than 4,300 seminary programs and 2,200 institutes of religion in operation around the world, and the Foundation for Ancient Research and Mormon Studies (FARMS) is a respected defender of the faith. The Church uses these vast resources to provide scriptural commentary and interpretation that is as reliable as that of any other Christian institution in the world today.

Buddhists & Hindus + Muslims have vast resources

All of this theological effort is laudable, but only insofar as it does not deny the preeminence of divine inspiration in formulating the most accurate interpretations of the Bible. The Bible teaches men and women to rely on the spirit of God for understanding, not on the wisdom of man (1 Corinthians 2:14). The authors of this book are no exception.

"test the spirits"

CHAPTER ORGANIZATION

Each chapter of this book, except this one and the last chapter, is organized into two main sections, Biblical Teaching and Mormon Understanding.

Biblical Teaching

The Biblical Teaching section of each chapter is arranged into major subtopics, each presenting key scriptures from the Bible with short explanations that relate to the chapter's topic. This methodology helps the reader understand the relationship of one scripture to another in context.

An effort was made to limit this section to the Mormon foundations that a reasonable person of any faith could find in the cited biblical quotations. To clarify these foundations, the authors provided explanatory notes in brackets within the biblical quotations.

This was an imperfect effort. Different interpretations are possible in many cases. But the authors were in search of the biblical foundations of Mormonism—not of Presbyterianism, Methodism, Catholicism, or some other branch of Christianity. The book reflects this focus.

Mormon Understanding

The Mormon Understanding section of each chapter briefly explains the doctrines of The Church of Jesus Christ of Latter-day Saints relating to the chapter's topic. These explanations are summaries written to facilitate understanding among Latter-day Saints and other Christians who have some familiarity with the Bible.

HOW TO USE THIS BOOK

Some will read this book from beginning to end, while others will go directly to a chapter or section that is of particular interest to them. The authors organized the book, particularly the table of contents and index, to accommodate either approach.

Because it links topics with biblical scripture and commentary, this book is an excellent reference. It is also a teaching manual. The table of contents constitutes a comprehensive lesson plan, which can be broken into logical parts as needed. Lessons can then be taught directly from the contents of the book.

The authors were careful to avoid argumentative references to other churches or their theological interpretations, doctrines, belief systems, or practices. Such references are both unnecessary and distracting, and they are not the point of this book. Differences do exist, and a few had to be pointed out to clarify the doctrines of The Church of Jesus Christ of Latter-day Saints. However, in most cases, such differences were not pertinent to the authors' exposition of the biblical foundations of Mormonism.

[right margin handwritten: Avoid common mis2 interpretations]

Conventions

This book is the original work of the authors except where quotations are indicated in the conventional ways: by indention or quotation marks. Citations for these quotations are given as endnotes at the end of the chapters.

Parenthetical references to where additional information can be found appear throughout the book. Most of these references are to Bible quotations and are given in full below the reference.

In many cases, the authors used references and content from *Catholic Roots, Mormon Harvest*, a book authored by Eric Shuster and edited by Charles Sale.

The authors did not intend to write a scholarly tome, but rather a simple exposition of basic Mormon beliefs and the foundations for them that can be found in the Bible. Accessibility took precedence over scholarly norms, even to the extent of removing verse numbers from biblical quotes to enhance readability.

The authors made a diligent effort to write what is consistent with the doctrines and practices of The Church of Jesus Christ of Latter-day Saints; however, this book is a private work and has not been reviewed or approved by Church authorities. Where a Church publication is quoted or reliance on it was particularly heavy, the publication is cited in the usual manner.

HUMBLE UNDERSTANDING

The Lord revealed to Isaiah that his thoughts are not man's thoughts, and his ways are not the ways of man (Isaiah 55:6–9). Jesus explained to Nicodemus that if he was not able to understand earthly things, he would not be able to understand heavenly things (John 3:12). Paul created the analogy of milk before meat. He urged believers to learn line upon line (Hebrews 5:12–14; 1 Corinthians 3:2). The ways of God will appear foolish to men, even those who consider themselves to be mighty and wise (1 Corinthians 1:27). This book is best read in light of these truths.

> ↳ What does that mean? Assume the authors are right or know more than me?

NOTE

1. David B. Barrett, *World Christian Encyclopedia* (New York: Oxford University Press, 2001), 10.

PREMORTAL LIFE

BIBLICAL TEACHING

The Father of All Spirits

God the Father is the father of all spirits, including the spirits of everyone who has been born or ever will be born on earth, (Hebrews 12:9). All men and women are the spirit offspring of God (Acts 17:29), chosen before the foundation of the world (Ephesians 1:3–4). Before Jeremiah was born, the Lord knew him, sanctified him, and ordained him a prophet (Jeremiah 1:5).

Handwritten margin notes:
who was chosen? Chosen for what?
Father = Creator. verse doesn't say "on earth"
offspring = creation. Gen 1:26
Before he was born, not conceived.

Hebrews 12:9

> Furthermore we have had fathers of our flesh which corrected us, and we gave them reverence: shall we not much rather be in subjection unto the Father of spirits, and live?

Acts 17:29

> Forasmuch then as we are the offspring of God [*the spirit children of God the Father*], we ought not to think that the Godhead is like unto gold, or silver, or stone, graven by art and man's device.

Ephesians 1:3–4

> Blessed be the God and Father of our Lord Jesus Christ, who hath blessed us with all spiritual blessings in heavenly places in Christ: According as he hath chosen us in him before the foundation of the world [*before the Creation, in the premortal realm*], that we should be holy and without blame before him in love.

Jeremiah 1:5

Before I formed thee in the belly [*before conception*] I knew thee; and before thou camest forth out of the womb [*before being born into mortality*] I sanctified thee, and I ordained thee a prophet unto the nations.

Sons of God

It is recorded in the Old Testament that the "sons of God," Satan among them, presented themselves to the Lord in a time and place not of this earth (Job 1:6; 2:1). It is recorded later that the "sons of God shouted for joy" when the corner stone (of creation) was laid (Job 38:7). It is recorded in the New Testament that all men should be "blameless and harmless, the sons of God" (Philippians 2:15; 1 John 3:1–2).

Implicit in the questions recorded in Job 38:4–7 is the presence of the sons of God before the creation of the earth. They "shouted for joy" when the corner stone of creation was laid. All this celebration occurred before earth and Adam were made. It was the celebration of a plan, a design, and a purpose.

Job 1:6 and 2:1

Now there was a day when the sons of God came to present themselves before the Lord, and Satan came also among them. . . . Again there was a day when the sons of God came to present themselves before the Lord, and Satan came also among them to present himself before the Lord. [*It is not clear from the text precisely when or where this gathering took place, but it is reasonably clear it was not on earth.*]

Job 38:4–7

Where wast thou when I laid the foundations of the earth? declare, if thou hast understanding. Who hath laid the measures thereof, if thou knowest? or who hath stretched the line upon it? Whereupon are the foundations thereof fastened? or who laid the corner stone thereof; When the morning stars sang together, and all the sons of God shouted for joy? [*God indicts Satan with these rhetorical questions, pointing out that Satan in his rebellion took no part in the creation and was not among those loyal "morning stars" and "sons of God" who "shouted for joy" when the corner stone of creation was laid. More to the point in this discussion, all these events clearly took place in a premortal realm—a realm in which the "sons of God" lived before the earth and Adam and Eve were created.*]

Handwritten annotations:
- See Judges 13; where God promises Samson's mother she will conceive & bear a son & he will begin to deliver Israel. In that sense, God "knew" Samson before he existed.
- Job 38:4-7 - Job didn't exist when the universe was created.
- In this context, it refers to angels/demons
- Humans ≠ Sons of God
- Angels were created before humans ←

In this context, it is Christians/believers. See John 1:12. Humans are children of God's wrath by nature (Eph. 2:2-3), but can become sons of God by receiving Jesus + being born again (John 3:5-8). Also John 8:44.

Philippians 2:15

That ye may be blameless and harmless, the sons of God [*men and women are the spirit children of God the Father*], without rebuke, in the midst of a crooked and perverse nation, among whom ye shine as lights in the world.

1 John 3:1–2

Behold, what manner of love the Father hath bestowed upon us, that we should be called the sons of God [*human beings are the children of God the Father*]: therefore the world knoweth us not, because it knew him not. Beloved, now are we the sons of God, and it doth not yet appear what we shall [*in the future*] be: but we know that, when he shall [*in the future*] appear, we shall be like him; for we shall see him as he is. [*This is one of the clearest accounts of eternal progression in the Bible.*] ↳ ? I don't see anything about eternal progression here. When Jesus returns, Christians on earth will be transformed (1 Cor. 15:51-53)

Job 38:4–7

Where wast thou when I laid the foundations of the earth? declare, if thou hast understanding. Who hath laid the measures thereof, if thou knowest? or who hath stretched the line upon it? Whereupon are the foundations thereof fastened? or who laid the corner stone thereof; When the morning stars sang together, and all the sons of God shouted for joy? [*See commentary in the previous section.*]

Lucifer Rebels

Isaiah told how Lucifer sought to exalt himself above God and how he will be punished for this (Isaiah 14:13–15). John the Revelator told how Lucifer gathered unto himself one-third of the stars of heaven (spirit children of God) and organized them to destroy the child (Jesus), who would be delivered through a revered woman (Mary) (Revelation 12:1–4).

Isaiah 14:13–15

For thou [*Lucifer*] hast said in thine heart, I will ascend into heaven, I will exalt my throne above the stars of God: I will sit also upon the mount of the congregation, in the sides of the north: I will ascend above the heights of the clouds; I will be like the most High. Yet thou shalt be brought down to hell, to the sides of the pit.

Revelation 12:1–4

And there appeared a great wonder in heaven; a woman [*Mary*]

[handwritten left margin: Angels who chose to follow Satan]

clothed with the sun, and the moon under her feet, and upon her head a crown of twelve stars: And she being with child [*Jesus*] cried, travailing in birth, and pained to be delivered. And there appeared another wonder in heaven; and behold a great red dragon [*Lucifer*], having seven heads and ten horns, and seven crowns upon his heads. And his tail drew the third part of the stars of heaven [*those spirit offspring of God the Father who chose to join with Lucifer*], and did cast them to the earth: and the dragon stood before the woman which was ready to be delivered, for to devour her child as soon as it was born.

Michael Leads

Michael the Archangel led the fight against Lucifer (Revelation 12:7). Lucifer and his followers were defeated and cast down to earth as bodiless spirits (Revelation 12:8–9). Following the victory, a loud voice proclaimed that Christ had prevailed and that the "accuser" (Lucifer) was cast out (Revelation 12:10–11).

Revelation 12:7–11

[handwritten left margin: Angels/demons are a different creation from humans]

And there was war in heaven: Michael and his angels fought against the dragon; and the dragon fought and his angels, And prevailed not; neither was their place found any more in heaven. [*Satan and his followers were cast out of heaven.*] And the great dragon was cast out, that old serpent, called the Devil, and Satan, which deceiveth the whole world: he was cast out into the earth, and his angels were cast out with him. [*Satan and his followers, denied physical bodies, were cast down to the earth.*] And I heard a loud voice saying in heaven, Now is come salvation, and strength, and the kingdom of our God [*God the Father*], and the power of his Christ [*Jesus*]: for the accuser of our brethren is cast down, which accused them before our God day and night. And they overcame him by the blood of the Lamb, and by the word of their testimony; and they loved not their lives unto the death.

[handwritten right margin: where did this idea come from?]

The Father Laments

God the Father lamented the loss of his spirit child Lucifer and of the spirit children Lucifer led into rebellion (Isaiah 14:12).

Isaiah 14:12

How art thou fallen from heaven, O Lucifer, son of the morning! how art thou cut down to the ground, which didst weaken the nations [*the nations of spirit children*]!

[handwritten bottom: What?? Nations are nations of humans, why are nations suddenly made up of "spirit children?"]

Jesus Is Recognized

Lucifer and the other rebellious spirit children of the Father were cast down to earth, where their memory of the premortal realm caused them to suffer (Matthew 8:28–29; Mark 1:23–25; 3:11–12; 5:7–8; Luke 4:33–34, 41; 8:28). When they encountered Jesus on earth, they recognized him as the only begotten Son of God (the only spirit offspring of the Father who is also the mortal offspring of the Father, through Mary) before Jesus intended to proclaim this publicly. Jesus was quick to silence these spirits as they sought to disrupt his mission on earth (Mark 1:34).

[handwritten: Once created, angels/demons are eternal. Since they don't have bodies, they don't die physically. The demons in these passages had known Jesus since they were created, so they recognized him on earth (esp. His power)]

Matthew 8:28–29

And when he was come to the other side into the country of the Gergesenes, there met him two possessed with devils, coming out of the tombs, exceeding fierce, so that no man might pass by that way. And, behold, they cried out, saying, What have we to do with thee, Jesus, thou Son of God? art thou come hither to torment us before the time? [*Jesus had not announced publicly his relationship to God the Father, yet the unclean spirit addressed him as the "Son of God"*]

Mark 1:23–25 (see also Mark 1:34; 3:11–12, and 5:7–8)

And there was in their synagogue a man with an unclean spirit; and he cried out, Saying, Let us alone; what have we to do with thee, thou Jesus of Nazareth? art thou come to destroy us? I know thee who thou art, the Holy One of God. [*Jesus had not announced publicly his relationship to God the Father, yet the unclean spirits knew him as the "Holy One of God."*] And Jesus rebuked him, saying, Hold thy peace, and come out of him.

Luke 8:28 (see also Luke 4:33–34, 41)

When he [*one of the spirit followers of Lucifer, a devil, an unclean spirit*] saw Jesus, he cried out, and fell down before him, and with a loud voice said, What have I to do with thee, Jesus, thou Son of God most high? I beseech thee, torment me not.

MORMON UNDERSTANDING

[handwritten: This whole section is made up. No basis in the Bible.]

Spirit Children

Every person born in the flesh on earth was first born in the premortal realm as a spirit offspring of God the Father. In this realm, all spirit children of the Father are endowed with unique talents and capabilities. Each has a specific purpose to fulfill. To fulfill this purpose *progress to what? What's wrong w/ their current state?*

and continue to (progress eternally,) each must choose freely to leave the premortal realm, take on a physical body, and live in mortality, with all its joys, sorrows, forgetting, and death. Those in the premortal realm who choose not to enter mortality must remain in the premortal realm, where their bodiless state prevents them from progressing further.

Life, a Test

Life on earth is a test. It is here that men and women struggle to discover their purpose, work to fulfill it as far as they are able, and gain strength in the struggle. People experience mortality, progress in knowledge and understanding, and gain a testimony of the Savior Jesus Christ, who was the firstborn spirit offspring of Heavenly Father. An essential part of this test requires men and women to proceed in mortality without memory of their premortal existence.

Life, a Choice

Because Heavenly Father knows the challenges men and women will face on earth, he gives them the ability to recognize eternal truths when they hear them in mortality with a humble and truth-seeking heart. He provided a savior, Jesus Christ, through whose atoning sacrifice all mankind can obtain forgiveness for sins and overcome physical and spiritual death. Heavenly Father presented this plan of salvation in the premortal realm, and in that realm, he made clear the challenges and rewards of undertaking life on earth. All men and women who are born on earth made a free and informed choice to enter mortality.

War in Heaven

There was a war in the premortal realm, and all the spirit children of Heavenly Father fought in this war, some on Heavenly Father's side, some on the side of Lucifer. Most of the hosts of heaven rejoiced in the plan of salvation, including moral agency (free will) and the Atonement of Jesus Christ. Lucifer, also a spirit child of Heavenly Father, rose up in rebellion against the plan of salvation and led away one-third of God's spirit children. Michael the Archangel led the loyal spirit children in the ensuing fight against Lucifer. Lucifer and his minions were cast down to earth, where they continue to fight as bodiless spirits.

The war is not over.

✿ 2 ✿

SATAN

BIBLICAL TEACHING

Fallen Spirit

Satan, whose birth name is Lucifer (meaning "light bearer" or "son of the morning"), fell from heaven and was cut down to the ground (Isaiah 14:12). Lucifer fell after rebelling against the Father (Revelation 12:10). He was defeated by Michael in the war in heaven (Revelation 12:7–8) and was cast out of heaven and down to the earth along with the one-third of the spirits of heaven who followed him (Revelation 12:4, 9). Satan's fall was witnessed by the angels, and he was given dominion over hell, the "bottomless pit" (Revelation 9:1).

Isaiah 14:12

> How art thou fallen from heaven, O Lucifer, son of the morning! how art thou cut down to the ground, which didst weaken the nations! [*Lucifer, one of the Father's spirit children, rebelled against the Father and was cast out of heaven.*]

Revelation 12:10

> And I heard a loud voice saying in heaven, Now is come salvation, and strength, and the kingdom of our God, and the power of his Christ: for the accuser of our brethren [*Satan*] is cast down, which accused them before our God day and night.

Revelation 12:7–8

> And there was war in heaven: Michael [*the Archangel*] and his

13

angels [*the loyal two-thirds of the Father's spirit offspring*] fought against the dragon [*Satan*]; and the dragon fought and his angels [*the rebellious one-third of the Father's spirit offspring*], And prevailed not; neither was their place found any more in heaven [*they were cast out*].

Revelation 12:4, 9

And his [*Satan's*] tail drew the third part of the stars of heaven [*the rebellious one-third of the Father's spirit offspring*], and did cast them to the earth: and the dragon [*Satan*] stood before the woman [*Mary*] which was ready to be delivered, for to devour her child [*Jesus, God the Son*] as soon as it was born. And the great dragon was cast out, that old serpent, called the Devil, and Satan, which deceiveth the whole world: he was cast out into the earth, and his angels were cast out with him.

Revelation 9:1

And the fifth angel sounded, and I saw a star [*Satan*] fall from heaven unto the earth: and to him was given the key of the bottomless pit [*hell*].

Satan in the Old Testament

Satan appears—though not under that name—for the first time in the third chapter of Genesis. His evil influence enters into the serpent to deceive Eve in the Garden of Eden (Genesis 3:1). The first use of the name Satan appears in the first book of Chronicles (1 Chronicles 21:1). Satan's birth-name, Lucifer, is revealed later by the prophet Isaiah. The term *devils* (plural) is used in the Old Testament; however, reference to Satan as "the Devil" (singular) does not begin until the book of Matthew in the New Testament (Matthew 4:1).

Genesis 3:1

Now the serpent [*the form taken by Satan in the Garden*] was more subtil than any beast of the field which the Lord God had made. And he said unto the woman [*Eve*], Yea, hath God said, Ye shall not eat of every tree of the garden?

1 Chronicles 21:1

And Satan stood up against Israel, and provoked David to number Israel. [*This is the first use of the name Satan in the Bible.*]

Matthew 4:1

Then was Jesus led up of the Spirit [*the Holy Ghost*] into the wilderness to be tempted of the devil. [*This is the first use of the word devil in the Bible.*]

Satan in the New Testament—Spirit of Many Names

The New Testament uses a host of names, labels, and metaphors in reference to Satan:

Abaddon ("destruction") and Apollyon ("destroyer") (Revelation 9:11)

the Accuser (Revelation 12:10);

the Adversary and the Roaring Lion (1 Peter 5:8);

the Angel of Light (2 Corinthians 11:14);

the Antichrist (1 John 4:3);

the Beast (Revelation 14:9–10);

Beelzebub (Matthew 12:24);

Belial (2 Corinthians 6:15);

chief (or ruler) of demons (Luke 11:15);

the Deceiver, Dragon, and Old Serpent (Revelation 12:9);

the Devil (1 John 3:8);

the Enemy (Matthew 13:39);

Evil or Evil One (John 17:15);

Father of Lies and Murderer (John 8:44);

God of this World (earth) (2 Corinthians 4:4);

Man of Sin and Son of Perdition (2 Thessalonians 2:3–4);

Power of Darkness (Colossians 1:13);

Prince or Ruler of this World (earth) (John 12:31);

Prince of the Power of the Air (Ephesians 2:1–2);

Ruler of the Darkness (Ephesians 6:12);

Satan (Mark 1:13);

Star (Revelation 9:1);

the Tempter (Matthew 4:3);

the Thief (John 10:10);

and Wicked (Ephesians 6:16).

The Millennium

Satan will lose his power to tempt the children of God during the Millennium (the one thousand years following the Second Coming of Christ). However, in the period between the close of the Millennium and the final judgment, Satan will rise up and usher in the final conflict. The "four quarters of the earth" will be involved in this conflict (Revelation 20:2–3, 7–8).

Satan will be defeated in this final conflict and be cast into the lake of fire and outer darkness for all eternity (Revelation 20:9–10).

Revelation 20:2–3, 7–8—The Final Conflict

And he laid hold on the dragon, that old serpent, which is the Devil, and Satan, and bound him a thousand years. And cast him into the bottomless pit, and shut him up, and set a seal upon him, that he should deceive the nations no more, till the thousand years should be fulfilled: and after that he must be loosed a little season. . . . And when the thousand years are expired, Satan shall be loosed out of his prison, And shall go out to deceive the nations which are in the four quarters of the earth, Gog and Magog, to gather them together to battle: the number of whom is as the sand of the sea.

Revelation 20:9–10—Satan is Defeated

And they went up on the breadth of the earth, and compassed the camp of the saints about, and the beloved city: and fire came down from God out of heaven, and devoured them. And the devil that deceived them was cast into the lake of fire and brimstone, where the beast and the false prophet are, and shall be tormented day and night for ever and ever.

Warnings

John the Revelator warned about Satan (Revelation 12:12), proclaiming that Satan is fallen (come down) to earth and enraged. The Apostle Peter warned that Satan "walketh about" ready to strike (1 Peter 5:8). Satan can enter into people (John 13:26–27). Men and women can make themselves vulnerable to Satan (Isaiah 47:10–14; Deuteronomy 18:9–12).

Revelation 12:12

Therefore rejoice, ye heavens, and ye that dwell in them. Woe to the inhabiters of the earth and of the sea! for the devil is come down unto you, having great wrath, because he knoweth that he hath but a short time.

1 Peter 5:8

Be sober, be vigilant; because your adversary the devil, as a roaring lion, walketh about, seeking whom he may devour.

John 13:26–27

Jesus answered, He it is, to whom I shall give a sop, when I have dipped it. And when he had dipped the sop, he gave it to Judas Iscariot, the son of Simon. And after the sop Satan entered into him. Then said Jesus unto him, That thou doest, do quickly.

Isaiah 47:10–14

For thou [*the unrepentant sinner*] hast trusted in thy wickedness:

thou hast said, None seeth me [*I sin in secret*]. Thy [*the sinner's*] wisdom and thy knowledge, it hath perverted thee; and thou hast said in thine heart, I am, and none else beside me [*there is no God*]. Therefore shall evil [*Satan*] come upon thee; thou shalt not know from whence it riseth: and mischief shall fall upon thee; thou shalt not be able to put it off: and desolation shall come upon thee suddenly, which thou shalt not know [*the influence of Satan and the wages of sin shall come upon the sinner*]. Stand now with thine enchantments, and with the multitude of thy sorceries, wherein thou hast laboured from thy youth; if so be thou shalt be able to profit, if so be thou mayest prevail. Thou art wearied in the multitude of thy counsels. Let now the astrologers, the stargazers, the monthly prognosticators, stand up, and save thee from these things that shall come upon thee. [*This is a facetious invitation to seek help where it cannot be found.*] Behold, they [*the aforementioned sorceries, enchantments, counsels, astrologers, stargazers, and prognosticators*] shall be as stubble; the fire shall burn them; they shall not deliver themselves from the power of the flame: there shall not be a coal to warm at, nor fire to sit before it.

Deuteronomy 18:9–12

When thou art come into the land which the Lord thy God giveth thee, thou shalt not learn to do after the abominations of those nations. There shall not be found among you any one that maketh his son or his daughter to pass through the fire, or that useth divination, or an observer of times, or an enchanter, or a witch, Or a charmer, or a consulter with familiar spirits, or a wizard, or a necromancer. For all that do these things are an abomination unto the Lord: and because of these abominations the Lord thy God doth drive them out from before thee.

Satan Remembers

Satan and his spirits remember the premortal realm and they use their memory of this realm to subvert men and women in mortality. See the chapter on the premortal life for details (Matthew 8:28–29; Mark 1:23–25; 3:11–12; 5:7–8; Luke 4:33–34, 41; 8:28).

The Imitator

Satan gave power to the sorcerers of Pharaoh, who cleverly imitated the miracles (spiritual gifts) of Aaron and Moses (Exodus 7:8–11, 17–22).

Exodus 7:8–11 (see also Exodus 17–22)

And the Lord spake unto Moses and unto Aaron, saying, When Pharaoh shall speak unto you, saying, Shew a miracle for you: then thou shalt say unto Aaron, Take thy rod, and cast it before Pharaoh, and it shall become a serpent. And Moses and Aaron went in unto Pharaoh, and they did so as the Lord had commanded: and Aaron cast down his rod before Pharaoh, and before his servants, and it became a serpent. Then Pharaoh also called the wise men and the sorcerers: now the magicians of Egypt, they also did in like manner with their enchantments [*imitated the gifts of the spirit manifested by Moses and Aaron*].

Rebuking Satan

[handwritten: Only Christian men & women John 8:34; Rom. 6:17-18]

Despite the fact that Satan and his followers are real and possess great power to tempt and try the hearts of men, God the Father has promised that men and women will never be tempted above their strength to overcome temptation (1 Corinthians 10:13). It is by putting on "the whole armour of God" that mortal humans become spiritually prepared to battle Satan and to rebuke his deceptive ways (Ephesians 6:10–18).

[handwritten: Christians - those who have placed their faith in Jesus for salvation.]

1 Corinthians 10:13

There hath no temptation taken you but such as is common to man: but God is faithful, who will not suffer you to be tempted above that ye are able; but will with the temptation also make a way to escape, that ye may be able to bear it.

Ephesians 6:10–18

Finally, my brethren, be strong in the Lord, and in the power of his might. Put on the whole armour of God, that ye may be able to stand against the wiles of the devil. For we wrestle not against flesh and blood, but against principalities, against powers, against the rulers of the darkness of this world, against spiritual wickedness in high places. Wherefore take unto you the whole armour of God, that ye may be able to withstand in the evil day, and having done all, to stand. Stand therefore, having your loins girt about with truth, and having on the breastplate of righteousness; And your feet shod with the preparation of the gospel of peace; Above all, taking the shield of faith, wherewith ye shall be able to quench all the fiery darts of the wicked. And take the helmet of salvation, and the sword of the Spirit, which is the word of God: Praying always with all prayer and supplication in the Spirit, and watching thereunto with all perseverance and supplication for all saints.

Casting Out Devils

Jesus rebuked Satan in the desert (Matthew 4:10) and cast out numerous evil spirits during his public ministry (Matthew 8:16, 31). The Savior's disciples cast out devils during their missionary work (Luke 10:17; Mark 6:12–13).

Matthew 4:10

> Then saith Jesus unto him, Get thee hence, Satan: for it is written, Thou shalt worship the Lord thy God, and him only shalt thou serve.

Matthew 8:16, 31

> When the even was come, they brought unto him many that were possessed with devils: and he cast out the spirits with his word, and healed all that were sick. . . . So the devils besought him, saying, If thou cast us out, suffer us to go away into the herd of swine.

Luke 10:17

> And the seventy returned again with joy, saying, Lord, even the devils are subject unto us through thy name.

Mark 6:12–13

> And they went out, and preached that men should repent. And they cast out many devils, and anointed with oil many that were sick, and healed them.

MORMON UNDERSTANDING

Origins of Rebellion

[handwritten: Do spirit offspring always exist or are they created at some point?]

Satan was among the spirit offspring of God the Father. Together with scriptures from the book of Revelation, modern scripture reveals that in the premortal Grand Council, Satan offered to be the savior of mankind. In this offer, which devolved into a demand, Satan took a stand against moral agency (free will) even though he knew this capacity was a key element of Heavenly Father's plan of salvation. In short, Satan proclaimed that he would establish a dictatorship of his own design and under his own absolute control, and he demanded that the glory for this achievement be granted to him alone.

In the same premortal Grand Council, Jesus Christ, the firstborn spirit offspring of God the Father, also offered to serve as the savior, but one of an entirely different sort. His offer, unlike Satan's, respected

Heavenly Father's absolute authority and Heavenly Father's desire that men have the gift of agency, the power to choose.

God the Father Chose Jesus to Be the Christ

Satan was enraged. He rebelled against Heavenly Father and the plan of salvation, and he convinced a third of the hosts of heaven, also spirit offspring of Heavenly Father, to follow him. Thus commenced the great war in heaven, which continues on earth.

Cast Out

After their rebellion, Satan and his minions were cast out of heaven and forever denied the opportunity to obtain physical bodies and the eternal progression and increase possible through such bodies when they are glorified. Having only spirit form and substance, these dark angels and their leader were cast down to earth, where they are permitted to tempt and torment men and women but not to compel them in anything. The ultimate punishment of Satan and his underlings is eternal separation from Heavenly Father with no possibility of forgiveness.

Satanic Methods and Means

Satan accomplishes his goals primarily through deception. The many names by which he is known are a reflection of his role as master deceiver. He is able to imitate the gifts of the spirit, including prophecy, tongues, healings, visions, and other miracles. Satan's army of seduced mortals includes false prophets, false healers and miracle workers, false fortune-tellers and mediums, and others who engage in deceptions that lead men and women away from Christ and Heavenly Father's plan of salvation.

Satan uses all means—some garishly blatant, others profoundly subtle—to deceive mankind. He hints that disobedience of God's laws is freedom, even a pathway to godhood. He encourages men and women to follow him in ways that have terrible consequences.

Perhaps Satan's most masterful deception is in convincing people, on the one hand, that he simply does not exist and, on the other hand, that he exists with powers far greater than what he really has.

Satan leverages human passions. He gives gentle nudges along the pathways already laid into human nature. For example, he leads men and women into violating the laws of chastity through fornication and adultery. Satan often accomplishes this in small steps, leading people into wearing immodest clothing, entertaining erotic thoughts, discoursing in vulgar language, viewing and listening to erotic movies and music, transforming dance into a coarse simulation of sexual intercourse, and entertaining the notion that, in matters of sex, some compulsions are so strong they cannot and should not be denied.

Remembering Heavenly Father and the premortal realm, Satan and the evil spirits that follow him suffer constantly from a grinding awareness of their loss, which they know is hopelessly eternal. They seek to persuade men and women in mortality to abandon Heavenly Father's plan of salvation, forgo the trials of eternal progression, and follow Satan into outer darkness.

Fighting Back

Heavenly Father gives clear guidance on how to avoid the temptations of Satan and the bondage that comes from yielding to them. First, he instructs men and women to trust in him—to trust that he will never allow them to be tempted beyond their capacity to resist. Second, he instructs men and women to struggle valiantly against evil, pray always for his help in resisting the temptations of Satan, and nurture their faith in the Atonement of Jesus Christ.

The Millennium

Satan will have this power to tempt and deceive until the Second Coming of Jesus Christ. During the thousand-year reign (known as the Millennium) of Christ before the final judgment, Satan will be bound by the righteousness of human beings on the earth. He will have no power to tempt or persuade during this time. At the end of the Millennium, however, Satan will be set free once again as part of the last epic struggle before the final judgment. In this final battle, Satan and his followers will be defeated and cast into outer darkness for all eternity.

❧ 3 ❧

ADAM AND EVE

BIBLICAL TEACHING

Creation and Communication

God the Father worked through Jesus Christ to create the earth (Hebrews 1:1–2), and together they created man (Genesis 1:26). The Lord God (the term for the Father in the first three chapters of Genesis) in the beginning communicated directly with Adam and Eve to provide instruction and guidance (Genesis 3:9, 13).

Hebrews 1:1–2

> God, who at sundry times and in divers manners spake in time past unto the fathers by the prophets, Hath in these last days spoken unto us by his Son, whom he hath appointed heir of all things, by whom also he made the worlds.

Genesis 1:26

> And God said, Let us make man in our [*plural*] image, after our likeness: and let them have dominion over the fish of the sea, and over the fowl of the air, and over the cattle, and over all the earth, and over every creeping thing that creepeth upon the earth.

Genesis 3:9, 13

> And the Lord God [*also translated "Yahweh"—meaning God the Creator or God the Father over all*] called unto Adam, and said unto him, Where art thou? . . . And the Lord God said unto the woman, What is this that thou hast done? And the woman said, The serpent beguiled me, and I did eat.

Deathless Bodies

Adam and Eve were created as physical beings "from the dust of the ground" (Genesis 2:7). The tree of life, whose fruit gave eternal life, was not forbidden to them in the beginning (Genesis 2:9, 16–17), as Adam and Eve were not yet subject to death. After the fall, God would not allow Adam and Eve to eat of the fruit of the tree of life because they would then live forever in a state of transgression (Genesis 3:22, 24).

Genesis 2:7

> And the Lord God formed man of the dust of the ground, and breathed into his nostrils the breath of life; and <u>man became a living soul.</u> This is the moment the first human existed, not before.

Genesis 2:9, 16–17

> And out of the ground made the Lord God to grow every tree that is pleasant to the sight, and good for food; the tree of life also in the midst of the garden, and the tree of knowledge of good and evil. . . . And the Lord God commanded the man, saying, Of every tree of the garden thou mayest freely eat: But of the tree of the knowledge of good and evil, thou shalt not eat of it: for <u>in the day that thou eatest thereof thou shalt surely die</u> [*become subject to mortal death*].

Genesis 3:22, 24

> At its worst, death is separation. Adam & Eve were separated from God spiritually when they ate the fruit.
>
> And the Lord God said, Behold, the man is become as one of us [*plural*], to know good and evil: and now, lest he put forth his hand, and take also of the tree of life, and eat, and live for ever [*eating of the tree of life would cause physical beings to live forever*]. . . . So he drove out the man; and he placed at the east of the garden of Eden Cherubims, and a flaming sword which turned every way, to keep the way of the tree of life. [*The tree was available for food when Adam and Eve were innocent and not subject to death. Now that they had transgressed and were subject to death, God kept the fruit of this tree from Adam and Eve to protect them from being in a state of transgression for eternity and also to maintain his truthfulness that they would die if they ate of the tree of the knowledge of good and evil.*]

Two Commandments

God told Adam and Eve to multiply and replenish the earth (Genesis 1:28) and to eat not of the tree of knowledge of good and evil (Genesis 2:17). While it is possible other commandments may have been given, these two are cited specifically in the Bible.

Genesis 1:28

> And God blessed them, and God said unto them, Be fruitful, and multiply, and replenish the earth . . .

Genesis 2:17

> But of the tree of the knowledge of good and evil, thou shalt not eat of it: for in the day that thou eatest thereof thou shalt surely die.

Eve is Beguiled, Adam Follows, Death Comes

Satan, by way of the serpent, beguiled Eve in the Garden of Eden, and she ate of the fruit of the tree of the knowledge of good and evil (Genesis 3:4–6). The serpent did not then beguile Adam (1 Timothy 2:14); rather, Adam observed Eve's decision. Eve gave Adam the fruit, and Adam chose to eat of the fruit (Genesis 3:6). From Adam and Eve's transgression came physical and spiritual death—ultimately resolved by the Atonement of Jesus Christ (Romans 5:12–17).

Genesis 3:4–6

> And the serpent said unto the woman, Ye shall not surely die: For God doth know that in the day ye eat thereof, then your eyes shall be opened, and ye shall be as gods, knowing good and evil. And when the woman saw that the tree was good for food, and that it was pleasant to the eyes, and a tree to be desired to make one wise, she took of the fruit thereof, and did eat.

1 Timothy 2:14

> And Adam was not deceived [*the serpent deceived Eve alone, and then Adam chose to eat to remain with Eve and have offspring*], but the woman being deceived was in the transgression.

Genesis 3:6

> And when the woman saw that the tree was good for food, and that it was pleasant to the eyes, and a tree to be desired to make one wise, she took of the fruit thereof, and did eat, and gave also unto her husband with her; and he did eat . . .

Romans 5:12–17

> Wherefore, as by one man sin entered into the world, and death by sin; and so death passed upon all men, for that all have sinned: (For until the law sin was in the world: but sin is not imputed when there is no law. Nevertheless death reigned from Adam to Moses, even over them that had not sinned after the

similitude of Adam's transgression, who is the figure of him that was to come. But not as the offence, so also is the free gift. For if through the offence of one many be dead, much more the grace of God, and the gift by grace, which is by one man, Jesus Christ, hath abounded unto many. And not as it was by one that sinned, so is the gift: for the judgment was by one to condemnation, but the free gift is of many offences unto justification. For if by one man's offence death reigned by one; much more they which receive abundance of grace and of the gift of righteousness shall reign in life by one, Jesus Christ.)

Innocence Lost

Before eating of the tree of knowledge of good and evil, Adam and Eve felt no shame and were unaware they were naked (Genesis 2:25). After eating of the tree, they lost their innocence, felt shame in nakedness (Genesis 3:7), and were cast out of the Garden of Eden (Genesis 3:23). After being cast out of the Garden, Eve conceived their firstborn son, Cain (Genesis 4:1).

Genesis 2:25

> And they were both naked, the man and his wife, and were not ashamed.

Genesis 3:7

> And the eyes of them both were opened [*after eating of the fruit of the tree of knowledge of good and evil*], and they knew that they were naked [*innocence was lost*]; and they sewed fig leaves together, and made themselves aprons [*shame arose from lost innocence*].

Genesis 3:23

> Therefore the Lord God sent him forth from the garden of Eden [*Adam and Eve were cast out*], to till the ground from whence he was taken.

Genesis 4:1

> And Adam knew [*had sexual intercourse with*] Eve his wife [*after expulsion from the garden*]; and she conceived, and bare Cain, and said, I have gotten a man [*a spirit son of the Father in the premortal existence*] from the Lord [*God the Father*].

Plan of Salvation Commenced

Jesus was ordained Savior before the foundation of the world

(1 Peter 1:19–20; John 17:24; Ephesians 1:3–5). God the Father, knowing all, knew there would be a need for redemption long before events in the Garden of Eden transpired.

The Fall brought about both physical and spiritual death, but the Atonement and Resurrection of Christ brought hope to all mankind that they might also be resurrected and return to the presence of Heavenly Father (1 Corinthians 15:22). *[handwritten: Humans are created at conception, so they don't return]*

Heavenly Father's plan of salvation includes men and women coming to the earth as mortal beings, having the hope of eternal life (1 Corinthians 15:44–45), having the opportunity to gain the ability to choose between good and evil (Genesis 3:22), and having the opportunity to be saved by the divine sacrifice of Jesus Christ.

[handwritten left margin: we don't come to earth. we are created by God at conception]

[handwritten: It's called "the fall" b/c we fell from right relationship w/ God, this was not a good thing. We know good/evil from the perspective of being evil.]

1 Peter 1:19–20

But with the precious blood of Christ, as of a lamb without blemish and without spot: Who verily was foreordained before the foundation of the world. [*Before the world was formed, Jesus was ordained to be the Savior of the World: God knew there would be a fall*] but was manifest in these last times for you.

John 17:24

Father, I will that they also, whom thou hast given me, be with me where I am; that they may behold my glory, which thou hast given me: for thou lovest me before the foundation of the world.

Ephesians 1:3–5

Blessed be the God and Father of our Lord Jesus Christ, who hath blessed us with all spiritual blessings in heavenly places in Christ: According as he hath chosen us in him before the foundation of the world, that we should be holy and without blame before him in love: Having predestinated us unto the adoption of children by Jesus Christ to himself, according to the good pleasure of his will.

1 Corinthians 15:22

For as in Adam all die, even so in Christ shall all be made alive [*both played their part in the plan of salvation*].

1 Corinthians 15:44–45

It is sown a natural body; it is raised a spiritual body. There is a natural body, and there is a spiritual body. And so it is written, The first man Adam was made a living soul; the last Adam was made a quickening spirit. [*Adam was a life-giving spirit; while his transgression*] *caused physical and spiritual death, his actions commenced the plan of salvation for all mankind to have the opportunity for eternal life.*]

Genesis 3:22

> And the Lord God said, Behold, the man is become as one of us, to know good and evil . . .

Direct Communication Ceases

In the first three chapters of Genesis, God is referred to as "Lord God." Thereafter, God is referred to as "Lord." It is the Lord God who speaks directly to Adam and Eve in the Garden. It is the Lord who speaks to them outside the Garden (see Genesis 4:6; 6:3, and so forth). Thus begins the role of Jesus Christ as the great mediator (1 Timothy 2:5).

Genesis 4:6

> And the Lord [*Jesus Christ as denoted by the use of "Lord" only*] said unto Cain, Why art thou wroth? and why is thy countenance fallen?

Genesis 6:3

> And the Lord [*Jesus Christ as denoted by the use of "Lord" only*] said, My spirit shall not always strive with man, for that he also is flesh: yet his days shall be an hundred and twenty years.

1 Timothy 2:5

> For there is one God, and one mediator between God and men, the man Christ Jesus;

MORMON UNDERSTANDING

Premortal Adam and Eve

nowhere in the Bible ↑

Adam and Eve were valiant spirits in the premortal realm, and they were given the assignment to be the first man and woman on earth. When they assumed their places in the Garden of Eden, Adam and Eve had physical bodies. However, they were not yet mortal: their bodies were not subject to death.

b/c they didn't have a prior life ↑

Memory Lost

God was with Adam and Eve in the Garden, as he had been in the premortal life, but Adam and Eve had no memory of their prior life, and they had no comprehension of good and evil. They did not know who they were or what role they were destined to play in the plan of salvation.

The Fall

God gave Adam and Eve two key commandments: first, multiply and replenish the earth; and second, don't eat of the tree of knowledge of good and evil. Satan entered the Garden of Eden to tempt Adam and Eve to join him in rebellion against God and thus disrupt the plan of salvation. When Adam learned that Satan had persuaded Eve to eat of the tree of knowledge of good and evil, he chose to do likewise and be cast out of the Garden with her. Had he not made this choice, he would have remained alone in the Garden, separated from Eve. He would have been incapable of producing offspring, and therefore unable to obey God's first commandment. *Adam's choice was not noble. It was the beginning of rampant evil.*

The Choice

Adam chose mortality and with it offspring, advancing physical infirmity and ultimately physical death. Adam and Eve took their first steps in fulfilling Heavenly Father's plan of salvation. They were not compelled in this: they willingly accepted their roles in the plan. *They didn't know their roles. They acted w/ pride + greed + selfishness*

Cast Out

The Fall made Adam and Eve and their descendants subject to physical and spiritual death. Physical death is separation of the spirit from the body. Spiritual death is separation from God. Satan works to keep men confined in both forms of death. Jesus Christ, through his Atonement, enables mankind to be freed from both kinds of death and, through repentance to return to Heavenly Father. *—> What is repentance in Mormonism?*

The Plan of Salvation

Despite the introduction of physical and spiritual death and its consequences, the Fall was part of Heavenly Father's plan of salvation. According to this plan, Adam and Eve and all their descendants obtained physical bodies of flesh and bone, the ability to know and to choose freely between good and evil, and the opportunity to take part in the unfolding of the Atonement and Resurrection of Jesus Christ.

Original Sin

Adam and Eve are accountable for their transgression and the Fall; their offspring are not. However, their offspring do inherit the consequences of the Fall, including all the blessings and hardships of mortality. Men and women are accountable for their own transgressions in mortality, not for those of Adam and Eve.

4

GOD THE FATHER

BIBLICAL TEACHING

Omniscient, Omnipotent, Omnipresent

God the Father has all power over heaven and earth and all things in them (Matthew 19:26). God the Father's dominion is incomprehensible to man (2 Corinthians 2:14; Matthew 6:8).

Matthew 19:26
> But Jesus beheld them, and said unto them, With men this is impossible; but with God all things are possible [*God is omnipotent*].

2 Corinthians 2:14
> Now thanks be unto God, which always causeth us to triumph in Christ, and maketh manifest the savour of his knowledge by us in every place [*God is omnipresent*]. Not what this verse is about.

Matthew 6:8
> Be not ye therefore like unto them: for your Father knoweth what things ye have need of, before ye ask him [*God is omniscient*].

Father of All

Every mortal human being has a biological father and mother, and through them acquires a body of flesh and bones. As the sons (and daughters) of God (Hosea 1:10), the spirits of men and women were created by God the Father in heaven through a process that is unknown (Hebrews 12:9). This intimate relationship with God the Father is illuminated in the Bible through references to him as "Abba,"

verse doesn't say this

Aramaic for "father" (Romans 8:15–16; Galatians 4:6–7).

Hosea 1:10

Yet the number of the children of Israel shall be as the sand of the sea, which cannot be measured nor numbered; and it shall come to pass, that in the place where it was said unto them, Ye are not my people, there it shall be said unto them, Ye are the sons of the living God.

Hebrews 12:9

Furthermore we have had fathers of our flesh which corrected us, and we gave them reverence: shall we not much rather be in subjection unto the Father of spirits, and live? [*God is the father of our spirits.*]

Romans 8:15–16

For ye have not received the spirit of bondage again to fear; but ye have received the Spirit of adoption, whereby we cry, Abba, Father. The Spirit itself beareth witness with our spirit, that we are the children of God.

Galatians 4:6–7

And because ye are sons, God hath sent forth the Spirit of his Son into your hearts, crying, Abba, Father. Wherefore thou art no more a servant, but a son; and if a son, then an heir of God through Christ.

Body and Spirit

Man was created in the image of God both spiritually and physically (Genesis 1:26–27). God's body is physical (Genesis 9:6), although perfected and glorified beyond all human comprehension (Hebrews 1:1–3). God the Father has substance and shape (John 5:37). Jesus proclaimed God the Father as one of the two witnesses testifying that Jesus was the Christ (John 8:17–18). God the Father has a spirit just as the men and women whom he created in his image have spirits (John 4:24).

God the Son, Jesus, was born in the flesh to Mary and lived among the men and women of his time. The form and appearance of Jesus was in the "express image of his [God the Father's] person" (Hebrews 1:1–3). Some men have seen God the Father (Acts 7:55–56). The physical nature of the Godhead has been revealed to mankind. (Exodus 24:10–11; 31:18; 33:11, 23; Numbers 22:9–12, 20; 23:4, 16; Deuteronomy 23:14; 1 Kings 9:2–3).

Genesis 1:26–27

And God said, Let us make man in our image, after our

likeness. . . . So God created man in his own image, in the image of God created he him; male and female created he them.

Genesis 9:6

Whoso sheddeth man's blood, by man shall his blood be shed: for in the image of God made he man.

Hebrews 1:1–3

God [*the Father*], who at sundry times and in divers manners spake in time past unto the fathers by the prophets, Hath in these last days spoken unto us by his Son [*Jesus*], whom he hath appointed heir of all things, by whom [*by God the Son, Jesus*] also he [*God the Father*] made the worlds; Who [*Jesus*] being the brightness of his glory, and the express image of his [*the Father's*] person [*Jesus, a physical person, is in the express image of the Father, a physical person*], and upholding all things by the word of his power, when he had by himself purged our sins, sat down on the right hand of the Majesty on high.

John 5:37 In context, ~~verse is~~ Jesus is saying they refused to

And the Father himself, which hath sent me, hath borne witness listen to of me. Ye have neither heard his [*physical*] voice at any time, nor seen his [*physical*] shape. What God said or "see" His character.

John 8:17–18

It is also written in your law, that the testimony of two men is true. I am one that bear witness of myself, and the Father that sent me beareth witness of me. [*The Father is given as the second person to bear witness, indicating that the image of God and man are sufficiently shared to satisfy the law.*]

John 4:24 (1 John 4:12; John 1:18; John 6:46)

God is a Spirit: and they that worship him must worship him in spirit and in truth.

Acts 7:55–56

But he, being full of the Holy Ghost, looked up stedfastly into heaven, and saw the glory of God, and Jesus standing on the right hand of God, And said, Behold, I see the heavens opened, and the Son of man standing on the right hand of God. [*God the Son, Jesus, and God the Father have form and substance and are both seen by Stephen.*]

John 14:9

Jesus saith unto him, Have I been so long time with you, and yet hast thou not known me, Philip? he that hath seen me hath seen the

Father; and how sayest thou then, Shew us the Father? [*The emphasis is on "seeing" and being "shown." That which can be seen or shown directly to the senses must have form and substance.*]

Exodus 24:10–11 (see also Exodus 31:18; 33:11, 23)

And they saw the God of Israel: and there was under his feet as it were a paved work of a sapphire stone, and as it were the body of heaven in his clearness. And upon the nobles of the children of Israel he laid not his hand: also they saw God, and did eat and drink.

We don't know what they saw. Theophany?

Numbers 22:9–12, 20 (see also Numbers 23:4, 16)

And God came unto Balaam, and said [*God did not merely speak to Balaam: he came to him, visited, and spoke to him*], What men are these with thee? And Balaam said unto God, Balak the son of Zippor, king of Moab, hath sent unto me, saying, Behold, there is a people come out [*to physically come out; see above*] of Egypt, which covereth the face of the earth: come now, curse me them; peradventure I shall be able to overcome them, and drive them out. And God said unto Balaam, Thou shalt not go with them; thou shalt not curse the people: for they are blessed. . . . And God came [*see above uses of "come"*] unto Balaam at night, and said unto him, If the men come [*meaning to visit in person*] to call thee, rise up, and go with them; but yet the word which I shall say unto thee, that shalt thou do.

theophany?

Deuteronomy 23:14

imagery

For the Lord thy God walketh in the midst of thy camp, to deliver thee, and to give up thine enemies before thee; therefore shall thy camp be holy: that he see no unclean thing in thee, and turn away from thee.

1 Kings 9:2–3:

That the Lord appeared to Solomon the second time, as he had appeared unto him at Gibeon. And the Lord said unto him, I have heard thy prayer and thy supplication, that thou hast made before me: I have hallowed this house, which thou hast built, to put my name there for ever; and mine eyes and mine heart shall be there perpetually.

theophany?

Adversity, Suffering, and Death

God the Father, working through his Son Jesus Christ (the God of the Old Testament), brought adversity to the Israelites as instruction, chastisement, and punishment (Exodus 32:14; Judges 9:23; 10:7; 1 Chronicles 21:14–15). David spoke of the trials that will come as a result of the Lord's ministry to man (Psalm 78:49–50; 119:75), while

Job experienced firsthand how the Lord allows certain afflictions to come upon mankind for what might appear at the time to be no reason at all (Job 12:14–25). God knows what is best for his children and will never give them more than they are capable of managing through reliance on him (1 Corinthians 10:13).

Because God is omniscient, omnipotent, and omnipresent, he can cause or prevent all adversity, suffering, and death. He cares for all of his children individually in ways that are inexplicable, and he causes or allows adversity, suffering, and death according to his infinite wisdom. God provides for his children the experiences needed to reach their full potential as his sons and daughters, and in this he preserves their free will.

Exodus 32:14

God's trying to help people see the consequences of their sin & the need for repentance to have a restored relationship w/ Him.

And the Lord repented of the evil which he thought to do unto his people.

Judges 9:23

Then God sent an evil spirit between Abimelech and the men of Shechem; and the men of Shechem dealt treacherously with Abimelech.

Judges 10:7

And the anger of the Lord was hot against Israel, and he sold them into the hands of the Philistines, and into the hands of the children of Ammon.

1 Chronicles 21:14–15

So the Lord sent pestilence upon Israel: and there fell of Israel seventy thousand men. And God sent an angel unto Jerusalem to destroy it: and as he was destroying, the Lord beheld, and he repented him of the evil, and said to the angel that destroyed, It is enough, stay now thine hand. And the angel of the Lord stood by the threshing floor of Ornan the Jebusite.

Psalm 78:49–50

He cast upon them the fierceness of his anger, wrath, and indignation, and trouble, by sending evil angels among them. He made a way to his anger; he spared not their soul from death, but gave their life over to the pestilence.

Psalm 119:75

I know, O Lord, that thy judgments are right, and that thou in faithfulness hast afflicted me.

In all passages above, God is responding w/ judgment in response to sin. It is not "inexplicable."

Job 12:14–25

Behold, he [*the Lord*] breaketh down, and it cannot be built again: he shutteth up a man, and there can be no opening. Behold, he withholdeth the waters, and they dry up: also he sendeth them out, and they overturn the earth. With him is strength and wisdom: the deceived and the deceiver are his. He leadeth counsellors away spoiled, and maketh the judges fools. He looseth the bond of kings, and girdeth their loins with a girdle. He leadeth princes away spoiled, and overthroweth the mighty. He removeth away the speech of the trusty, and taketh away the understanding of the aged. He poureth contempt upon princes, and weakeneth the strength of the mighty. He discovereth deep things out of darkness, and bringeth out to light the shadow of death. He increaseth the nations, and destroyeth them: he enlargeth the nations, and straiteneth them again. He taketh away the heart of the chief of the people of the earth, and causeth them to wander in a wilderness where there is no way. They grope in the dark without light, and he maketh them to stagger like a drunken man.

1 Corinthians 10:13

this is written to Christians, not unbelievers

There hath no temptation taken you but such as is common to man: but God is faithful, who will not suffer you to be tempted above that ye are able; but will with the temptation also make a way to escape, that ye may be able to bear it.

Incomprehensible God

I think God was using Samson's out-of-control sex drive to accomplish His purpose b/c He had already committed to using Samson

God the Father fulfills his purposes in ways that are incomprehensible to man. God's wisdom and understanding are infinite. His goals and purposes are infinite. Human understanding cannot encompass them.

For example, Samson pursued women who were not of his faith, vexing his mother and father and violating the Mosaic law. Nevertheless, what Samson was doing "was of the Lord" (Judges 14:3–4).

God does not fail in his purposes, however incomprehensible his methods and however distant from human understanding his goals. Whether it be allowing the transgression of Adam and Eve in the Garden of Eden or using the sinful nature of man to carry out judgments against an offending nation, God's purposes will be satisfied. He does not wait upon human understanding.

Judges 14:3–4

Then his father and his mother said unto him, Is there never a woman among the daughters of thy brethren, or among all my people, that thou goest to take a wife of the uncircumcised Philistines? And Samson said unto his father, Get her for me; for she pleaseth me well. But his father and his mother knew not that it was of the Lord, that he sought an occasion against the Philistines: for at that time the Philistines had dominion over Israel. [*Despite God's admonition that the Israelites should marry their own, Samson was led to marry a Philistine to fulfill God's purposes.*]

The Family of God

The family is ordained of God both in heaven and on earth (Ephesians 3:14–15). Mankind is taught to pray that God's will "be done in earth, as it is in heaven" (Matthew 6:9–10). According to conventions of the period, women are referred to directly in the scriptures much less frequently than men. Yet no one supposes that women did not play a vital role in the family, or that family did not play a vital role in the culture (1 Samuel 8:1–2).

Ephesians 3:14–15

For this cause I bow my knees unto the Father of our Lord Jesus Christ, Of whom the whole family in heaven [*God's family in heaven*] and earth [*God's family on earth*] is named. → *probably referring to angels & believers who are dead. Could also mean all created beings*

Matthew 6:9–10

After this manner therefore pray ye: Our Father which art in heaven, Hallowed be thy name. Thy kingdom come. Thy will be done in earth, as it is in heaven.

1 Samuel 8:1–2

And it came to pass, when Samuel was old, that he made his sons judges over Israel. Now the name of his firstborn was Joel; and the name of his second, Abiah: they were judges in Beer-sheba. [*Samuel's wife is not mentioned in the Bible, but no one supposes his sons had no mother. The importance of family is reflected in the emphasis on order of birth and lineage throughout the Bible.*]

MORMON UNDERSTANDING

Unity and Supremacy

The Godhead consists of three personages:

* God the Father, who is a divine personage with a glorified body of flesh and bones and the supreme member of the Godhead;

not found in the Bible

[handwritten: Jesus is the firstborn among the dead, i.e. the first to rise from the dead — Col. 1:18, Rev.1:5, Rom. 8:25]

- Jesus Christ, who is a divine personage with a glorified body of flesh and bones, the first-born spirit son of God the Father, and the only begotten (mortal) son of God the Father; and

- The Holy Ghost, who is a personage of spirit in the form of a man. *[handwritten: What? Where did this come from?]*

[handwritten: Isa.45:5, Isa.46:9] These three personages are in such perfect harmony and are so divinely unified in purpose and divine love that they are correctly referred to as one God. While the tangible bodies of God the Father *[handwritten: nope]* and his son Jesus Christ resemble those of men, they are glorified and perfected beyond human comprehension.

[handwritten: no biblical basis] God the Father is the creator of all things. All men and women, whether in the premortal, mortal, or postmortal realms, are the spiritual sons and daughters of God the Father.

Free Will *[handwritten: ↳ creation]*

[handwritten: human] God the Father knows intimately each ~~one of his spirit children.~~ He gives to each of them moral agency (free will), the most precious of all spiritual capacities. Exercising this capacity, all men and women choose for themselves in their ~~premortal,~~ mortal, and eternal states. God the Father knows, loves, and teaches each *[handwritten: human]* ~~of his spirit children;~~ however, he does not compel them. *[handwritten: ↳ big difference between believers/unbelievers. Those who refuse to repent will be cut off from God's love when they die,]*

Eternal Progression

[handwritten: no biblical basis] Some of Heavenly Father's spirit children choose to enter mortality, the state through which all who seek eternal progression and increase must pass. Adversity, joy, suffering, and death are encountered in mortality. Heavenly Father causes or allows these and other conditions of mortality to befall his spirit children. His purpose is for men and women, by their own choice, ~~to progress toward perfection.~~ His methods of instruction are often incomprehensible to man. *[handwritten: Not even close.]* *[handwritten: Heb. 10:14 - by one sacrifice He has made perfect those who]*

Eternal Increase *[handwritten: are being made holy.]*

God the Father is the father of all, and, like a righteous and loving father on earth, he is willing to bequeath the power of eternal increase (eternal procreation) to those of his children who are willing to pass through the trials necessary to be become worthy of this power.

[handwritten: Completely made up!]

5

JESUS CHRIST

BIBLICAL TEACHING

Firstborn of All

Jesus Christ is not the firstborn in the flesh (that would be Adam), but he is the "firstborn of every creature," meaning the firstborn spirit offspring of God the Father (Colossians 1:15; Hebrews 1:5–6). Jesus is also the only begotten son of God the Father by the Holy Ghost through Mary. All other men and women on earth, while also spirit offspring of God the Father, are begotten by mortal parents. Jesus is the elder brother among brethren, the spirit offspring of God the Father (Romans 8:29).

Colossians 1:15

Who [*Jesus Christ*] is the image of the invisible God [*the Father*], the (firstborn) of every creature [*every spirit offspring of the Father*].

Refers to Christ's position as heir & Lord. The next verse says all things created by Him, which implies He is not created.

Hebrews 1:5–6

For unto which of the angels said he [*God the Father*] at any time, Thou art my Son, this day have I begotten thee? And again, I *Ps. 89:27* will be to him a Father, and he shall be to me a Son? And again, when he bringeth in the (first begotten) [*Jesus, the firstborn spirit offspring of the Father*] into the world [*into the flesh, through Mary*], he saith, And let all the angels of God worship him. *Same as firstborn. Since Jesus is firstborn among the dead (Col 1:18; Rev 1:5), it is possible that every*

Romans 8:29 reference to Him as firstborn/begotten is referring to

For whom he did foreknow, he also did predestinate to be con- *His resurrection* formed to the image of his Son, that he might be the firstborn among many brethren. *definitely referring to His resurrection & the promise that all believers will be raised w/ new, glorified bodies (1 Cor. 15:20;42-44)*

37

Creator of Worlds

God the Father is the one supreme being and creator of all things; however, God the Son (Jesus Christ), acting on direction from and in perfect harmony with the Father, created the earth and worlds without end (Colossians 1:16; Hebrews 1:2).

Colossians 1:14–16

Who [*God the Father*] hath delivered us from the power of darkness, and hath translated us into the kingdom of his dear Son [*Jesus*]:

In whom we have redemption through his blood, even the forgiveness of sins: Who [*Jesus*] is the image of the invisible God [*the Father*], the firstborn of every creature [*Jesus, the firstborn spirit of the Father*]: For by him [*Jesus, the Father's delegate*] were all things created, that are in heaven, and that are in earth, visible and invisible, whether they be thrones, or dominions, or principalities, or powers: all things were created by him, and for him.

discussed before ↗

Hebrews 1:2

Hath in these last days spoken unto us by his Son, whom he hath appointed heir of all things, by whom also he made the worlds.

God of the Old Testament

As explained in the chapter on Adam and Eve, God the Father limited his direct communication with man after the Fall of Adam. He delegated the bulk of such communication to Jesus Christ.

I don't know enough about this

This delegation is first evidenced by the abrupt change in terminology from "Lord God" (God the Father) in chapters 1, 2, and 3 of Genesis to "Lord" (Jesus Christ) only in chapter 4. This change is coincident with the expulsion of Adam and Eve from the Garden. "Lord" denotes Jesus Christ when the term *God* does not immediately follow. (See chapter on Adam and Eve.)

In various ways and in various contexts, the Old Testament gives evidence that God the Son is the God most frequently referred to in that testament:

- Old Testament passages refer to God as the Savior and Redeemer (See Isaiah 43:3; 45:21–22; 49:26; 60:16; 63:16; Hosea 13:4);
- Old Testament passages use atonement imagery in

reference to God (see Isaiah 43:25; 50:6) and tell of the coming of Christ (Malachi 3:1);

- Old Testament passages use the term *Jehovah* to refer to God (see Genesis 22:14; Exodus 6:2–3; Psalm 83:18; Isaiah 12:2; and Isaiah 26:4); and
- Old Testament passages report that Jesus, God the Son, spoke about God the Father as separate from himself (see Exodus 34:14).

Paul links Jesus to Moses (see Hebrews 11:24–26; 1 Corinthians 10:9). Finally, Jesus plainly declares his place in Old Testament events when he declares, "Verily, verily, I say unto you, Before Abraham was, I am" (see John 8:58).

Mortal Son of the Father

The conception of Jesus was accomplished by the Holy Ghost overshadowing Mary (Luke 1:35; Matthew 1:20, 23). Jesus thus became the only begotten son of God the Father (John 1:14; John 3:16). "Begotten" in this context means "born in the flesh."

Luke 1:35

And the angel answered and said unto her [*Mary*], The Holy Ghost shall come upon thee, and the power of the Highest shall overshadow thee: therefore also that holy thing which shall be born of thee shall be called the Son of God.

Matthew 1:20, 23

But while he thought on these things, behold, the angel of the Lord appeared unto him in a dream, saying, Joseph, thou son of David, fear not to take unto thee Mary thy wife: for that which is conceived in her is of the Holy Ghost. . . . Behold, a virgin shall be with child, and shall bring forth a son, and they shall call his name Emmanuel, which being interpreted is, God with us.

John 1:14

And the Word was made flesh [*reinforcing Jesus as the only begotten*], and dwelt among us, (and we beheld his glory, the glory as of the only begotten of the Father,) full of grace and truth.

John 3:16

> Only human besides Adam created w/o an earthly father.

For God so loved the world, that he gave his only begotten Son, that whosoever believeth in him should not perish, but have everlasting life.

The Atoner

The ancient Israelites were given the law of the atonement as a similitude of Christ's sacrifice to come (Exodus 29:33, 36–37). Jesus atoned for the sins of all humankind. The Atonement of Christ eradicates the spiritual effects of sin and with repentance enables full reconciliation with God the Father (Romans 5:10–11). God the Son was perfect in every way, the unspotted sacrificial lamb, and thus the only one capable of performing the infinite Atonement (1 Peter 1:19).

The Atonement began in the Garden of Gethsemane, where Jesus took upon him the sins of the world and suffered pain "even unto death." His sweat became as drops of blood, and he begged God the Father, if it was the Father's will, to allow him to forgo the agony of the Atonement (Matthew 26:38–39; Mark 14:34–36). But Jesus moved forward despite his fears and was ministered to by an angel (Luke 22:42–44).

Jesus completed the Atonement by dying on the cross (John 19:17–18; Matthew 27:33, 35, 46, 50; Mark 15:22, 25, 34, 37; Luke 23:33, 46).

Where thousands throughout history have been crucified, only one of them was both God and man. Only one went to his death voluntarily to atone for the sins of the world.

Exodus 29:33, 36–37

And they shall eat those things wherewith the atonement was made, to consecrate and to sanctify them: but a stranger shall not eat thereof, because they are holy. . . . And thou shalt offer every day a bullock for a sin offering for atonement: and thou shalt cleanse the altar, when thou hast made an atonement for it, and thou shalt anoint it, to sanctify it. Seven days thou shalt make an atonement for the altar, and sanctify it; and it shall be an altar most holy: whatsoever toucheth the altar shall be holy [*One of the many Old Testament passages mentioning an atonement—a similitude of the Atonement of Jesus Christ that would come in the meridian of time*].

Romans 5:10–11

For if, when we were enemies, we were reconciled to God by the death of his Son, much more, being reconciled, we shall be saved by his life. And not only so, but we also joy in God through our Lord Jesus Christ, by whom we have now received the atonement.

1 Peter 1:19

But with the precious blood of Christ, as of a lamb without blemish and without spot:

Matthew 26:38–39 (see also Mark 14:34–36)

Then saith he unto them, My soul is exceeding sorrowful, even unto death: tarry ye here, and watch with me. And he went a little further, and fell on his face, and prayed, saying, O my Father, if it be possible, let this cup pass from me: nevertheless not as I will, but as thou wilt.

Luke 22:42–44

[*Jesus speaking*] Saying, Father, if thou be willing, remove this cup from me: nevertheless not my will, but thine, be done. And there appeared an angel unto him from heaven, strengthening him. And being in an agony he prayed more earnestly: and his sweat was as it were great drops of blood falling down to the ground.

John 19:17–18

And he bearing his cross went forth into a place called the place of a skull, which is called in the Hebrew Golgotha: Where they crucified him.

Matthew 27:33, 35, 46, 50 (see also Mark 15:22, 25, 34, 37)

And when they were come unto a place called Golgotha, that is to say, a place of a skull. . . . And they crucified him. . . . And about the ninth hour Jesus cried with a loud voice, saying, Eli, Eli, lama sabachthani? that is to say, My God, my God, why hast thou forsaken me? . . . Jesus, when he had cried again with a loud voice, yielded up the ghost.

Luke 23:33, 46

And when they were come to the place, which is called Calvary, there they crucified him. . . . And when Jesus had cried with a loud voice, he said, Father, into thy hands I commend my spirit: and having said thus, he gave up the ghost.

The Resurrected

Three days after his death, Jesus was resurrected through an integrated physical and spiritual process that is beyond human comprehension (Mark 16:6). The spirit of Jesus was reunited with his body in perfection and glory. Jesus showed his disciples his glorified physical body, but they feared he was a ghost (a spirit). He told them that a spirit did not have flesh and bones as he did, and he invited them to touch him to confirm this (Mark 16:6, 9, 12, 14; Luke 24:36–40). To further prove the resurrection of his physical body, Jesus ate a meal with his apostles (Luke 24:41–43) and declared that he would drink the fruit of the vine in his Father's kingdom (Mark 14:25). After his Ascension to God the Father (Acts 1:9–11), Jesus returned and revealed his resurrected physical body to a chosen few (Acts 7:55–56).

Mark 16:6, 9, 12, 14

[*An angel speaking*] And he saith unto them, Be not affrighted: Ye seek Jesus of Nazareth, which was crucified: he is risen; he is not here: behold the place where they laid him. Now when Jesus was risen early the first day of the week, he appeared first to Mary Magdalene, out of whom he had cast seven devils. . . . After that he appeared in another form unto two of them, as they walked, and went into the country . . . Afterward he appeared unto the eleven as they sat at meat, and upbraided them with their unbelief and hardness of heart, because they believed not them which had seen him after he was risen.

Luke 24:36–40

And as they [*the apostles*] thus spake, Jesus himself stood in the midst of them, and saith unto them, peace be unto you. But they were terrified and affrighted, and supposed that they had seen a spirit. And he said unto them, Why are ye troubled? and why do thoughts arise in your hearts? Behold my hands and my feet, that it is I myself: handle me, and see; for a spirit hath not flesh and bones, as ye see me have. And when he had thus spoken, he shewed them his hands and his feet.

Luke 24:41-43

And while they yet believed not for joy, and wondered, he said unto them, Have ye here any meat? And they gave him a piece of a broiled fish, and of an honeycomb. And he took it, and did eat before them.

Mark 14:25

Verily I say unto you, I will drink no more of the fruit of the vine, until that day that I drink it new in the kingdom of God.

Acts 1:9–11

And when he [*Jesus*] had spoken these things, while they beheld, he was taken up; and a cloud received him out of their sight. And while they looked stedfastly toward heaven as he went up, behold, two men stood by them in white apparel; Which also said, Ye men of Galilee, why stand ye gazing up into heaven? this same Jesus, which is taken up from you into heaven, shall so come in like manner as ye have seen him go into heaven.

Acts 7:55–56

But he [*Stephen*], being full of the Holy Ghost, looked up sted-fastly into heaven, and saw the glory of God, and Jesus standing [*a* Not *physical body "stands"*] on the right hand of [*in a physical position to* necessarily, *the right of*] God [*in a physical body with right and left sides*], And said, Could be Behold, I see the heavens opened, and the Son of man standing on Shekinah the right hand of God. glory.

The Millennial King

Jesus will come again to rule and reign on the earth in what is referred to as the Second Coming (Isaiah 11:11; Hebrews 9:28). He will return the same way he departed: in all glory and splendor (Revelation 1:7).

No man knows when the Second Coming will take place (1 Thessalonians 5:2), not even Jesus. Only the Father knows (Mark 13:32). The Second Coming of Jesus is described as both great and terrible (2 Peter 3:10–13)—great in that the faithful will reign with Christ during the Millennium, and terrible for those who are unprepared at his coming.

Isaiah 11:11

And it shall come to pass in that day, that the Lord shall set his hand again the second time to recover the remnant of his people, which shall be left, from Assyria, and from Egypt, and from Path-ros, and from Cush, and from Elam, and from Shinar, and from Hamath, and from the islands of the sea.

Hebrews 9:28

So Christ was once offered to bear the sins of many; and unto them that look for him shall he appear the second time without sin unto salvation.

Revelation 1:7

Behold, he cometh with clouds; and every eye shall see him, and they also which pierced him: and all kindreds of the earth shall wail because of him. Even so, Amen.

1 Thessalonians 5:2

For yourselves know perfectly that the day of the Lord so cometh as a thief in the night.

Mark 13:32

But of that day and that hour knoweth no man, no, not the angels which are in heaven, neither the Son, but the Father.

2 Peter 3:10–13

But the day of the Lord will come as a thief in the night; in the which the heavens shall pass away with a great noise, and the elements shall melt with fervent heat, the earth also and the works that are therein shall be burned up. Seeing then that all these things shall be dissolved, what manner of persons ought ye to be in all holy conversation and godliness, Looking for and hasting unto the coming of the day of God, wherein the heavens being on fire shall be dissolved, and the elements shall melt with fervent heat? Nevertheless we, according to his promise, look for new heavens and a new earth, wherein dwelleth righteousness.

Man of Many Names

Jesus is called Savior, Redeemer, and the Son of God in the Bible. He also shares names that are usually reserved for the Father. For example, Jesus is called Everlasting Father, Immanuel, and Mighty God in the Bible.

The choice of names or labels for Jesus is usually based on delegation: When Jesus acts for the Father, he may be called "father," just as the copilot of an aircraft is called the "pilot" whenever he is at the controls, whether or not he is the senior officer. Names, then, can also signify function or esteem.

Here are some of the names for Jesus:

Alpha and Omega, Almighty
(Revelation 1:8)
Bread of Life (John 6:35)
The Bright and Morning Star
(Revelation 22:16)
Chief Corner Stone
(Ephesians 2:20)
Christ (Matthew 16:16)
Counsellor, the Mighty God,
the Everlasting Father, the
Prince of Peace (Isaiah 9:6)
Deliverer (Romans 11:26)

Good Shepherd (John 10:11)
Head of the Church
(Ephesians 5:23)
The Holy One (Acts 3:14)
Immanuel (Isaiah 7:14)
Jehovah (Exodus 6:3)
King of Kings, Lord of Lords
(Revelation 19:16)
The Lamb of God (John 1:29)
Light of the World (John 8:12)
Lion of the Tribe of Judah
(Revelation 5:5)

Lord (Matthew 22:43–44)

Master (Mark 5:35)

Mediator (1 Timothy 2:5)

Messiah (Messias)
  (John 4:25–26)

Prince of Life (Acts 3:15)

Rabbi (John 1:38)

Redeemer (Titus 2:14)

Savior (Saviour) (Luke 2:11)

Son of David (Matthew 15:22)

Son of God (Mark 1:1)

Son of Man (Matthew 8:20)

The Way, the Truth, and the
  Life (John 14:6)

The Word (John 1:1)

The Word of God
  (Revelation 19:13)

MORMON UNDERSTANDING

Plan of Salvation

The mission of Jesus Christ—his role in the Creation, his role in the salvation of mankind, and his role in the Millennium and the final judgment—was ordained in the premortal realm, long before Jesus came to the earth.

God the Father's plan of salvation provided the opportunity for all his spirit offspring to choose to leave him and their premortal existence, come to the earth, and take on bodies of flesh and bone. The plan anticipated that the first man and woman, Adam and Eve, would leave the Garden of Eden and make themselves subject to the joys and sorrows of mortality, including procreation and death. *[No biblical basis]* *[Why is Jesus any better than the other Spirit children?]*

Finally, the plan called for Jesus Christ, the firstborn spirit child of Heavenly Father, to come to the earth, to be born to the Virgin Mary as the only begotten (born in the flesh) son of Heavenly Father, and to suffer and die for the redemption of mankind. Jesus knowingly and willingly accepted this mission despite the suffering he knew he would endure. *[Why must his birth be different?]*

Jesus is the literal savior of all mankind. Without his Atonement (his suffering in the Garden of Gethsemane, his death on the cross, and his resurrection), no man or woman could return from mortality to the presence of God the Father in heaven. *[Why not? What would happen to them?]*

Firstborn of All

Jesus Christ is the firstborn of all creation, the first spirit child born to Heavenly Father in the premortal existence. The Father delegated to Jesus Christ the task of creating the world. Jesus, also by delegation, was the God of the Old Testament before coming to the earth in the flesh to be the savior of mankind.

Born of a Virgin

The spirit of the Holy Ghost came upon Mary and the power of God overshadowed her, and Jesus was born of the Virgin Mary. Through God his father, Jesus, the "only begotten son of God" (John 3:18) retained his divinity; from his human mother he inherited mortality.

Although little is known about his youth, we know Jesus "grew and waxed strong in spirit, filled with wisdom" (Luke 2:40), and at twelve years old, he had knowledge of his divine mission (Luke 2:46–49).

Public Ministry

At about thirty years of age, Jesus was baptized "to fulfill all righteousness" (Matthew 3:15). After his baptism, Jesus fasted in the wilderness for forty days. During this fast, Satan tempted Jesus. All of this was to prepare Jesus to begin his public ministry.

During his public ministry, Christ set an example of service, performed a variety of stirring miracles, established his church, and taught the gospel to all who would hear.

Although he declared himself to be "the way, the truth, and the life" (John 14:6), Jesus always referred deferentially to God the Father. Jesus proclaimed, "I came down from heaven, not to do mine own will, but the will of him that sent me" (John 6:38). Jesus said it was the will of his father "that every one which seeth the Son, and believeth on him, may have everlasting life: and I will raise him up at the last day" (John 6:40).

The Atonement

At the end of his public ministry, Jesus went into the garden of Gethsemane, and there took upon himself the sins of every human who has ever lived or will ever live on the earth.

It was there that Jesus endured what no other mortal could endure, saying, "My soul is exceeding sorrowful unto death" (Mark 14:34).

The pain Jesus suffered in the garden was beyond what is humanly imaginable. Though he was the very Son of God, the creator of worlds, Jesus came to a moment in which he "fell on his face, and prayed, saying, O my Father, if it be possible, let this cup pass from me: nevertheless not as I will, but as thou wilt" (Matthew 26:39).

Significant in this prayer is Christ's expression of unwavering deference and loyalty to the Father—and to Christ's role as savior: The deferential conditions, "if it be possible" and "not as I will, but as thou wilt," surround the request and are clearly superior to it. There was a job to be done. Jesus was the only one who could do it. How it was to be done was left to the Father.

After enduring the suffering of Gethsemane, Jesus allowed himself to be taken by the Pharisees and the Romans, physically and verbally brutalized, and crucified on the hill of Calvary.

Jesus was both God and man. He knew this. Unlike other men, he remembered clearly having been with his Heavenly Father in the premortal realm. Throughout his ministry, he testified of his Heavenly Father being with him, supporting him: "The words that I speak unto you I speak not of myself: but the Father that dwelleth in me, he doeth the works" (John 14:10).

Therefore, Jesus—alone among all men—knew fully and could suffer fully in the brief interval of separation from the comforting spirit of the Father. In that moment, at his ninth hour upon the cross, Jesus sensed what it was like to die a spiritual death, to be separated from God. In that ultimate agony, he cried out with a loud voice, "My God, my God, why hast thou forsaken me?" (Matthew 27:46).

There could be no greater suffering. Voluntarily confined in a dying human body and fully sensing what it was like to be separated from the divine, Jesus completed his mission.

God the Father accepted Jesus' suffering on the cross: "At-one-ment" between God the Father and every man and woman born into mortality was achieved.

Death and Resurrection

The body of Jesus was placed in a sealed tomb. During the three days before his Resurrection, his spirit entered the spirit world to organize and commence the teaching of his gospel to those who had died before him and would die in the future without the gospel (1 Peter 3:18–20). Reading into passage

Most likely, passage means Noah spoke by the same spirit to the people of his time, but they were disobedient + their spirits are now in prison.

After three days, Jesus was resurrected. His spirit and his body were reunited in a perfection and glory no human could comprehend. Through the fulfillment of his mission, Jesus made it possible for every man and woman to be resurrected into immortality. He gave every person who accepts the Atonement the opportunity to be saved from spiritual death.

Following his Resurrection, Jesus appeared to many individuals and groups, including his apostles in Jerusalem and people in the Americas,

not in the Bible

Gentiles, not Americans

who were his "other sheep" (John 10:16). He taught and strengthened those in need.

The Ascension

Following this brief period on earth after his Resurrection, Jesus ascended into heaven and now sits at the right hand of God the Father, serving him as he has from the beginning. Jesus Christ will come again in fulfillment of scriptural prophecies, will reign in righteousness during the Millennium, and will oversee the final judgment.

❧ 6 ❧

THE HOLY GHOST

BIBLICAL TEACHING

Personage of Spirit

The Holy Ghost is a personage of spirit. Unlike the other two personages of the Godhead, he does not occupy a glorified physical body; however, he can manifest himself in various ways, including appearing in the form of a dove (Luke 3:21–22). The Holy Ghost communicates directly, spirit-to-spirit, with the spirits of men and women, according to their worthiness and his divine will (Acts 13:2; 15:28).

Luke 3:21–22

> Now when all the people were baptized, it came to pass, that Jesus also being baptized, and praying, the heaven was opened, And the Holy Ghost descended in a bodily shape like a dove upon him, and a voice [*Heavenly Father's voice*] came from heaven, which said, Thou art my beloved Son; in thee I am well pleased.

Acts 13:2

> As they ministered to the Lord, and fasted, the Holy Ghost [*invisible, yet present*] said, Separate me Barnabas and Saul for the work whereunto I have called them.

Acts 15:28

> For it seemed good to the Holy Ghost [*an objective entity, a personage of spirit*], and to us, to lay upon you no greater burden than these necessary things.

Spirit of Many Names

There are many names or titles given to the Holy Ghost in the Bible. They range from the simple, "the Spirit," to the complex, "the Spirit of Knowledge and of the Fear of the Lord." Many of the names associated with the Holy Ghost incorporate the names of God the Father and Jesus Christ. This naming reflects the divine unity of the individual members of the Godhead.

Here are some Bible passages where different names and titles are used for the Holy Ghost:

The Comforter (John 14:26)

The Eternal Spirit (Hebrews 9:14)

The Holy Spirit (Luke 11:13)

The Holy Spirit of Promise (Ephesians 1:13)

The Spirit (Romans 8:16)

The Spirit of Christ (Romans 8:9)

The Spirit of Glory and of God (1 Peter 4:14)

The Spirit of God (Genesis 1:2)

The Spirit of Grace (Hebrews 10:29)

The Spirit of His Son (Galatians 4:6)

The Spirit of Holiness (Romans 1:4)

The Spirit of Judgment and the

Spirit of Burning (Isaiah 4:4)

The Spirit of Life (Romans 8:2)

The Spirit of the Lord (Acts 5:9)

The Spirit of the Lord God (Isaiah 61:1)

The Spirit of the Oil of Gladness (Hebrews 1:9)

The Spirit of Truth (John 14:17)

The Spirit of Wisdom and Understanding, the Spirit of Counsel and Might, and the Spirit of Knowledge and of the Fear of the Lord (Isaiah 11:2)

The Spirit of Your Father (Matthew 10:20)

The Testifier

Before Jesus ascended to his Father, he assured the apostles that the Holy Ghost (the Spirit of Truth) would be sent to them and would testify of him (John 15:26). The Holy Ghost, who proceeds from the Father, gave Peter his testimony of Jesus being the Christ (Matthew 16:16–17). While the children of God can witness under the influence of the Holy Ghost that Jesus is the Christ, it is the Holy Ghost alone who testifies of the divinity of Jesus Christ to the hearts of men (1 Corinthians 12:3, 11).

John 15:26

But when the Comforter is come, whom I will send unto you from the Father, even the Spirit of truth, which proceedeth from the Father, he shall testify of me.

Matthew 16:16–17

> And Simon Peter answered and said, Thou art the Christ, the Son of the living God. And Jesus answered and said unto him, Blessed art thou, Simon Barjona: for flesh and blood hath not revealed it unto thee, but my Father which is in heaven. [*Jesus praises Peter for listening to Spirit, who is not flesh and blood, and hearing through the Spirit the message of the Father.*]

1 Corinthians 12:3, 11

> Wherefore I give you to understand, that no man speaking by the Spirit of God calleth Jesus accursed: and that no man can say that Jesus is the Lord, but by the Holy Ghost . . . But all these worketh that one and the selfsame Spirit, dividing to every man severally as he will.

The Divine Communicator

The Holy Ghost is the primary channel from which divine communication flows. The Holy Ghost is the great teacher (John 14:16, 26; Luke 12:12); he reminds men and women of spiritual truths they have been given (John 14:16); he is the revealer of God's most sacred truths (1 Corinthians 2:9–14; Luke 2:25–26); he is the provider of spiritual power (1 Thessalonians 1:5–6); he witnesses on behalf of the Father (Hebrews 10:15); he is the provider of the law (Acts 1:2); and he is the guide and director of the disciples of Christ (Acts 13:4; 16:6).

John 14:16, 26

> And I will pray the Father, and he shall give you another Comforter, that he may abide with you for ever . . . But the Comforter, which is the Holy Ghost, whom the Father will send in my name, he shall teach you all things [*the Holy Ghost teaches*], and bring all things to your remembrance [*the Holy Ghost helps man remember important spiritual truths*], whatsoever I have said unto you.

Luke 12:12

> For the Holy Ghost shall teach you in the same hour what ye ought to say.

1 Corinthians 2:9–14

> But as it is written, Eye hath not seen, nor ear heard, neither have entered into the heart of man, the things which God hath prepared for them that love him. But God hath revealed them unto us by his Spirit [*the Holy Ghost*]: for the Spirit searcheth all things, yea,

the deep things of God. For what man knoweth the things of a man, save the spirit of man which is in him? even so the things of God knoweth no man, but the Spirit of God. Now we have received, not the spirit of the world, but the spirit which is of God; that we might know the things that are freely given to us of God. Which things also we speak, not in the words which man's wisdom teacheth, but which the Holy Ghost teacheth; comparing spiritual things with spiritual. But the natural man receiveth not the things of the Spirit of God: for they are foolishness unto him: neither can he know them, because they are spiritually discerned.

Luke 2:25–26

And, behold, there was a man in Jerusalem, whose name was Simeon; and the same man was just and devout, waiting for the consolation of Israel: and the Holy Ghost was upon him. And it was revealed unto him by the Holy Ghost, that he should not see death, before he had seen the Lord's Christ.

1 Thessalonians 1:5–6

For our gospel came not unto you in word only, but also in power, and in the Holy Ghost, and in much assurance [*the Holy Ghost provides power and assurance*]; as ye know what manner of men we were among you for your sake. And ye became followers of us, and of the Lord, having received the word in much affliction, with joy of the Holy Ghost. [*The Holy Ghost delivers the word of God.*] Not what's being said, they received the word from the apostles with joy. Their joy was from the Holy Spirit.

Hebrews 10:15

Whereof the Holy Ghost also is a witness to us: for after that he had said before. In context, verse is saying the HS in our heart is a witness to us that b/c of Jesus' work, we are perfect in His sight.

Acts 1:2

Until the day in which he was taken up, after that he through the Holy Ghost had given commandments [*God's laws*] unto the apostles whom he had chosen. In this context, just means instructions.

Acts 13:4

So they, being sent forth by the Holy Ghost, departed unto Seleucia; and from thence they sailed to Cyprus.

Acts 16:6

Now when they had gone throughout Phrygia and the region of Galatia, and were forbidden of the Holy Ghost to preach the word in Asia.

[handwritten top margin: Apostles are never distinguished from other Christians as having a special priesthood (1 Peter 2:9)]

Gift of the Holy Ghost

[handwritten: Not true. Eph 1:13]

The gift of the Holy Ghost is given to the faithful by those who hold the (priesthood) authority to do so (Acts 8:18–20). This is done by the laying on of hands (Acts 8:15–17). Although the Holy Ghost is given, he must also be received in faith (Acts 2:38)—even bestowed (or poured) upon those who are desirous to receive him (Acts 10:45). The gift of the Holy Ghost manifests (its) greatest influence when (it) is a constant companion to those who allow the Holy Ghost to dwell within them (1 Corinthians 6:19–20) as they live worthily so their body can be a holy temple for the Holy Ghost (2 Timothy 1:14).

[handwritten left margin: Only given to believers]

[handwritten right margin: Not required Acts 10:44-46]

[handwritten: →? His; —He; All Christians have HS in their heart, no non-Christians have HS in their heart.]

[handwritten below: None of us are worthy (Rom 3:23). We can quench HS — 1 Thess 5:19, Eph 4:30. Acts 8:18-20 but He still lives in every Christian]

Now when the apostles which were at Jerusalem heard that

Acts 8:18–20

And when Simon saw that through laying on of the apostles' hands the Holy Ghost was given, he offered them money, Saying, Give me also this power, that on whomsoever I lay hands, he may receive the Holy Ghost. But Peter said unto him, Thy money perish with thee, because thou hast thought that the gift of God may be purchased with money.

Acts 8:15–17

Now when the apostles which were at Jerusalem heard that Samaria had received the word of God, they sent unto them Peter and John: Who, when they were come down, prayed for them, that they might receive the Holy Ghost: (For as yet he was fallen upon none of them: only they were baptized in the name of the Lord Jesus.) Then laid they their hands on them, and they received the Holy Ghost.

Acts 2:38

Then Peter said unto them, Repent, and be baptized every one of you in the name of Jesus Christ for the remission of sins, and ye shall *receive* the gift of the Holy Ghost [*emphasis added*].

[handwritten right margin: Laying on of hands not required. Repentance & faith required.]

Acts 10:45

And they of the circumcision which believed were astonished, as many as came with Peter, because that on the Gentiles also was poured out the gift of the Holy Ghost.

1 Corinthians 6:19–20

What? know ye not that your body is the temple of the Holy Ghost which is in [*a constant companion with*] you, which ye have of God, and ye are not your own? For ye are bought with a price: therefore glorify God in your body, and in your spirit, which are God's.

2 Timothy 1:14

That good thing which was committed unto thee keep by the Holy Ghost which dwelleth in us.

Gifts of the Spirit

With the Holy Ghost as a constant companion, a man or woman can develop unique gifts of the Spirit. There are spiritual gifts without number which include wisdom, knowledge, faith, healing, the working of miracles, prophecy, discernment, and the speaking in and interpretation of tongues (1 Corinthians 12:4–10). Because Satan is the great deceiver, he offers counterfeit gifts of the spirit that may seem divine in nature but arise from the powers of darkness to fool and entrap the children of God to their destruction (Exodus 7:11–12, 20–22).

1 Corinthians 12:4–10

Now there are diversities of gifts, but the same Spirit. And there are differences of administrations, but the same Lord. And there are diversities of operations, but it is the same God which worketh all in all. But the manifestation of the Spirit is given to every man to profit withal. For to one is given by the Spirit the word of wisdom; to another the word of knowledge by the same Spirit; To another faith by the same Spirit; to another the gifts of healing by the same Spirit; To another the working of miracles; to another prophecy; to another discerning of spirits; to another divers kinds of tongues; to another the interpretation of tongues: But all these worketh that one and the selfsame Spirit, dividing to every man severally as he will.

Exodus 7:11–12, 20–22

Then Pharaoh also called the wise men and the sorcerers: now the magicians of Egypt, they also did in like manner with their enchantments. For they cast down every man his rod, and they became serpents: but Aaron's rod swallowed up their rods. . . . And Moses and Aaron did so, as the Lord commanded; and he lifted up the rod, and smote the waters that were in the river, in the sight of Pharaoh, and in the sight of his servants; and all the waters that were in the river were turned to blood. And the fish that was in the river died; and the river stank, and the Egyptians could not drink of the water of the river; and there was blood throughout all the land of Egypt. And the magicians of Egypt did so with their enchantments: and Pharaoh's heart was hardened.

The Unforgiveable Sin

Insulting deity, showing a lack of reverence for sacred things, or falsely claiming to posses the attributes of deity is blasphemy. Jesus said those who blaspheme against him will be forgiven, but those who blaspheme against the Holy Ghost will not be forgiven for all eternity (Matthew 12:31–32). Paul warned that those who know the truth (are partakers of the Holy Ghost) but rebel against it cannot be "renew[ed] . . . again" (Hebrews 6:4–6).

Matthew 12:31–32

Wherefore I say unto you, All manner of sin and blasphemy shall be forgiven unto men: but the blasphemy against the Holy Ghost shall not be forgiven unto men. And whosoever speaketh a word against the Son of man, it shall be forgiven him: but whosoever speaketh against the Holy Ghost, it shall not be forgiven him, neither in this world, neither in the world to come.

what do Mormons think will happen to such a person in the world to come?

Hebrews 6:4–6

For it is impossible for those who were once enlightened, and have tasted of the heavenly gift, and were made partakers of the Holy Ghost, And have tasted the good word of God, and the powers of the world to come, If they shall fall away, to renew them again unto repentance; seeing they crucify to themselves the Son of God afresh, and put him to an open shame.

There is debate over whether this is about Christians or non.

MORMON UNDERSTANDING

Personage of the Godhead

The Holy Ghost is one of the three personages (Father, Son, and Holy Ghost) who constitute the Godhead. He is referred to variously as the Comforter, the Holy Spirit, the Spirit of God, the Spirit of the Lord, or simply the Spirit.

The Holy Ghost is a member of the Godhead (1 John 5:7). He is a spirit that has the form and likeness of a man. He can be in only one place at a time, but his influence can be everywhere at the same time. The Holy Ghost is our Heavenly Father's messenger and is a special gift to us. The mission of the Holy Ghost is to bear witness of the Father and the Son and of the truth of all things.[1]

What? No biblical basis

Doesn't make sense bc He is in every believer

The Comforter

Before his departure from the earth, Jesus promised that the Holy

Ghost would come as a comforter to the faithful. The Holy Ghost testifies of all truth. He gives instruction, divine revelation, and loving support. He whispers comfort and gives the power of discernment, teaches according to the will of Heavenly Father, and guides men and women according to the plan of salvation.

Gift of the Holy Ghost

The Holy Ghost may give guidance and comfort to any man or woman he chooses; however, the gift of the Holy Ghost—his constant companionship—is available only to those who have been baptized and confirmed in The Church of Jesus Christ of Latter-day Saints by the authority of the priesthood of God. To enjoy the benefits of this companionship, men and women must exercise faith, live worthily, maintain a sincere desire to receive guidance, and learn to feel and heed the promptings of the Holy Ghost.

[handwritten note in margin: No biblical basis]

In the ordinance of confirmation, the gift of the Holy Ghost is given through the laying on of hands by men who hold the Melchizedek Priesthood. Confirmation can take place immediately following baptism, later the same day, or a few days after. The gift of the Holy Ghost brings peace to the souls of all who accept it. By this gift, men and women may be granted a new understanding of the deep things of God and the ability to use the gifts of the Spirit.

Gifts of the Spirit

The Gifts of the Spirit include:

> The Gift of Tongues; the Gift of Interpretation of Tongues; the Gift of Translation; the Gift of Wisdom; the Gift of Knowledge; the Gift of Teaching Wisdom and Knowledge; the Gift of Knowing that Jesus Christ Is the Son of God; the Gift of Believing the Testimony of Others; the Gift of Prophecy; the Gift of Healing; the Gift of Working Miracles; and the Gift of Faith.[2]

Every man and woman on earth has one or more of these gifts of the Spirit. It is the duty of human beings to recognize, develop, and use these gifts while in mortality. Satan has his own imitations of these gifts, usually exaggerations, and hopes to use these imitations to deceive the children of God.

[handwritten note above line: Only Christians]

[handwritten note at bottom: Why don't Mormons call themselves Christians? Acts 11:26; 26:28; 1 Cor. 7:15; 1 Peter 4:16; 2 Peter 1:7; Acts 16:1; 1 Cor. 7:39; Rom. 16:7,11]

NOTES

1. *Gospel Principles* (Salt Lake City: Intellectual Reserve, 2009), 32.
2. Ibid., 125–130.

❦ 7 ❧

THE GODHEAD

BIBLICAL TEACHING

According to Paul

The Apostle Paul used the word *Godhead* to warn against idolatry
(Acts 17:29; Romans 1:20–23; Colossians 2:8–9), specifying the idolatry of vain conceit, vain imaginings, and human philosophy as well as
the idolatry of objects. He taught the hierarchy of God the Father, God
the Son, and men and women (1 Corinthians 11:3).

Paul did not deny the supremacy of God the Father, a supremacy
Jesus had repeatedly declared. Rather, Paul saw in Jesus Christ the full
delegated authority of God the Father. Paul's reference to Christ as God
was an affirmation of this authority, not a denial of it.

Acts 17:29

> Forasmuch then as we are the offspring of God, we ought not to
> think that the Godhead is like unto gold, or silver, or stone, graven
> by art and man's device.

Romans 1:20–23

> For the invisible things of him from the creation of the world
> are clearly seen, being understood by the things that are made, even
> his eternal power and Godhead; so that they are without excuse:
> Because that, when they knew God, they glorified him not as God,
> neither were thankful; but became vain in their imaginations, and
> their foolish heart was darkened. Professing themselves to be wise,
> they became fools,
> And changed the glory of the uncorruptible God into an image

made like to corruptible man, and to birds, and fourfooted beasts, and creeping things.

Colossians 2:8–9

Beware lest any man spoil you through philosophy and vain deceit, after the tradition of men, after the rudiments of the world, and not after Christ. For in him dwelleth all the fulness of the Godhead bodily.

1 Corinthians 11:3

But I would have you know, that the head of every man is Christ; and the head of the woman is the man; and the head of Christ is God [*the Father*].

Three Beings

The authors of the New Testament frequently referred to the Godhead as three individual beings having a perfect unity of love and purpose. Nowhere is God described in this testament as the mystical union of three divine "persons" or personalities in a single divine being.

After the Ascension, the disciples frequently mentioned Jesus and God the Father separately in the same passages (1 Corinthians 8:6; 2 Corinthians 5:19–21; 1 Timothy 1:2; Hebrews 3:1–2; Ephesians 5:5; Romans 8:39; 2 Thessalonians 2:16; Colossians 1:2; 1 John 4:1–2; 2 John 1:9). Biblical authors frequently mention all three members of the Godhead in the same passages (Acts 10:38; 5:30–32; 2 Corinthians 13:14; Jude 1:20–21). Finally, Peter (1 Peter 3:22), Paul (Colossians 3:1; Hebrews 10:10–12), Mark (Mark 16:19), and Luke (Acts 7:55–56) all testified of the Savior being on the "right hand" of God in the heavens.

1 Corinthians 8:6

But to us there is but one God, the Father, of whom are all things, and we in him; and one Lord Jesus Christ, by whom are all things, and we by him.

2 Corinthians 5:19–21

To wit, that God was in Christ, reconciling the world unto himself, not imputing their trespasses unto them; and hath committed unto us the word of reconciliation. Now then we are ambassadors for Christ, as though God did beseech you by us: we pray you in Christ's stead, be ye reconciled to God. For he [*God the Father*] hath made him [*God the Son, Jesus*] to be sin for us, who knew no sin; that we might be made the righteousness of God in him.

1 Timothy 1:2

Unto Timothy, my own son in the faith: Grace, mercy, and peace, from God our Father and [*in addition*] Jesus Christ our Lord. [*A greeting from both the Father and the Son.*]

Hebrews 3:1–2

Wherefore, holy brethren, partakers of the heavenly calling, consider the Apostle and High Priest of our profession, Christ Jesus; Who was faithful to him [*God the Father*] that appointed him [*Jesus, who was faithful to his Heavenly Father*], as also Moses was faithful in all his house.

Ephesians 5:5

For this ye know, that no whoremonger, nor unclean person, nor covetous man, who is an idolater, hath any inheritance in the kingdom of Christ and of God.

Romans 8:39

Nor height, nor depth, nor any other creature, shall be able to separate us from the love of God, which is in Christ Jesus our Lord.

2 Thessalonians 2:16

Now our Lord Jesus Christ himself, and God, even our Father, which hath loved us, and hath given us everlasting consolation and good hope through grace.

Colossians 1:2

To the saints and faithful brethren in Christ which are at Colosse: Grace be unto you, and peace, from God our Father and the Lord Jesus Christ.

1 John 4:1–2

Beloved, believe not every spirit, but try the spirits whether they are of God: because many false prophets are gone out into the world. Hereby know ye the Spirit of God: Every spirit that confesseth that Jesus Christ is come in the flesh is of God.

2 John 1:9

Whosoever transgresseth, and abideth not in the doctrine of

Christ, hath not God. He that abideth in the doctrine of Christ, he hath both the Father and the Son.

Acts 10:38

How God [*the Father*] anointed Jesus of Nazareth with the Holy Ghost and with power: [*God the Father anoints Jesus with the Holy Ghost*] who went about doing good, and healing all that were oppressed of the devil; for God was with him.

Acts 5:30–32

The God of our fathers raised up Jesus, whom ye slew and hanged on a tree. Him [*Jesus*] hath God [*the Father*] exalted with his right hand to be a Prince and a Saviour [*God the Father exalts his son, Jesus Christ*], for to give repentance to Israel, and forgiveness of sins. And we are his witnesses of these things; and so is also [*in addition*] the Holy Ghost [*the Holy Ghost is a separate witness of Christ*], whom God hath given to them that obey him. [*God the Father gives the Holy Ghost to those who obey him.*]

2 Corinthians 13:14

The grace of the Lord Jesus Christ [*God the Son*], and the love of God [*God the Father*], and the communion of the Holy Ghost [*God the Holy Ghost*], be with you all. Amen. [*Three distinct gifts from three distinct personages are offered in blessing.*]

Jude 1:20–21

But ye, beloved, building up yourselves on your most holy faith, praying in the Holy Ghost, Keep yourselves in the love of God [*God the Father*], looking for the mercy of our Lord Jesus Christ [*God the Son*] unto eternal life. [*Seek something different from each of the three distinct members of the Godhead.*]

1 Peter 3:22

Who is gone into heaven, and is on the right hand of God; angels and authorities and powers being made subject unto him.

Colossians 3:1

If ye then be risen with Christ, seek those things which are above, where Christ sitteth on the right hand of God.

Hebrews 10:10–12

By the which will we are sanctified through the offering of the body of Jesus Christ once for all. And every priest standeth daily ministering and offering oftentimes the same sacrifices, which can never take away sins: But this man, after he had offered one sacrifice for sins for ever, sat down on the right hand of God.

Mark 16:19

So then after the Lord had spoken unto them, he was received up into heaven, and sat on the right hand of God.

Acts 7:55–56

But he [*Stephen*], being full of the Holy Ghost, looked up stedfastly into heaven, and saw the glory of God, and Jesus standing on the right hand of God, And said, Behold, I see the heavens opened, and the Son of man standing on the right hand of God.

One God

The oneness shared by the Godhead is beyond all human comprehension. Jesus said of a man and woman who marry, "And they twain shall be one flesh" (Matthew 19:5)—not one flesh physically, but in love, commitment, and covenant. Although such a union in marriage can be close—where husband and wife speak for one another, act for one another, and in all things are one in purpose—they are still individual beings. No less is the individuality of the personages of the Godhead.

This perfect oneness is described by Jesus in the Garden of Gethsemane where he prays to the Father that his disciples would be one just as he (Jesus) and God the Father are one (John 17:11; 17:21–23). Elsewhere in the Bible, Jesus proclaimed that he and the Father were one, that he dwelled in the Father, and the Father dwelled in him (John 10:15, 25, 30, 38; 14:18–20). John later expounded on dwelling within another person without becoming that person (1 John 4:13).

Jesus was with God in the beginning, was and is in perfect purpose with God, and can be called God (John 1:1–2). Jesus revealed how such a union can be achieved in faith and unity. He prayed that mankind would share in this unity to fulfill his purposes on earth and in heaven. God the Father, Jesus Christ, and the Holy Ghost can witness as three individual beings but still maintain a complete and perfect accord as one in purpose (1 John 5:7).

Matthew 19:5

And said, For this cause shall a man leave father and mother, and shall cleave to his wife: and they twain shall be one flesh?

John 17:11

And now I am no more in the world, but these are in the world, and I come to thee. Holy Father, keep through thine own name those whom thou hast given me, that they may be one, as we are.

John 17:21–23

That they all may be one; as thou, Father, art in me, and I in thee, that they also may be one in us [*One in purpose, love, commitment, and covenant—as in a marriage*]: that the world may believe that thou hast sent me. And the glory which thou gavest me I have given them; that they may be one, even as we are one: I in them, and thou in me, that they may be made perfect in one; [*one in purpose, love, commitment, and covenant*] and that the world may know that thou hast sent me, and hast loved them, as thou hast loved me.

John 10:15, 25, 30, 38

As the Father knoweth me, even so know I the Father: and I lay down my life for the sheep. . . . Jesus answered them, I told you, and ye believed not: the works that I do in my Father's name, they bear witness of me. . . . I and my Father are one. . . . But if I do, though ye believe not me, believe the works: that ye may know, and believe, that the Father is in me, and I in him.

John 14:18–20

I will not leave you comfortless: I will come to you. Yet a little while, and the world seeth me no more; but ye see me: because I live, ye shall live also. At that day ye shall know that I am in my Father, and ye in me, and I in you. [*Not one in being, but in purpose, love, commitment, and covenant.*]

1 John 4:13

Hereby know we that we dwell in him, and he in us, because he hath given us of his Spirit. [*Confirming the doctrine of being in purpose by dwelling in one another as Jesus describes in John 17.*]

John 1:1–2

In the beginning was the Word, and the Word was with God, [*God and Jesus Christ were together*] and the Word was God [*one in perfect purpose in the Godhead*]. The same was in the beginning with God.

1 John 5:7

For there are three that bear record in heaven, the Father, the Word, and the Holy Ghost: and these three are one.

The Father, Jesus, and Adam

Jesus Christ was the firstborn spirit offspring of God the Father (Colossians 1:15; Hebrews 1:5–6). Jesus was foreordained to become the mortal son of God (Luke 1:32). God the Father declared that man would be made "in our image" (Genesis 1:26), that is, the image of himself and of Jesus Christ. God the Father declared that Adam would "become as one of us" (Genesis 3:22) after his fall. Speaking through the prophet Isaiah, Jesus proclaimed that God the Father gave him many gifts and supported him in his saving work on behalf of mankind (Isaiah 50:1, 4–5, 7, 9).

Colossians 1:15

Who is the image of the invisible God, the firstborn of every creature.

Hebrews 1:5–6

For unto which of the angels said he at any time, Thou art my Son, this day have I begotten thee? And again, I will be to him a Father, and he shall be to me a Son? And again, when he bringeth in the firstbegotten [*Jesus is the first born spirit of Heavenly Father*] into the world, he saith, And let all the angels of God worship him.

Luke 1:32

He shall be great, and shall be called the Son of the Highest: and the Lord God shall give unto him the throne of his father David.

Genesis 1:26

And God said, Let us [*God the Father and Jesus Christ*] make man in our [*plural*] image, after our [*plural*] likeness.

Genesis 3:22

And the Lord God said, Behold, the man is become as one of us [*God the Father and Jesus Christ*], to know good and evil.

Isaiah 50:1, 4–5, 7, 9

Thus saith the Lord [*Jesus Christ speaking because of the single "Lord" reference*] . . . The Lord God [*God the Father because of the "Lord" plus "God" reference*] hath given me [*Jesus Christ, God the Son*] the tongue of the learned, that I should know how to speak a word in season to him that is weary: he wakeneth morning by morning, he wakeneth mine ear to hear as the learned. The Lord God hath opened mine ear, and I was not rebellious, neither turned away back . . . For the Lord God will help me; therefore shall I not be confounded: therefore have

I set my face like a flint, and I know that I shall not be ashamed. . . .
Behold, the Lord God will help me; who is he that shall condemn me?
lo, they all shall wax old as a garment; the moth shall eat them up.

Jesus Defers to the Father

From an early age, Jesus recognized his role as the only begotten
son of God. Jesus sought to do the Father's will and found favor in the
Father's sight (Luke 2:49; 2:52). Throughout his public ministry, Jesus
acknowledged the Father as his father and frequently reminded his disciples that he was sent by the Father (John 7:28–29; 5:37). Jesus made
it clear that it was the will of the Father that he was fulfilling, not his
own will (John 14:23; Matthew 16:27; 16:17; John 4:34). Jesus repeatedly confirmed that he was the "son of God" (Mark 14:61–62) and
that his father bore witness of him as part of the testimony of two witnesses—Jesus Christ being one witness and his Heavenly Father being
the other (John 8:17–18).

Luke 2:49

> And he said unto them, How is it that ye sought me? wist ye not
> that I must be about my Father's business?

Luke 2:52

> And Jesus increased in wisdom and stature, and in favour with
> God and man.

John 7:28–29

> Then cried Jesus in the temple as he taught, saying, Ye both
> know me, and ye know whence I am: and I am not come of myself,
> but he that sent me is true, whom ye know not. But I know him: for
> I am from him, and he hath sent me. [*God is the Father of Jesus Christ;
> Christ is from God; Christ was sent from God and is there for God the
> Father, not for himself.*]

John 5:37

> And the Father himself, which hath sent me, hath borne witness
> of me. Ye have neither heard his voice at any time, nor seen his shape.
> [*Jesus clarifies that he and the Father are separate personages.*]

John 14:23

> Jesus answered and said unto him, If a man love me, he will
> keep my words: and my Father will love him, and we [*God the Father
> and Jesus Christ*] will come unto him, and make our [*plural*] abode
> with him.

Matthew 16:27

> For the Son of man shall come in the glory of his Father [*bearing not his own glory but that of the Father*] with his angels; and then he shall reward every man according to his works.

Matthew 16:17

> And Jesus answered and said unto him, Blessed art thou, Simon Bar-jona: for flesh and blood hath not revealed it unto thee, but my Father which is in heaven. [*Jesus did not reveal it; the Father revealed it through the Spirit.*]

John 4:34

> Jesus saith unto them, My meat is to do the will of him that sent me, and to finish his work. [*Jesus is the delegate of the Father.*]

Mark 14:61–62

> But he held his peace, and answered nothing. Again the high priest asked him, and said unto him, Art thou the Christ, the Son of the Blessed? And Jesus said, I am [*he is the son of God the Father, a separate being*]: and ye shall see the Son of man [*Jesus or God the Son*] sitting on the right hand of power [*God the Father*], and coming in the clouds of heaven.

John 8:17–18

> It is also written in your law, that the testimony of two men is true. I [*Jesus, God the Son*] am one that bear witness of myself, and the Father [*God the Father*] that sent [delegated to] me beareth witness of me. [*Two "men"—meaning two individual beings bearing witness.*]

Jesus and the Holy Ghost

Jesus Christ spoke of the Holy Ghost with reverence. Before going into the wilderness to fast for forty days and be tempted by Satan, Jesus was "full of the Holy Ghost" (Luke 4:1). Thus it was that Jesus and the Holy Ghost, two personages of the Godhead, endured these trials together. Jesus taught that blasphemy against himself (one personage of the Godhead) could be forgiven, but that blasphemy against the Holy Ghost (a separate and different personage of the Godhead) could not be forgiven in this life or the next (Matthew 12:31–32). Before he ascended into heaven, Jesus told his apostles that the Holy Ghost (the Comforter) would take his place when he left (John 16:7). As long as Jesus was on the earth, there was little need for the Holy Ghost among the children of men (John 7:39).

Luke 4:1

> And Jesus being full of the Holy Ghost [*Jesus was not full of himself, but rather of another personage of the Godhead*] returned from Jordan, and was led by the Spirit into the wilderness. [*Jesus did not lead himself. He was led by another, the Holy Ghost, a separate personage.*]

Matthew 12:31–32

> Wherefore I say unto you, All manner of sin and blasphemy shall be forgiven unto men: but the blasphemy against the Holy Ghost shall not be forgiven unto men. And whosoever speaketh a word against the Son of man [*Jesus, a personage of the Godhead*], it shall be forgiven him: but whosoever speaketh against the Holy Ghost [*a different personage of the Godhead*], it shall not be forgiven him, neither in this world, neither in the world to come.

John 16:7

> Nevertheless I tell you the truth; It is expedient for you that I go away: for if I go not away, the comforter [*the Holy Ghost*] will not come unto you; but if I depart, I will send him unto you. [*When Jesus departs, he will send another to take his place. Jesus is not playing a trick—he is leaving and then coming back in a different form.*]

John 7:39

> But this spake he [*Jesus*] of the Spirit, which they that believe on him should receive: for the Holy Ghost was not yet given; because that Jesus was not yet glorified [*returned to the Father.*]

Together: Father, Son, and Holy Ghost

All three members of the Godhead were present at the baptism of Jesus. When the Savior came out of the water, the Holy Ghost descended in the form of a dove and Heavenly Father spoke from heaven (Mark 1:10–11; Matthew 3:16–17). Jesus spoke of God the Father and the Holy Ghost together (John 14:26; 16:13–15), acknowledging both their divine individuality and their divine unity.

Mark 1:10–11

> And straightway coming up out of the water, he [*Jesus*] saw the heavens opened, and the Spirit [*Jesus saw the Spirit, a separate entity, not an altered form of himself*] like a dove descending upon him: And there came a voice from heaven, saying [*speaking to Jesus*], Thou art my beloved Son, in whom I am well pleased. [*God the Father speaking, the Holy Ghost descending, and Jesus coming out of the water.*]

Matthew 3:16–17

And Jesus, when he was baptized, went up straightway out of the water: and, lo, the heavens were opened unto him, and he saw the Spirit of God descending like a dove, and lighting upon him: And lo a voice from heaven, saying, This is my beloved Son, in whom I am well pleased. [*Three entities acting individually in close cooperation.*]

John 14:26

But the Comforter, which is the Holy Ghost, whom the Father will send in my name [*clear reference to three individual entities*], he shall teach you all things, and bring all things to your remembrance, whatsoever I have said unto you.

John 16:13–15

Howbeit when he, the Spirit of truth [*the Holy Ghost*], is come, he will guide you into all truth: for he shall not speak of himself; but whatsoever he shall hear, that shall he speak: and he will shew you things to come. He shall glorify me [*the Holy Ghost will glorify Christ, not himself*]: for he shall receive of mine, and shall shew it unto you. All things that the Father hath are mine [*Christ received what he has from God the Father*]: therefore said I, that he shall take of mine, and shall shew it unto you.

Jesus Pled with the Father

During the events of the Atonement, Jesus was particularly close to his divine father—and then horribly separated from him. Chapter 17 of John details the great intercessory prayer, where Jesus poured out his heart to God the Father and pled on behalf of the apostles and all believers that they might come to know "the only true God" and Jesus Christ (John 17:3). This was not an internal dialogue. Jesus was imploring another being, not merely some aspect of his own personhood. He was imploring his Heavenly Father.

In the Garden of Gethsemane, Jesus pled with his Heavenly Father—calling him by the intimate "Abba," meaning "father"— asking him if it might be according to the Father's will to "take away this cup from me" (Mark 14:36). Jesus remained in this intimacy with the Father throughout the events leading up to his death on the cross. He pled with his father to forgive those who were crucifying him (Luke 23:24); he cried out in agony to his father when death was imminent (Matthew 27:46); and he commended his spirit into the hands of his father when the work was finished (Luke 23:46).

John 17:3

And this is life eternal, that they might know thee the only true God, and [*in addition to*] Jesus Christ, whom thou hast sent. [*Men and women are to know both God the Father and God the Son, not one or the other or two mystical aspects of a single divine being.*]

Mark 14:36

And he [*Jesus*] said, Abba, Father, [*calling on a separate and superior divine being*] all things are possible unto thee; take away this cup from me: nevertheless not what I [*Jesus, God the Son*] will, but what thou [*God the Father, a separate and superior divine being*] wilt.

Luke 23:34

Then said Jesus, Father, [*calling on a separate divine being*] forgive them; for they know not what they do. And they parted his raiment, and cast lots.

Matthew 27:46

And about the ninth hour Jesus cried with a loud voice, saying, Eli, Eli, lama sabachthani? That is to say, My God, my God, why hast thou forsaken me? [*calling out to a separate and superior divine being, his God, God the Father*].

Luke 23:46

And when Jesus had cried with a loud voice, he said, Father, into thy hands I commend my spirit [*submitting himself to a separate and superior personage of the Godhead*]: and having said thus, he gave up the ghost.

The Personage of Jesus

Paul, Luke, and Peter all referred repeatedly to Jesus as being the son of God the Father (Galatians 4:4, 6; Ephesians 1:2–3; 3:14; Acts 3:13; 1 Peter 5:10). Jesus is described as the image of God (2 Corinthians 4:4), who was made manifest of God in the flesh (1 Timothy 3:16) to be the one and only mediator between God (the Father) and man (1 Timothy 2:5).

Galatians 4:4, 6

But when the fulness of the time was come, God sent forth his Son, made of a woman, made under the law. . . . And because ye are sons, God hath sent forth the Spirit of his Son into your hearts, crying, Abba, Father.

Ephesians 1:2–3

Grace be to you, and peace, from God our Father, and from the Lord Jesus Christ. Blessed be the God and Father of our Lord Jesus Christ, who hath blessed us with all spiritual blessings in heavenly places in Christ.

Ephesians 3:14

For this cause I bow my knees unto the Father of our Lord Jesus Christ.

Acts 3:13

The God of Abraham, and of Isaac, and of Jacob, the God of our fathers, hath glorified his Son Jesus; whom ye delivered up, and denied him in the presence of Pilate, when he [*Pilate*] was determined to let him go.

1 Peter 5:10

But the God of all grace, who hath called us unto his eternal glory by Christ Jesus, [*God the Father is the God of all grace, the Father of Jesus Christ*] after that ye have suffered a while, make you perfect, stablish, strengthen, settle you.

2 Corinthians 4:4

In whom the god of this world hath blinded the minds of them which believe not, lest the flight of the glorious gospel of Christ, who is the image of [*resembles*] God [*the Father*], should shine unto them.

1 Timothy 3:16

And without controversy great is the mystery of godliness: God [*the Son*] was manifest in the flesh [*mortal flesh*], justified in the Spirit, seen of angels, preached unto the Gentiles, believed on in the world, received up into glory.

1 Timothy 2:5

For there is one God, and one mediator between God and men, the man Christ Jesus.

Father and Son Differ in Knowledge

Although being divinely one in purpose, God the Father has

understanding and knowledge that his son Jesus does not (Mark 13:32), at least while Jesus occupied the mortal realm.

Mark 13:32

> [*Jesus speaking*] But of that day and that hour knoweth no man, no, not the angels which are in heaven, neither the Son [*Jesus*], but the Father.

Father and Son Differ in Power and Dominion

Jesus said during his public ministry that his father (God the Father) had greater power and dominion than he (John 10:29; John 13:16). The doctrine that Jesus taught was that of his father (John 7:16). Jesus deferred to God the Father in matters of heavenly decision making (Matthew 20:23) and accepted commandments given by his father (John 10:18). Jesus ultimately gained all that his father had (John 5:26–27; 17:22), but he still acted upon the will of his father in all things (John 5:19, 21; 5:30), despite having his moral agency to do otherwise.

John 10:29

> My Father, which gave them me, is greater than all; and no man is able to pluck them out of my Father's hand.

John 13:16

> Verily, verily, I [*Jesus*] say unto you, The servant [*Jesus*] is not greater than his lord [*the Father*]; neither he that is sent [*Jesus*] greater than he that sent him [*the Father*].

John 7:16

> Jesus answered them, and said, My doctrine is not mine, but his that sent me.

Matthew 20:23

> And he saith unto them, Ye shall drink indeed of my cup, and be baptized with the baptism that I am baptized with: but to sit on my right hand, and on my left, is not mine to give, but it shall be given to them for whom it is prepared of my Father. [*Jesus must defer to God the Father for this decision.*]

John 10:18

> No man taketh it from me, but I lay it down of myself. I have power to lay it down, and I have power to take it again. This commandment have I received of my Father.

John 5:26–27

 For as the Father [*God the Father*] hath life in himself; so hath he given to the Son [*God the Son*] to have life in himself [*two individual beings: the first, God the Father, superior to the second, God the Son, and giving him life*]; And hath given him authority to execute judgment also, because he is the Son of man. [*God the Father gave Jesus authority.*]

John 17:22

 And the glory which thou [*God the Father*] gavest me [*Jesus, God the Son*] I have given them; that they may be one [*in purpose, commitment, love—not in person or being*], even as [*in the same way as*] we are one [*in purpose, commitment, love—not in person or being*].

John 5:19, 21

 Then answered Jesus and said unto them, Verily, verily, I say unto you, The Son [*Jesus*] can do nothing of himself, but what he seeth the Father do: for what things soever he [*God the Father*] doeth, these also doeth the Son likewise. . . . For as the Father raiseth up the dead, and quickeneth them; even so the Son quickeneth whom he will. [*Christ takes his direction from the Father and will not deviate because they are one in purpose; however, Christ declares that ultimately he can choose for himself.*]

John 5:30

 I [*Jesus*] can of mine own self do nothing: as I hear, I judge: and my judgment is just; because I seek not mine own will, but the will of the Father [*God the Father*] is which hath sent me. [*Christ declares his separateness from and subordination to the Father even as he declares their perfect unity of purpose and commitment. They are one.*]

The Father Is God to the Son

The prophet Micah prophesied that Christ would be born "in the majesty of the name of the Lord his God" (Micah 5:4). Jesus referred to God the Father as God (Luke 18:19; Matthew 19:17; John 17:3), called upon God during his crucifixion (Mark 15:34; Matthew 27:46), and referred to God after his resurrection (John 20:17). Paul then confirms the doctrine of God the Father being the God of Jesus Christ in his letters to the Ephesians (Ephesians 1:17) and the Corinthians (1 Corinthians 11:3).

Within the Godhead, God the Father, Jesus Christ, and the Holy

Ghost are divinely unified. By the delegated authority of the Father, Jesus can stand in the place of God, act for God, and be called God. However, the Bible points out that God the Father is still the God of Jesus, a separate and superior member of the Godhead.

Micah 5:4

And he [*Jesus Christ*] shall stand and feed in the strength of the Lord [*God the Father*], in the majesty of the name of the Lord his God [*God the Father*]; and they [*both Jesus Christ and God the Father*] shall abide: for now shall he [*Jesus*] be great unto the ends of the earth.

Luke 18:19

And Jesus said unto him, Why callest thou me good? none is good, save one, that is, God [*God the Father is Jesus' God*].

Matthew 19:17

And he said unto him, Why callest thou me good? there is none good but one, that is, God [*God the Father*].

John 17:3

And this is life eternal, that they might know thee the only true God, and Jesus Christ, whom thou hast sent.

Mark 15:34 (see also Matthew 27:46)

And at the ninth hour Jesus cried with a loud voice, saying, Eloi, Eloi, lama sabachthani? which is, being interpreted, My God, my God, why hast thou forsaken me?

John 20:17

Jesus saith unto her [*Mary Magdalene*], Touch me not; for I am not yet ascended to my Father: but go to my brethren, and say unto them, I ascend unto my Father, and your Father [*Jesus is our brother and Savior*]; and to my God, and your God [*we share the same God*].

Ephesians 1:17

That the God of our Lord Jesus Christ, the Father of glory, may give unto you the spirit of wisdom and revelation in the knowledge of him.

1 Corinthians 11:3

But I would have you know, that the head of every man is Christ; and the head of the woman is the man; and the head of Christ is God.

MORMON UNDERSTANDING

The Godhead

The Latter-day Saint doctrine of the Godhead can be summarized in a quote from the writings of Gordon B. Hinckley, the late prophet and past president of The Church of Jesus Christ of Latter-day Saints:

> They [*the Godhead*] are distinct beings, but they are one in purpose and effort. They are united as one in bringing to pass the grand, divine plan for the salvation and exaltation of the children of God. In His great, moving prayer in the garden before His betrayal, Christ pleaded with His Father concerning the Apostles, whom He loved, saying: "Neither pray I for these alone, but for them also which shall believe on me through their word; That they all may be one; as thou, Father, art in me, and I in thee, that they also may be one in us" (John 17:20–21). It is that perfect unity between the Father, the Son, and the Holy Ghost that binds these three into the oneness of the divine Godhead.[1]

God the Father, Jesus Christ, and the Holy Ghost are three distinct beings who are one in purpose. Mormons believe that this conception of the Godhead is fully supported by an unencumbered reading of the plain language of the Bible, particularly the words of Jesus himself.

Council of Nicaea

The Roman Emperor Constantine I convened the Council of Nicaea in A.D. 325. This council was the first significant effort of the Christian church to arrive at a consensus on various points of doctrine.

At that time there was widespread dispute about the nature of the Godhead. Many Christians believed then—as Latter-day Saints do today—that the Godhead consisted of three separate personages united in purpose but not in being. For the majority of the council, however, this conception bore an uncomfortable resemblance to the pagan Greek and Roman conception of multiple gods.

The council majority came up with a compromise conception, declaring that there were indeed three "persons"—Father, Son, and Holy Ghost—but that these persons were not separate entities, not persons in the usual sense, but instead persons who were without substance, essence, or individual existence. These newly defined persons combined to form one essence, the "Triune God" (the Trinity).

The Triune God

The Council of Nicaea declared the Triune God in A.D. 325. This declaration became the essence of what is known as the Nicene Creed.

By this declaration, the Council brought unity to the Christian world, protected monotheism from polytheistic encroachment, and gave to the Roman Emperor Constantine the political stability he was seeking. It brought peace on many fronts.

The Nicene doctrine of the Trinity or the Triune God has endured. The vast majority of Christians today subscribe to this dogma.

Latter-day Saints do not.

Mormon Rejection

This Mormon rejection of the Triune-God conception has led many Christians to deny the Christian label of The Church of Jesus Christ of Latter-day Saints. Mormons could reach the reverse conclusion, but they have not—perhaps because of their Eleventh Article of Faith:

> We claim the privilege of worshiping Almighty God according to the dictates of our own conscience, and *allow all men the same privilege, let them worship how, where, or what they may.* [Emphasis added]

The three personages of the Godhead and their individual natures are clearly defined in the Bible: before Christ came to the earth, during Christ's public ministry, through events surrounding the Atonement (the passion) of Christ, and after the Ascension of Christ to the Father.

The Bible is clear that there are differences in knowledge between God the Father and Jesus Christ, differences in power and dominion, differences in the consequences of blasphemy, and differences in the references made by these personages to one another. For example, Jesus refers to Heavenly Father as his "God" on many occasions documented in the Bible. Because of this abundance of unambiguous biblical evidence for the divine individuality of God the Father, Jesus Christ, and the Holy Ghost, Latter-day Saints cannot accept the findings of the Council of Nicaea. This refusal has created a divide, but not one that warrants the conclusion that Mormons are not followers of Christ.

While the divine individuality of the three personages of the Godhead is biblically clear, so also is their divine unity. They are one in purpose. Their divine integration of reason, intention, drive, objective, and other qualities of character and action is beyond human comprehension. Thus, it is fair in the limited coinage of human language to refer to them collectively as one God, and this is done in the Bible, in the Book of Mormon, and other modern scripture. But fairness of reference does not alter the truth of the matter to which reference is made. The Council of Nicaea made a convenient decision, in part to end a distracting theological debate. Latter-day Saints simply believe it was the wrong decision.

Divine Unity

The perfect oneness of the Godhead is defined clearly in John 17. Jesus, praying to Heavenly Father, said, "That they all may be one; as thou, Father, art in me, and I in thee, that they also may be one in us" (John 17:20–21). Jesus Christ is the Son of God. He is the divine redeemer and savior. He is the only begotten of God the Father and the firstborn spirit offspring of the Father. Jesus Christ is in perfect oneness with the Father and sits on his right hand. The Holy Ghost is the third personage of the Godhead. Together they form one divinely unified God over the universe and all things in it.

NOTE

1. Gordon B. Hinckley, "The Father, Son, and Holy Ghost," *Ensign*, Mar. 1998, 2.

8

MARY

BIBLICAL TEACHING

Righteous Woman

The Bible provides no indication of Mary's age when she conceived Jesus. However, given the Jewish customs of the day regarding betrothal, she was probably between fourteen and sixteen when she was visited by an angel and given the news that she would conceive a child who would be the "Son of the Highest" and whose kingdom would have no end (see Luke 1:30–35).

Mary humbly submitted, saying, "Behold, the handmaid of the Lord" (see Luke 1:38). In accepting her role, she faced a whirlwind of community criticism and ridicule, including the justified doubts of her fiancé, Joseph.

Nevertheless, Mary confidently persevered in serving as the vessel of the Savior. While visiting her cousin Elizabeth, Mary bore testimony of Jesus Christ and his celestial commission (See Luke 1:46–55), demonstrating her prophetic faith.

Virgin

The miraculous conception and birth of Jesus to the virgin Mary was prophesied centuries before it occurred (Isaiah 7:14). Through the power of the Holy Ghost in a manner unfathomable to man, Mary became pregnant and bore the only begotten son of God the Father (Luke 1:35). She gave birth to the Savior of the world.

Isaiah 7:14

> Therefore the Lord himself shall give you a sign; Behold, a virgin shall conceive, and bear a son, and shall call his name Immanuel.

Luke 1:35

> And the angel answered and said unto her, The Holy Ghost shall come upon thee, and the power of the Highest shall overshadow thee: therefore also that holy thing which shall be born of thee shall be called the Son of God.

Mother

After the birth of Jesus, Mary had a normal marital relationship according to the Jewish tradition. However, Joseph "knew [had sexual intercourse with] her not until she had brought forth her firstborn son" (Matthew 1:24–25). Mary and Joseph then had other sons and possibly daughters. The sons named in the Bible are James, Joses, Simon, and Judas (Matthew 13:55–56; Mark 6:3).

Both Luke and Mark wrote of an occasion when Mary and her sons and perhaps daughters attempted to come to Jesus but were blocked by the crowd (Luke 8:19–21; Mark 3:31–35). Paul in his letter to the Galatians wrote specifically of James, the brother of Jesus (Galatians 1:19).

Matthew 1:24–25

> Then Joseph being raised from sleep did as the angel of the Lord had bidden him, and took unto him his wife: And knew her not till she had brought forth her firstborn [*"firstborn" implies other children were born later*]: and he called his name Jesus.

Matthew 13:55–56

> Is not this the carpenter's son? is not his mother called Mary? and his brethren, James, and Joses, and Simon, and Judas? And his sisters, are they not all with us? Whence then hath this man all these things?

Mark 6:3

> Is not this the carpenter, the son of Mary, the brother of James, and Joses, and of Juda, and Simon? and are not his sisters here with us? And they were offended at him.

Luke 8:19–21

> Then came to him his mother and his brethren, and could not come at him for the press. And it was told him by certain which said,

Thy mother and thy brethren stand without, desiring to see thee. And he answered and said unto them, My mother and my brethren are these which hear the word of God, and do it.

Mark 3:31–35

There came then his brethren and his mother, and, standing without, sent unto him, calling him. And the multitude sat about him, and they said unto him, Behold, thy mother and thy brethren without seek for thee. And he answered them, saying, Who is my mother, or my brethren? And he looked round about on them which sat about him, and said, Behold my mother and my brethren! For whosoever shall do the will of God, the same is my brother, and my sister, and mother.

Galatians 1:19

But other of the apostles saw I none, save James the Lord's brother. [*While every man could be referenced metaphorically as the "Lord's brother," this reference is specific, especially when added to Matthew 13:55–56 and Mark 6:3, which call out James as the brother of Jesus.*]

MORMON UNDERSTANDING

Mary in the Garden of Eden

The book of Genesis contains the earliest prophetic scriptural reference to Mary. The Lord said to the serpent in the Garden of Eden, "And I will put enmity between thee and the woman, and between thy seed and her seed [*Jesus*]; it [*the enmity, Jesus*] shall bruise thy head, and thou shalt bruise his [*Jesus'*] heel" (Genesis 3:15). The seed of the woman is Jesus, who will bruise the head of the serpent. About seven hundred years before the birth of Christ, the prophet Isaiah prophesied that a virgin would conceive and give birth to a son whose name would be Immanuel, meaning "God with us."

The Visitation

The angel told Mary, "The Holy Ghost shall come upon thee, and the power of the Highest [God the Father] shall overshadow thee: therefore also that holy thing which shall be born of thee shall be called the Son of God" (Luke 1:35).

Aware of the spiritual and temporal consequences, Mary acted in faith on the words of the angel: she agreed to become the virgin mother of Jesus. Thus, God the Father became the father of Jesus, bringing him into mortality through the body of Mary by processes not disclosed in scripture.

Other Children

Mary, with her mortal husband Joseph, had other children after Jesus was born. The Bible makes clear that Jesus was raised among sibling brothers. Their names were James, Joses, Simon, and Judas. While biblical references suggest Mary and Joseph also had daughters, the names of these offspring are not given in the New Testament. This is not surprising—details about women were often omitted from the Bible because of the social norms of the day.

≪ 9 ≫

SCRIPTURE

BIBLICAL TEACHING

Records Should Be Kept

The holy scriptures are the work of inspired authors who have "written for our learning, that we through patience and comfort of the scriptures might have hope" (Romans 15:4). Men have been commanded by the Lord (see Revelation 1:11) to keep records so that the children of men will have a remembrance (see Malachi 3:16) written for the generations to come (see Psalm 102:16–18).

Record Keepers

The Lord directed Moses to keep records (see Exodus 24:4; 34:27; Deuteronomy 31:9). Samuel, Isaiah, John, and the apostles and elders all kept scriptural records (see 1 Samuel 10:25; Isaiah 8:1–2; 30:8; John 21:24; and Acts 15:23, respectively). Jeremiah directed Baruch quite specifically in the keeping of records (see Jeremiah 36:4).

The Stick of Judah

The Lord told Ezekiel to write upon "one stick" the record of the tribe of Judah (the Jews in the Middle East). The stick of Judah is a figurative reference to the Bible (Ezekiel 37:15–16).

The Bible is fundamentally a record of the twelve tribes of Israel, but most specifically the tribe of Judah. Jesus was from the tribe of Judah (Hebrews 7:14).

Ezekiel 37:15–16

The word of the Lord came again unto me, saying, Moreover, thou son of man, take thee one stick, and write upon it, For Judah, and for the children of Israel his companions [*the record of the Jews, or the Bible*].

Hebrews 7:14

For it is evident that our Lord sprang out of Judah.

The Stick of Ephraim

The Lord told Ezekiel to write upon "another stick" the record of the tribe of Joseph (the Jews who would migrate from the Middle East). The stick of Ephraim is believed by Latter-day Saints to be the Book of Mormon (Ezekiel 37:16).

Ephraim was a son of Joseph of the tribe of Israel. Ephraim and Joseph were promised great blessings by Jacob, Joseph's father, who was also called Israel (Genesis 48:17–19; 49:22–16). Jeremiah also wrote of blessings that would come to Joseph and his entire family (Jeremiah 31:9, 20).

Like the Bible (see Judges 20:21, 25, 46), the Book of Mormon gives an account of many wars. However, the wars chronicled in the Book of Mormon took place on the American continent.

Isaiah prophesied that a voice would speak from the dust and would have "a familiar spirit" (Isaiah 29:4) and that the Lord would proceed to do a "marvelous work and a wonder" among the people that would confound the wise and prudent and help the deaf hear and the blind see (Isaiah 29:14, 18). David wrote that "truth shall spring out of the earth" (Psalm 85:11). Isaiah wrote of the words of a sealed book (Isaiah 29:11).

Many believe these prophecies refer to the Book of Mormon and the manner in which it came forth.

Ezekiel 37:16

Then take another stick, and write upon it, For Joseph, the stick of Ephraim, and for all the house of Israel his companions.

Genesis 48:17–19

And when Joseph saw that his father laid his right hand upon the head of Ephraim, it displeased him: and he held up his father's hand, to remove it from Ephraim's head unto Manasseh's head. And Joseph said unto his father, Not so, my father: for this is the firstborn; put thy right hand upon his head. And his father refused, and said, I know it, my son, I know it: he also shall become a people, and he also shall be great: but truly his younger brother shall be greater than he, and his seed shall become a multitude of nations.

Genesis 49:22–26

Joseph is a fruitful bough, even a fruitful bough by a well; whose branches run over the wall: The archers have sorely grieved him, and shot at him, and hated him: But his bow abode in strength, and the arms of his hands were made strong by the hands of the mighty God of Jacob; (from thence is the shepherd, the stone of Israel:) Even by the God of thy father, who shall help thee; and by the Almighty, who shall bless thee with blessings of heaven above, blessings of the deep that lieth under, blessings of the breasts, and of the womb: The blessings of thy father have prevailed above the blessings of my progenitors unto the utmost bound of the everlasting hills: they shall be on the head of Joseph, and on the crown of the head of him that was separate from his brethren.

Jeremiah 31:9, 20

They shall come with weeping, and with supplications will I lead them: I will cause them to walk by the rivers of waters in a straight way, wherein they shall not stumble: for I am a father to Israel, and Ephraim is my firstborn. . . . Is Ephraim my dear son? is he a pleasant child? for since I spake against him, I do earnestly remember him still: therefore my bowels are troubled for him; I will surely have mercy upon him, saith the Lord.

Isaiah 29:4

And thou shalt be brought down, and shalt speak out of the ground, and thy speech shall be low out of the dust, and thy voice shall be, as of one that hath a familiar spirit, out of the ground, and thy speech shall whisper out of the dust.

Isaiah 29:14, 18

Therefore, behold, I will proceed to do a marvellous work among this people, even a marvellous work and a wonder: for the wisdom of their wise men shall perish, and the understanding of their prudent men shall be hid. . . . And in that day shall the deaf hear the words of the book, and the eyes of the blind shall see out of obscurity, and out of darkness.

Psalm 85:11

Truth shall spring out of the earth; and righteousness shall look down from heaven.

Isaiah 29:11

And the vision of all is become unto you as the words of a book that is sealed, which men deliver to one that is learned, saying, Read this, I pray thee: and he saith, I cannot; for it is sealed.

Bible Linked to the Book of Mormon

Ezekiel foretells of the stick of Judah (the Bible) and the stick of Ephraim (the Book of Mormon) coming together to become "one stick" or "one in thine hand" (Ezekiel 37:15–20). The joining of these two records to validate each other accomplishes the Lord's law of two witnesses (Matthew 18:16; 2 Corinthians 13:1)—the Bible witnessing for the Book of Mormon and the Book of Mormon witnessing for the Bible.

Many Latter-day Saint scholars and prophets believe that the combination of the Bible and the Book of Mormon constitutes fulfillment of Ezekiel's prophecy.

Ezekiel 37:15–20

The word of the Lord came again unto me, saying, Moreover, thou son of man, take thee one stick, and write upon it, For Judah, and for the children of Israel his companions [*the record of the Jews, or the Bible*]: then take another stick, and write upon it, For Joseph, the stick of Ephraim, and for all the house of Israel his companions [*the record of the house of Joseph, or the Book of Mormon*]: And join them one to another into one stick [*the Bible and the Book of Mormon combined*]; and they shall become one in thine hand. And when the children of thy people shall speak unto thee, saying, Wilt thou not shew us what thou meanest by these? Say unto them, Thus saith the Lord God; Behold, I will take the stick of Joseph, which is in the hand of Ephraim [*the Book of Mormon*], and the tribes of Israel his fellows, and will put them with him, even with the stick of Judah [*the Bible*], and make them one stick, and they shall be one in mine hand. And the sticks whereon thou writest shall be in thine hand before their eyes.

Matthew 18:16

But if he will not hear thee, then take with thee one or two more, that in the mouth of two or three witnesses every word may be established.

2 Corinthians 13:1

This is the third time I am coming to you. In the mouth of two or three witnesses shall every word be established.

New Scripture

Many non-Mormon scholars argue that the book of Revelation forbids the addition of any scripture to the Bible (Revelation 22:18).

This argument is weakened by the likelihood, supported by most biblical scholars, that John wrote the book of Revelation before he wrote his gospel, thus violating his own rule if he intended this rule to apply to the Bible as a whole. It is fatally weakened by the fact the Bible of today did not exist during the lifetime of John.

It is noteworthy also that the book of Deuteronomy contains multiple prohibitions against adding to the words and commandments therein (Deuteronomy 4:2; Deuteronomy 12:32). All of this strongly suggests that these prohibitions apply to the particular book or chapter in which the prohibitions appear, not to the entire canon.

Revelation 22:18

For I testify unto every man that heareth the words of the prophecy of this book [*the Book of Revelation, since there was at that time no Bible*], If any man shall add unto these things [*"these things" refers to things immediate and specific, not the whole Bible*], God shall add unto him the plagues that are written in this book [*the Book of Revelation, since there was at that time no Bible and John had yet to write his gospel, which would be an addition*].

Deuteronomy 4:2

Ye shall not add unto the word which I command you, neither shall ye diminish ought from it, that ye may keep the commandments of the Lord your God which I command you.

Deuteronomy 12:32

What thing soever I command you, observe to do it: thou shalt not add thereto, nor diminish from it.

Open Canon

The Lord revealed to Daniel that "knowledge shall be increased" in the last days (Daniel 12:4). Paul testified of an open canon by referring to "all scripture" at a time when the only scriptures in existence were those contained in the Old Testament. He referred to scripture as that which is "given by inspiration of God" (2 Timothy 3:16).

Daniel 12:4

But thou, O Daniel, shut up the words, and seal the book, even to the time of the end: many shall run to and fro, and knowledge shall be increased [*more knowledge will come forth from revealed scriptures*].

2 Timothy 3:16

All scripture is given by inspiration of God, and is profitable for doctrine, for reproof, for correction, for instruction in righteousness [*emphasis added*]. [*Scripture is ongoing, since the New Testament had not yet been compiled.*]

Scripture Study

The Lord commanded Israel to keep his words in their heart and to teach them to their children day and night (see Deuteronomy 6:6–7). Joshua told Israel to meditate on the commandments of God with the same frequency (see Joshua 1:8), and Isaiah told the children of God to seek and read (see Isaiah 34:16). Jesus admonished the disciples to "search the scriptures" (see John 5:39). Paul wrote that the people of Berea were "noble" and "searched the scriptures daily" (Acts 17:10–11).

MORMON UNDERSTANDING

Eighth Article of Faith

The eighth article of faith of The Church of Jesus Christ of Latter-day Saints states: "We believe the Bible to be the word of God as far as it is translated correctly; we also believe the Book of Mormon to be the word of God."

The Bible

From earliest times, the Lord has commanded his prophets to keep records, both historical and spiritual. Often, but not always, these records have become scripture. The Bible is an example of such scripture.

The Bible records the lives of people living in the Middle East. It is a collection of separate writings authored by separate individuals. Authorship in some cases is debated to this day.

The Bible is not a single book with multiple coauthors. In some cases there is evidence of collaboration while in many cases there is no such evidence. Furthermore, the collection of writings that came to be called the Bible was not compiled by the authors or by contemporary editors. Rather, it was compiled by various ecclesiastical authorities over a period of hundreds of years after the writings were made.

Inspired prophets and apostles wrote most of the works that were eventually selected to form the Bible. Their writings went through an unknown—and perhaps unknowable—number of cycles of translation, transcription, and compilation before being bound into what is known today as the Bible. Numerous scholars and organizations participated in this translating, transcribing, and compiling. They worked from the original Greek and Hebrew found in documents that may themselves have been through many cycles of transcription, if not revision. Finally, the Bible was split off into many versions, each translated into many languages. The work of revision and clarification goes on unceasingly to this day.

Books Rejected

In the process of compiling the Bible, scholars and clerics rejected many books, including the book of Jubilees, the epistle of Barnabas, the shepherd of Hermas, Paul's epistle to the Laodiceans, writings attributed to Clement (believed to be a coworker with Peter), and some of the writings of Peter.

There have been many reasons offered for these and other rejections. Prominent among these was the suspicion of forgery or findings by clerics of the time that the writings were inconsistent with other more cherished writings or with well accepted church doctrines or widely held beliefs.

For example, the Roman Catholic version of the Bible includes the Apocrypha, seven books in the Catholic version of the Old Testament that are not found in non-Catholic versions, including the King James Version. These seven books were adopted at the Council of Trent in 1546 and remain part of the Catholic version of the Old Testament to this day.

Thus, if you are a Catholic holding a non-Catholic Bible, something has been taken away. On the other hand, if you are a non-Catholic holding a Catholic Bible, something has been added.

The Bible Story

The Bible as we know it today begins with the Creation and ends shortly after the Ascension of Christ. The thirty-nine books of the Old Testament foretell of the coming of the Savior, while the twenty-seven books of the New Testament provide a record of the life of the Savior, with an emphasis on his public ministry.

Compilation and Canonization

The integrated Bible as we know it today was compiled by committee at the (Catholic) Council of Carthage in A.D. 397; however, it was not until the Council of Trent in 1546 that the Roman Catholic

Church formally acknowledged the doctrinal authority of the Bible and canonized it as sacred scripture.

King James Version—Latter-day Saint Edition

The Church of Jesus Christ of Latter-day Saints uses the King James Version of the Bible without content editing or revision of any kind.

On October 15, 1982, the Layman's National Bible Committee presented an award to The Church of Jesus Christ of Latter-day Saints for outstanding service to the Bible cause through the publication of a new edition (again, not a revision—no content was edited) of the King James Version. This edition featured interpretive chapter headings, a simplified footnote system, and the linking of references to all other Latter-day Saint scriptures—thereby, greatly enhancing Bible study. President Gordon B. Hinckley accepted the award and explained that the extraordinary efforts of the Church on the Bible project were to "help the people become better Bible scholars" leading to "a personal witness that Jesus is the Christ."[1]

Mormons revere the Bible as they do the Book of Mormon. Both are essential parts of the Christian canon.

The Book of Mormon

The coming forth of the Book of Mormon was the fulfillment of the blessings promised to Joseph and Ephraim. The Book of Mormon complements the Bible in providing a record of a people living in the Americas approximately from 2,200 B.C. to A.D. 400. The Book of Mormon testifies of the Bible, and the Bible testifies of the Book of Mormon. The subtitle of the Book of Mormon stresses that it is "Another Testament of Jesus Christ," providing in particular a record of the visit of Jesus to the inhabitants of the Americas shortly after his Resurrection. Like the Bible, the Book of Mormon is a compilation of separate writings by separate inspired individuals. These writings were abridged and etched onto gold plates to ensure their preservation. The prophet Joseph Smith translated the Book of Mormon into English from the original reformed Egyptian text on these gold plates. Following the successful translation of the Book of Mormon, the plates were taken in the same way they were delivered—through the angel Moroni. The Book of Mormon was later translated from English into many different languages.

Doctrine and Covenants

The Doctrine and Covenants (D&C) is a collection of revelations given to Joseph Smith and other modern prophets. It was compiled from 1823 to 1978. The purpose of the Doctrine and Covenants is to prepare the inhabitants of the earth for the Second Coming of Jesus Christ by providing direction and guidance. The Doctrine and Covenants includes details for the organization and operation of the Church and the offices of the priesthood and associated ecclesiastical and spiritual functions.

Pearl of Great Price

The Pearl of Great Price contains three different works: the book of Moses, the book of Abraham, and a collection of inspired writings by the prophet Joseph Smith. The book of Moses is a work revealed to Joseph Smith pertaining to visions and writings of Moses. It focuses on the creation of the earth. The book of Abraham is a translation from a papyrus scroll originating from the Egyptian catacombs and translated by Joseph Smith. It contains insights and information on the Creation, the priesthood, the gospel, and the nature of God. The writings of Joseph Smith include a portion of Joseph Smith's inspired translation of the Bible, a brief history of the Church, and the Articles of Faith.

Continuing Revelation: The Open Canon

The words of the living prophets, when spoken or written within the purview of their prophetic calling, are considered scripture. Such words can come to Latter-day Saints (and all mankind) through Church publications, conferences, and other forms of inspired instruction. While the inspired words of prophets, ancient and modern, are considered scripture, they are not part of the canon unless and until they are ratified by the First Presidency and the Quorum of the Twelve Apostles. Latter-day Saints believe that God can choose to speak to his prophets today just as he did in biblical times and that there can be additions to canonical scripture. Thus, The Church of Jesus Christ of Latter-day Saints is said to have an open canon.

Carefully Examining the Scriptures

To the inattentive eye or the error-seeking mind, there are plenty of troublesome issues raised in the scriptures. Variations in account, teaching, and translation can be confusing. Diligence and careful attention to context are necessary when studying the scriptures.

Variations in Account

For example, 1 Kings chapter 1 describes how Adonijah attempts to usurp the throne from Solomon and how Solomon works with Nathan to secure the throne. This is interesting in light of the fact that 1 Chronicles 29 details the same events without saying anything about the struggle with Adonijah. Similarly, 1 Kings 11 details how Solomon turned to the worshipping idols, while 2 Chronicles 9 provides a record of the same time period without any mention of Solomon worshipping idols.

In Matthew 5:3, Jesus tells his disciples, "Blessed are the poor in spirit: for theirs is the kingdom of heaven," while in Luke 6:20 he says, "Blessed be ye poor: for yours is the kingdom of God." These scriptures are close but different.

Variations in Teaching

Two different scriptures can provide different teachings on the same doctrine when examined in isolation. For example, John 1:7 states: "But if we walk in the light, as he is in the light, we have fellowship one with another, and the blood of Jesus Christ his Son cleanseth us from *all sin*" (emphasis added). Matthew 12:32 states: "And whosoever speaketh a word against the Son of man, it shall be forgiven him: but whosoever speaketh against the Holy Ghost, *it shall not be forgiven him*, neither in this world, neither in the world to come" (emphasis added). John wrote that all sin can be forgiven through Christ, while Matthew wrote that there is at least one sin that cannot be forgiven.

Variations in Translation

Dozens of English translations of the Bible have been created over the last several centuries. An estimated sixteen English translations are still in widespread circulation. These include the English Standard Version, Good News Bible, Holman Christian Standard Bible, J. B. Phillips New Testament, King James Version, the Living Bible, the Message, New American Bible, New American Standard Bible, New International Version, (New) Jerusalem Bible, New King James Bible, New Living Translation, (New) Revised Standard Version, Today's English Version, and Today's New International Version.

This proliferation of translations both helps and hurts human understanding of God's message to mankind. The various translations can be seen as useful commentary and in that way add to understanding, or they can be seen as rooms in a figurative tower of Babel, creating confusion if not profound misunderstanding.

The multiple translations of John 3:16 are interesting. For example, the King James Version (KJV) records this: "For God so loved the world, that he gave his only begotten Son, that whosoever believeth in him should not perish, but have everlasting life." The New International Version (NIV) records this: "For God so loved the world, that He gave his one and only Son that whoever believes in him shall not perish but have eternal life." The difference between "begotten" and "one and only" is significant, and it is easy to suspect revisionism at work in the later translation.

Another example is 2 Chronicles 26:5. The KJV records this: "And he sought God in the days of Zechariah, who had understanding in the visions of God: and as long as he sought the Lord, God made him to prosper." The NIV records this: "He sought God during the days of Zechariah, who instructed him in the fear of God. As long as he sought the Lord, God gave him success." Was the "he" in these passages instructed by Zechariah or did he merely live in the days of Zechariah? If he was instructed, did Zechariah teach him to fear God or to understand the visions of God?

Paradox

Paradox is the foundation of discovery. There are perceived paradoxes within scripture that require careful study and examination. An excellent example in the Bible is the following:

Luke 9:49–50
> And John answered and said, Master, we saw one casting out devils in thy name; and we forbad him, because he followeth not with us. And Jesus said unto him, *Forbid him not: for he that is not against us is for us* [emphasis added].

Compared to this:

Mark 9:38–40
> And John answered him, saying, Master, we saw one casting out devils in thy name, and he followeth not us: and we forbad him, because he followeth not us. But Jesus said, Forbid him not: for there is no man which shall do a miracle in my name, that can lightly speak evil of me. *For he that is not against us is on our part* [emphasis added].

Contrasted with this:

Matthew 12:30
> *He that is not with me is against me*; and he that gathereth not with me scattereth abroad [emphasis added].

So which is it? For him if not against him? Or against him if not for him? The answer is . . . both.

Comment

Christ is saying in the aggregate that a man has to be more than merely not with him to be against him. A child might say it this way: "Jesus will take me with him even if I don't know all about him, even if I am still learning, even if I am wrong sometimes. He will do this because he loves me."

The child would be right.

The apostles wanted to consider themselves an exclusive club; Christ reminded them to cast the net wider, to be more inclusive.

Penetrating the seeming contradiction in these passages, and others like them, can reward the patient reader with a joyful shock of new understanding. This is how the Master teaches, knowing that without something to puzzle over, men often will hear only words—and be unavailable to any shock of new understanding.

Interpretation

Sincere scholars and clerics study painstakingly and write prolifically on matters of interpretation. They often reach far different conclusions from the same evidence. This should be no surprise. It occurs in science, history, philosophy, engineering, and other disciplines as well. Scholarship in any discipline, including theology, proceeds by fits and starts. In matters of religion, it can be a worthwhile pursuit, but it cannot stop the constant flow of revealed communication. The best ancient manuscript is no match for the still small voice of the Spirit or the teachings of a living prophet.

This does not make things easier; it makes them infinitely harder. But the Lord did not promise it would be easy to discover him; he only promised it would be worth the effort.

Personal and Family Scripture Study

Church members are exhorted to study the scriptures every day, as individuals and as families. In doing so, Church members are told they can avoid evil and grow closer to God—especially when they read the scriptures in conjunction with pondering, praying, and asking God for further understanding through the Holy Ghost.

NOTE

1. Robert J. Matthews, "I Have a Question," *Ensign*, July 1985, 17–19.

✵ 10 ✵

APOSTASY AND RESTORATION

BIBLICAL TEACHING

Early Warnings of Apostasy

Pride, a forerunner of apostasy, arose among the early apostles and their families as they attempted to position themselves with the Savior for the privileges of heaven (Luke 22:24; Mark 10:35–37, 41; Matthew 20:20–21, 24). This manifestation of pride, however, was recorded long before the public ministry of Christ. The Lord revealed it to Isaiah when he had a vision of a land "utterly emptied and utterly spoiled . . . because they have transgressed the laws, changed the ordinance, broken the everlasting covenant" (Isaiah 24:1–6). Through the prophet Amos, the Lord prophesied of a "famine in the land . . . of hearing the words of the Lord" (Amos 8:11).

Luke 22:24

> And there was also a strife among them [*the apostles*], which of them should be accounted the greatest.

Mark 10:35–37, 41

> And James and John, the sons of Zebedee, come unto him, saying, Master, we would that thou shouldest do for us whatsoever we shall desire. And he said unto them, What would ye that I should do for you? They said unto him, Grant unto us that we may sit, one on thy right hand, and the other on thy left hand, in thy glory. . . .

And when the ten heard it, they began to be much displeased with James and John.

Matthew 20:20–21, 24

Then came to him the mother of Zebedee's children with her sons, worshipping him, and desiring a certain thing of him. And he said unto her, What wilt thou? She saith unto him, Grant that these my two sons may sit, the one on thy right hand, and the other on the left, in thy kingdom. . . . And when the ten heard it, they were moved with indignation against the two brethren.

Isaiah 24:1–6

Behold, the Lord maketh the earth empty, and maketh it waste, and turneth it upside down, and scattereth abroad the inhabitants thereof. And it shall be, as with the people, so with the priest; as with the servant, so with his master; as with the maid, so with her mistress; as with the buyer, so with the seller; as with the lender, so with the borrower; as with the taker of usury, so with the giver of usury to him. The land shall be utterly emptied, and utterly spoiled: for the Lord hath spoken this word. The earth mourneth and fadeth away, the world languisheth and fadeth away, the haughty people of the earth do languish. The earth also is defiled under the inhabitants thereof; because they have transgressed the laws, changed the ordinance, broken the everlasting covenant. Therefore hath the curse devoured the earth, and they that dwell therein are desolate: therefore the inhabitants of the earth are burned, and few men left. [*Before the Second Coming, it is clear than an apostasy of the laws, ordinances, and covenants of the gospel will have taken place.*]

Amos 8:11

Behold, the days come, saith the Lord God, that I will send a famine in the land, not a famine of bread, nor a thirst for water, but of hearing the words of the Lord.

Jesus Warned of Apostasy

Jesus prophesied of terrible things before his Second Coming, including the rise of false prophets and deceptions (Matthew 24:4–14). Paul later reiterated this (2 Timothy 3:1–5).

Matthew 24:4–14

And Jesus answered and said unto them, Take heed that no man deceive you. For many shall come in my name, saying, I am Christ;

and shall deceive many. And ye shall hear of wars and rumours of wars: see that ye be not troubled: for all these things must come to pass, but the end is not yet. For nation shall rise against nation, and kingdom against kingdom: and there shall be famines, and pestilences, and earthquakes, in divers places. All these are the beginning of sorrows. Then shall they deliver you up to be afflicted, and shall kill you: and ye shall be hated of all nations for my name's sake. And then shall many be offended, and shall betray one another, and shall hate one another. And many false prophets shall rise, and shall deceive many. And because iniquity shall abound, the love of many shall wax cold. But he that shall endure unto the end, the same shall be saved. And this gospel of the kingdom shall be preached in all the world for a witness unto all nations; and then shall the end come. [*Before the Second Coming, there will be a falling away of epic proportions, followed by the preaching of the gospel before the end of the world.*]

2 Timothy 3:1–5

This know also, that in the last days perilous times shall come. For men shall be lovers of their own selves, covetous, boasters, proud, blasphemers, disobedient to parents, unthankful, unholy, Without natural affection, trucebreakers, false accusers, incontinent, fierce, despisers of those that are good, Traitors, heady, highminded, lovers of pleasures more than lovers of God; Having a form of godliness, but denying the power thereof: from such turn away.

Later Warnings of Apostasy

After the Ascension of Christ, the apostles prophesied that when they were departed, trials and false teachings would arise (Acts 20:28–30). Paul was clear in his warnings of the pending apostasy. He told Timothy about a time of unsound doctrine (2 Timothy 4:3–4) and departure from the faith (1 Timothy 4:1–2). He warned the Galatians that they were already falling away from the true gospel (Galatians 1:6–9). He told the Thessalonians that before the Second Coming there would be a falling away (2 Thessalonians 2:3). And he warned the Ephesians of the ease of drifting from the true faith into all manner of false doctrines (Ephesians 4:14).

Acts 20:28–30

[*Paul speaking*] Take heed therefore unto yourselves, and to all the flock, over the which the Holy Ghost hath made you overseers, to feed the church of God, which he hath purchased with his own blood. For I know this, that after my departing shall grievous wolves enter in among you, not sparing the flock. Also of your own selves shall men arise, speaking perverse things, to draw away disciples after them. [*Shortly after the departure of the apostles, the apostasy will begin.*]

2 Timothy 4:3–4

For the time will come when they will not endure sound doctrine; but after their own lusts shall they heap to themselves teachers, having itching ears; And they shall turn away their ears from the truth, and shall be turned unto fables.

1 Timothy 4:1–2

Now the Spirit speaketh expressly, that in the latter times some shall depart from the faith, giving heed to seducing spirits, and doctrines of devils; Speaking lies in hypocrisy; having their conscience seared with a hot iron.

Galatians 1:6–9

I marvel that ye are so soon removed from him that called you into the grace of Christ unto another gospel: Which is not another; but there be some that trouble you, and would pervert the gospel of Christ [*apostasy was already happening among the disciples of Christ*]. But though we, or an angel from heaven, preach any other gospel unto you than that which we have preached unto you, let him be accursed. As we said before, so say I now again, If any man preach any other gospel unto you than that ye have received, let him be accursed. [*Paul feared apostasy.*]

2 Thessalonians 2:3

Let no man deceive you by any means: for that day shall not come, except there come a falling away first, and that man of sin be revealed, the son of perdition.

Ephesians 4:14

That we henceforth be no more children, tossed to and fro, and carried about with every wind of doctrine, by the sleight of men, and cunning craftiness, whereby they lie in wait to deceive. [*Paul expresses his concerns that the saints would drift away from the true doctrine of Christ.*]

Early Promises of Restoration

The Bible reassures its readers that this apostasy would be followed by a restoration and that the everlasting gospel would be brought to all the people of the earth (Revelation 14:6). The Lord prophesied through Isaiah that although there would be an apostasy that caused men to be removed from God (Isaiah 29:13), the Restoration would come forth and lay waste to the wisdom of the world (Isaiah 29:14). The prophet Joel wrote that the Lord will "pour out his spirit" at the Second Coming as a continuation of the restoration that would precede the millennial reign (Joel 2:28).

Revelation 14:6

> And I saw another angel fly in the midst of heaven, having the everlasting gospel to preach unto them that dwell on the earth, and to every nation, and kindred, and tongue, and people. [*John the Revelator saw in a vision an angel coming to the earth with the everlasting gospel. If the everlasting gospel was already on the earth, there would have been no need for the angel to bring it.*]

Isaiah 29:13–14

> Wherefore the Lord said, Forasmuch as this people draw near me with their mouth, and with their lips do honour me, but have removed their heart far from me, and their fear toward me is taught by the precept of men: Therefore, behold, I will proceed to do a marvellous work among this people, even a marvellous work and a wonder: for the wisdom of their wise men shall perish, and the understanding of their prudent men shall be hid. [*Because of the apostasy that brought about the corruption of man, the Lord will bring forth the restoration, which will be a marvelous work; however, the wise of the world will reject it and therefore perish spiritually.*]

Joel 2:28

> And it shall come to pass afterward, that I will pour out my spirit upon all flesh; and your sons and your daughters shall prophesy, your old men shall dream dreams, your young men shall see visions. [*This scripture is generally associated with the events following the Second Coming, but its tone suggests a continuing of the Restoration whereby prophesies, dreams, and visions flow freely in the kingdom.*]

Later Promises of Restoration

Jesus used the parable of the cloth and the wine bottles to reveal how a restoration is accomplished (Luke 5:36–38). He described it as requiring an entirely new vessel because the existing vessels could not complete the work necessary or withstand the trials that would follow. Peter and John preached of a "restitution of all things" before the Second Coming of Christ (Acts 3:19–21). Paul prophesied that there would come a dispensation in time where a gathering in Christ would take place (Ephesians 1:10).

Luke 5:36–38

> And he spake also a parable unto them; No man putteth a piece of a new garment upon an old; if otherwise, then both the new maketh a rent, and the piece that was taken out of the new agreeth not with the old. And no man putteth new wine into old bottles; else the new wine will burst the bottles, and be spilled, and the bottles shall perish. But new wine must be put into new bottles; and both are preserved. [*A preview of the restoration suggests that it could only be achieved through a completely new vessel, not something already in place.*]

Acts 3:19–21

> Repent ye therefore, and be converted, that your sins may be blotted out, when the times of refreshing shall come from the presence of the Lord; And he shall send Jesus Christ, which before was preached unto you: Whom the heaven must receive until the times of restitution of all things, which God hath spoken by the mouth of all his holy prophets since the world began.

Ephesians 1:10

> That in the dispensation of the fulness of times [*the times we are currently in*] he might gather together in one all things in Christ, both which are in heaven, and which are on earth; even in him

The Restoration and Miracles

Miracles are by definition inexplicable.

Some say that miracles are simply events that violate the laws of nature as they are known at the time of the event. Thus, by this definition, today's miracle is tomorrow's commonplace. For example, today a man standing in his living room in New York can know precisely the thoughts of a man standing in his living room in Tokyo—while the man in Tokyo is having those thoughts. Little more than a hundred years ago, this would have been in fact miraculous. The invention of the telephone changed a miracle into a commonplace.

However, mortal men and women will never catch up with miracles of another kind—those that are the work of God operating freely according to his will outside the laws of nature.

The Bible is a record of both kinds of miracles, with some metaphor and allegory thrown in to challenge discernment and make for lively debate.

The Restoration, modern revelation, and modern scripture are the same. Each of them contains elements of the miraculous.

Old Testament Miracles

The building of Noah's ark and the flooding of the earth (see Genesis 6–8), the confounding of language at the tower of Babel (see Genesis 11:5–7), and the captivity of Jonah in the belly of a fish for three days (see Jonah 1:17) are among the many miracles recorded in the Old Testament.

The Lord physically appearing to men is miraculous. These appearances are painstakingly recorded in the Old Testament (see Genesis 12:7; 18:1). The appearance to Ezekiel is particularly rich in detail (see Ezekiel 1:26–28).

New Testament Miracles

The transfiguration of Jesus includes the bodily appearance of the deceased Moses and Elias and God speaking to all present (Mark 9:2–7; Luke 9:28–35; Matthew 17:1–5). The appearance and verbal admonition of the resurrected and ascended Jesus Christ to Saul of Damascus, later to become Paul the apostle (Acts 9:3–6; 22:6–10), leaves no doubt that God can appear to men when and where he chooses.

Mark 9:2–7 (see also Matthew 17:1–5)

And after six days [*Luke reported eight days*] Jesus taketh with him Peter, and James, and John, and leadeth them up into an high mountain apart by themselves: and he was transfigured before them. And his raiment became shining, exceeding white as snow; so as no fuller on earth can white them. And there appeared unto them Elias with Moses: and they were talking with Jesus. And Peter answered and said to Jesus, Master, it is good for us to be here: and let us make three tabernacles; one for thee, and one for Moses, and one for Elias. For he wist not what to say; for they were sore afraid. And there was a cloud that overshadowed them: and a voice came out of the cloud, saying, This is my beloved Son: hear him.

Luke 9:28–35

And it came to pass about an eight days [*Mark and Matthew report six days*] after these sayings, he took Peter and John and James, and went up into a mountain to pray. And as he prayed, the fashion of his countenance was altered, and his raiment was white and glistering. And, behold, there talked with him two men, which were Moses and Elias: Who appeared in glory, and spake of his decease which he should accomplish at Jerusalem. But Peter and they that were with him were heavy with sleep: and when they were awake, they saw his glory, and the two men that stood with him. And it came to pass, as they departed from him, Peter said unto Jesus, Master, it is good for us to be here: and let us make three tabernacles; one for thee, and one for Moses, and one for Elias: not knowing what he said. While he thus spake, there came a cloud, and overshadowed them: and they feared as they entered into the cloud. And there came a voice out of the cloud, saying, This is my beloved Son: hear him.

Acts 9:3–6

And as [*Saul*] journeyed, he came near Damascus: and suddenly there shined round about him a light from heaven: And he fell to the earth, and heard a voice saying unto him, Saul, Saul, why persecutest thou me? And he said, Who art thou, Lord? And the Lord said, I am Jesus whom thou persecutest: it is hard for thee to kick against the pricks. And he trembling and astonished said, Lord, what wilt thou have me to do? And the Lord said unto him, Arise, and go into the city, and it shall be told thee what thou must do. [*Paul describes seeing Jesus Christ. Interestingly, this description is slightly different from the one he gave to King Agrippa (below).*]

Acts 22:6–10

And it came to pass, that, as I made my journey, and was come nigh unto Damascus about noon, suddenly there shone from heaven a great light round about me. And I fell unto the ground, and heard a voice saying unto me, Saul, Saul, why persecutest thou me? And I answered, Who art thou, Lord? And he said unto me, I am Jesus of Nazareth, whom thou persecutest. And they that were with me saw indeed the light, and were afraid; but they heard not the voice of him that spake to me. And I said, What shall I do, Lord? And the Lord said unto me, Arise, and go into Damascus; and there it shall be told thee of all things which are appointed for thee to do. [*Given the abundant biblical precedents, the honest skeptic must allow, at least, that if God did not appear to the Mormon prophet Joseph Smith, it was not because he was unable to do so.*]

MORMON UNDERSTANDING

Christ Establishes His Church

Jesus organized his church and ordained apostles before ascending to take his seat at the right hand of God his father. To aid his disciples in building his church, Jesus promised the gift of the Holy Ghost, granted his disciples the power of the priesthood, and left a legacy of teachings that would form the foundation of the New Testament as we know it today.

Persecution

The church Christ established was engaged in an intense struggle for survival from its very beginnings. That it did survive is a historical anomaly. The early Christian church was persecuted as heretical by Jewish authorities and as inconsistent with cultural and philosophical traditions by Roman authorities. It was not until the fourth century that Christianity was finally legalized and then accepted by the Roman Emperors Galerius and Constantine.

What Survived

But what price was paid for this legalization and worldly acceptance? Indeed, what Christian church was legalized and accepted? Was there really an unbroken chain of apostolic succession from Peter? Were the doctrines and forms established by Christ sustained in the various ecumenical councils that followed Roman acceptance? Did these doctrinal and ecclesiastical derivatives remain true to the teachings of Christ and the church he established during his life?

Apostasy

Apostasy grew over the centuries after the Ascension of Christ. In this falling-away, inconsistent philosophies and base motivations of men corrupted many tenets of the gospel of Jesus Christ. The doctrine, organization, and priesthood ordinances established by Christ were corrupted. Soon, the Lord withdrew the authority of the priesthood from the earth. He left men to work out spiritual matters on their own, granting to worthy individuals the inspiration of the Holy Ghost from time to time. However, he preserved the framework of

Christianity because he knew he would restore his church before the Second Coming.

Evidence of Apostasy

Historical events provide compelling evidence of the apostasy. These events include institutional and doctrinal disputes within the Catholic Church, the largest Christian sect that has endured since the Ascension of Christ, and a wide range of political events associated with that church. These events included the Crusades of the late eleventh century, the great Schism of 1054, the Medieval Inquisition of 1184, the Spanish Inquisition of 1478, the Roman Inquisition of 1542, and the silencing of Galileo in the seventeenth century.

Many respected religious authorities, including Eusebius, bishop of Caesarea in Palestine (-275–May 30, 339); Martin Luther (November 10, 1483–February 18, 1546); John Wesley (June 17, 1703–March 2, 1791); and others wrote of the apostasy. Indeed, the Protestant reformation grew out of the Apostasy.

Upon This Rock

A common misconception about the Apostasy centers on the term *rock*. The name Peter in Greek is *petros* (a detached stone or small rock), and the word for rock is *petra* (meaning a mass of rock). Taken from the original Greek text of the New Testament, Matthew 16:18 should be read, "Thou art Peter [petros, or a small rock], and upon this rock [petra, or foundation of rock] I will build my church." The rock upon which the Lord intended his church to be built was and is today the rock of revelation—not the person or personality of an apostle or some other ecclesiastical authority. It was upon continuous revelation from God the Father and the Lord Jesus Christ that the Church of Jesus Christ would be built.

Men and their institutions, both religious and secular, can be led astray. Apostles and prelates may fall away or die, church buildings may crumble, doctrines may be distorted, scriptural records may be lost, and many lies may be told. But the Church of Jesus Christ, founded on the rock of continuous revelation, is unassailable. Men may cut themselves off from it, but their separation from it does not alter its presence.

Reformation Not Enough

John Lathrop, Roger Williams, Martin Luther, Henry VIII, and many others attempted reformation—some with pure intentions. But this purity of intention—where it existed—did not trump the Lord's intention. It was not the Lord's will that something new be made out of something broken (Matthew 9:16–17; Mark 2:21–22). Christ's church had not been improved during the apostasy, and Christ had not fumbled when he first established his church. It was restoration of the original, not reformation of a broken copy, that the Lord intended.

The Place, the Time, the Man

The land chosen for the Restoration was America, a country founded on the principle of religious freedom. The time chosen was the Second Great Awakening (1820–1835), when religious awareness was at a fever pitch in America. The individual chosen to lead the Restoration was a young boy without religious bias or strong religious affiliation. That boy was Joseph Smith.

The Lord could have chosen otherwise—a different place, a different time, and a different person. But it was this particular intersection of the vectors of place, time, and vessel that suited the Lord's purpose. It was in America during the nineteenth century and by this otherwise unremarkable man that the Lord chose to restore his church.

Amidst the fervor of the Second Great Awakening in the spring of 1820, Joseph Smith, a fourteen-year-old boy of meager circumstances and little education, knelt and prayed in a grove of trees in Palmyra, New York. There he was visited by God the Father and his son Jesus Christ. Joseph asked them which church he should join. He was told to join none of them. "They [the churches of Joseph's time] draw near to me [God] with their lips, but their hearts are far from me, they teach for doctrines the commandments of men, having a form of godliness, but they deny the power thereof" (Joseph Smith—History 1:19).

The First Vision (as this event has since come to be known) was a miraculous occurrence, not unlike miraculous occurrences recorded in the Bible. After the First Vision, Joseph was visited by the Angel Moroni, a messenger sent from the Lord. In the biblical tradition of ministering angels, the Angel Moroni instructed Joseph over a period of about seven years. During this period of preparation, Joseph was taught and sometimes admonished by the Lord. Under divine tutelage, the boy became a mature man of God. Joseph's thoughts and actions were refined according to the Lord's will. The instruction and admonishment Joseph received and the adversity he and his loved ones endured prepared him to be the first prophet of the Restoration.

Imperfect Man on a Perfect Mission

Joseph was not a perfect man, but he was God's perfect choice for this mission. He led the world into the dispensation of the fulness of times: the restoration of the Church of Jesus Christ was accomplished and final preparations for the return of the Savior commenced.

❧ 11 ❧

REVELATION AND PROPHETS

BIBLICAL TEACHING

Revelation

God communicates to man through revelation. According to his will and purpose, he communicates directly to individuals, or through the scriptures, or through prophets and others he has chosen.

Revelations edify a person or group of people (1 Corinthians 14:26), can come to any individual at any time (1 Corinthians 14:30), and are usually preceded by faith and a strong desire to understand the deep mysteries of God (1 Corinthians 2:9–10, Ephesians 3:3–4).

1 Corinthians 14:26

> How is it then, brethren? when ye come together, every one of you hath a psalm, hath a doctrine, hath a tongue, hath a revelation, hath an interpretation. Let all things be done unto edifying.

1 Corinthians 14:30

> If any thing be revealed to another that sitteth by, let the first hold his peace. [*Revelations can be delivered at any time and by unlikely messengers, but all that are true come through the Holy Ghost.*]

1 Corinthians 2:9–10

> But as it is written, Eye hath not seen, nor ear heard, neither have entered into the heart of man, the things which God hath prepared for them that love him. But God hath revealed them unto us

by his Spirit: for the Spirit searcheth all things, yea, the deep things of God. [*Through the ministrations of the Holy Ghost, God reveals himself to those who search for him.*]

Ephesians 3:3–4

How that by revelation he made known unto me the mystery; (as I wrote afore in few words, Whereby, when ye read, ye may understand my knowledge in the mystery of Christ).

Prophets

Prophets are inspired men who reveal God's will. Prophets warn, teach, testify of Christ, and denounce sin. Sometimes they reveal coming events, particularly events that flow from rebelling against God's will. When prophets speak, they do so with clarity and boldness.

The Lord speaks to his prophets, his prophets speak to the people, and the people who choose to follow God follow the teachings of the prophets (Haggai 1:12). The Lord does not withhold his guidance from mankind (Amos 3:7). Prophets such as Judas and Silas continued to reveal the will of the Lord after Christ ascended into heaven (Acts 15:32). Paul wrote often of prophets in the present tense, acknowledging prophetic callings in his own time and in times to come (Ephesians 3:5; 1 Corinthians 14:29; 12:28). John made it clear that prophets would be on the earth as the servants of God during the Second Coming (Revelation 10:7). God will not leave men in darkness; he will always send his prophets (plural) because he desires clarity over confusion and peace over strife among his people (1 Corinthians 14:31–33).

Haggai 1:12

Then Zerubbabel the son of Shealtiel, and Joshua the son of Josedech, the high priest, with all the remnant of the people, obeyed the voice of the Lord their God, and the words of Haggai the prophet, as the Lord their God had sent him, and the people did fear before the Lord.

Amos 3:7

Surely the Lord God will do nothing, but he revealeth his secret unto his servants the prophets.

Acts 15:32

And Judas and Silas, being prophets also themselves, exhorted the brethren with many words, and confirmed them.

Ephesians 3:5

Which in other ages was not made known unto the sons of men, as it is now [*in the present age*] revealed unto his holy apostles and prophets by the Spirit.

1 Corinthians 14:29

Let the prophets speak two or three, and let the other judge.

1 Corinthians 12:28

And God hath set some in the church, first apostles, secondarily prophets, thirdly teachers, after that miracles, then gifts of healings, helps, governments, diversities of tongues.

Revelation 10:7

But in the days of the voice of the seventh angel, when he shall begin to sound, the mystery of God should be finished, as he hath declared to his servants the prophets.

1 Corinthians 14:31–33

For ye may all prophesy one by one, that all may learn, and all may be comforted. And the spirits of the prophets are subject to the prophets. For God is not the author of confusion, but of peace, as in all churches of the saints.

The Gift of Prophecy

Prophecy is a gift of the spirit that can edify many people, thus surpassing in importance all other spiritual gifts (1 Corinthians 14:1–6 and 1 Corinthians 12:10). Prophecy benefits the believer (1 Corinthians 14:22–24) and is a gift that is to be desired—even coveted (1 Corinthians 14:39). The gift of prophecy is not only given to men but to women also (1 Corinthians 11:5).

1 Corinthians 14:1–6

Follow after charity, and desire spiritual gifts, but rather that ye may prophesy. For he that speaketh in an unknown tongue speaketh not unto men, but unto God: for no man understandeth him; howbeit in the spirit he speaketh mysteries. But he that prophesieth speaketh unto men to edification, and exhortation, and comfort. He that speaketh in an unknown tongue edifieth himself; but he that prophesieth edifieth the church. I would that ye all spake with tongues, but rather that ye prophesied: for greater is he that prophesieth than he that speaketh with tongues, except he interpret, that the church may receive edifying. Now, brethren, if I come unto you speaking with tongues, what shall I profit you, except I shall speak to you either by revelation, or by knowledge, or by prophesying, or by doctrine?

1 Corinthians 12:10

To another the working of miracles; to another prophecy; to another discerning of spirits; to another divers kinds of tongues; to another the interpretation of tongues.

1 Corinthians 14:22–24

Wherefore tongues are for a sign, not to them that believe, but to them that believe not: but prophesying serveth not for them that believe not, but for them which believe. If therefore the whole church be come together into one place, and all speak with tongues, and there come in those that are unlearned, or unbelievers, will they not say that ye are mad? But if all prophesy, and there come in one that believeth not, or one unlearned, he is convinced of all, he is judged of all.

1 Corinthians 14:39

Wherefore, brethren, covet to prophesy.

1 Corinthians 11:5

But every woman that prayeth or prophesieth with her head uncovered dishonoureth her head: for that is even all one as if she were shaven.

Ambiguity and Interpretation

The recognition, interpretation, and application of revelations are the works of the men and women who receive them. Sometimes these interpretations are not inspired by the Holy Ghost. Sometimes they are inspired, but it is the Lord's will that the meaning and application be thoughtfully worked out through prayer and study. Disputes over meaning and application do arise.

For example, Psalm 69 is a Messianic prophecy that includes images of the crucifixion. Jesus prayed that the Father would forgive those who crucified him (see Luke 23:24); however, Psalm 69:28 says that those responsible would be "blotted out of the book of the living."

Which is it? "Blotted out of the book of the living" or forgiven? And what does it mean to be "blotted out" of the book of the living?

Another example is Deuteronomy 28:58–61, which speaks of

plagues, sickness, and diseases that will come upon those (and their children) who "wilt not observe to do all the words of this law that are written in this book." This prophecy could apply to a specific law; the book of Deuteronomy; the Old Testament; the entire Bible; or all scripture, ancient and modern. The terrible things spoken of could apply to the Israelites only, or to all people on the earth, then and now.

Cultural Noise

Revelations can be distorted by compelling aspects of culture, and they can apply in one age but not in another. For example, Paul wrote that women should be silent in church (see 1 Corinthians 14:34–35). Was this written only for women of Paul's day? Does it have any application today? Was it merely a local administrative ruling based on a local problem? Or was Paul merely incorrect and not speaking as a prophet in this case?

The Problem of Fulfillment

Some prophecies are not fulfilled, at least according to any standard interpretation of the words used to express them. Others are "fulfilled" only by a tortured interpretation of the words of the prophecy. For example, Ezekiel predicted that king Nebuchadnezzar would destroy Tyrus beyond reconstruction and would gain riches from the siege (see Ezekiel 26:3–14). While some claim the prophecy was fulfilled, historical evidence suggests that while the king did indeed attack the city, he probably failed in his attempt to destroy it, and he did not gain riches in the victory.

Available evidence is seldom subject to only one interpretation, and new evidence can appear, seemingly turning a cherished belief on its head. The point is this: the judgment that a prophecy has or has not been fulfilled is frequently based on faith in the first case or skepticism in the second.

For example, Jesus told his disciples of his Second Coming in considerable detail (see Matthew 24:29–35; Mark 13:24–31; Luke 21:25–33). Matthew, Mark, and Luke all report that Jesus said "this generation" would not pass away until "these things be fulfilled."

Jesus did not come again in his generation, and he has still not come, more than two thousand years later. Does this mean his prophecy was not fulfilled? Does it mean he made a mistake? Does it mean the Bible authors or their translators made a mistake? Does it mean that Jesus used the word *generation* to mean all human life on this planet? The atheist will answer one way. The biblical literalist will answer another. The poet another. The archeologist will search for lost texts. A few will agonize, even fall away, but the faithful will move on, unperturbed.

Prophets Not Infallible

The Lord recognizes human limitations in his children, even in his prophets. Prophets are not infallible. They suffer from the same mortal infirmities as all humans, despite their divine calling. The prophet Elisha in response to the children who mocked him and made fun of his baldness "cursed them in the name of the Lord" and caused two bears to come from the woods and tear the children apart (see 2 Kings 2:23–24).

This seems a bit harsh. Are these the actions of a prophet acting as a prophet, or a prophet acting as a petulant old man?

On the one hand, the Lord promised that a prophet "shall die" if he speaks falsely or with blasphemy (see Deuteronomy 18:20–22). On the other hand, the Lord told the people "not to be afraid" of (not to be concerned about or fearful of) such a prophet (see Deuteronomy 18:21–22).

MORMON UNDERSTANDING

Profile of a Prophet

A prophet is not a prophet because he says he is. He is a prophet because he has been called of God by priesthood authority. A prophet is also not a perfect human being, and his utterances and writings are prophetic only when he is speaking and acting authoritatively within the scope of his assigned role.

A prophet is an inspired teacher, a servant of the Lord chosen by the Lord to declare to the people the knowledge and will of the Lord. "Members of The Church of Jesus Christ of Latter-day Saints . . . are blessed to be led by living prophets—inspired men called to speak for the Lord, just as Moses, Isaiah, Peter, Paul, Nephi, Mormon, and other prophets of the scriptures."[1]

A prophet is an accredited witness, one who is given by God to know and to testify of the truth with authority. A prophet is also a special witness of Christ, testifying of his divinity and teaching his gospel. A prophet teaches truth and interprets the word of God. He calls the unrighteous to repentance. He receives revelations and direction from the Lord for the benefit of the people.

From time to time, a prophet may foretell coming events so that the world may be warned.[2] Several Old Testament prophets predicted the coming of Christ, in some cases hundreds of years before his birth, and modern prophets have made important predictions about his Second Coming. Indeed, it could be said that prophetic warnings frequently contain implicit predictions of the consequences of ignoring those warnings. Nevertheless, teaching and leading rather than predicting are the primary duties of a prophet.

Living Prophets

Prophets have been on the earth from the earliest of days. The profile of a prophet, then and now, varies dramatically in terms of age, education, vocation, family upbringing, and other characteristics. Prophets come from all walks of life.

Members of the First Presidency and the Quorum of the Twelve Apostles of The Church of Jesus Christ of Latter-day Saints are called and sustained as prophets, seers, and revelators.

> NOTE: The terms *seer* and *revelator* are used to explain or give emphasis to the term *prophet*. These terms do not denote special powers in addition to those denoted by the term *prophet*.

The president of the Church and the prophets, seers, and revelators under him give vital contemporary guidance and instruction from the Lord. Their presence and their devoted service are a constant reminder that God lives and speaks to his people through his prophets.

While Latter-day Saints greatly revere the prophets of the Old and New Testaments and of the early days of the Restoration, they listen to the living prophets, particularly the prophet of the Church, and follow them carefully and assiduously.

Prophets of The Church of Jesus Christ of Latter-day Saints address the world during semi-annual conferences, regular firesides, weekly appearances across the world, and through a wide variety of official Church publications. All of God's children, those who are members of the Church and those who are not, are counseled to follow the inspired teachings of these prophets in order to avoid the snares of the world and enjoy the blessings of the gospel of Jesus Christ.

The Prophet of the Church

Although all three members of the First Presidency of the Church and all members of the Quorum of the Twelve Apostles are prophets, seers, and revelators, the terms *prophet of the Church* and *the prophet* refer specifically the President of the Church.

The President of the Church is the presiding high priest: only he can receive revelations for the Church as a whole, provide binding interpretations of scripture, or change existing doctrines of the Church. Only he holds the "keys to the kingdom" with the power to loose or bind in all temporal and spiritual matters of the Church (Matthew 16:19).

The Lord has established a pattern in which the most senior member of the Quorum of the Twelve becomes the prophet of the Church upon the death of the current prophet. This pattern ensures there is continuity in leadership without political maneuvering or elections of any kind. The new prophet, like his predecessor, serves for life.

Some well-known prophets of The Church of Jesus Christ of Latter-day Saints include Joseph Smith, Brigham Young, Ezra Taft Benson, Gordon B. Hinckley, and Thomas S. Monson, who was the prophet at the time of this writing.

Limitations of Stewardship

Authoritative revelation comes to the seeking individual according to his or her stewardship. A stake president can receive revelation for his stake. A bishop can receive revelation for his ward. Parents can receive revelation for the families they lead. Individuals can receive revelation for themselves.

The Gift of Prophecy

The Lord's house is a house of order. He does not leave his people to stumble blindly through empty and darkened hallways. He sends prophets to guide and teach. He grants the gift of prophecy and understanding to those who seek him diligently, and he reveals himself to all who have eyes to see and ears to hear.

NOTES

1. *True to the Faith: A Gospel Reference* (Salt Lake City: Intellectual Reserve, 2004), 129.
2. *Gospel Principles* (Salt Lake City: Intellectual Reserve, 2009), 39.

❦ 12 ❧

JOSEPH SMITH

*L*atter-day Saints believe that Joseph Smith was given a divine mission, and that through him, the Book of Mormon was brought forth, the priesthood and the true church of Jesus Christ were restored to the earth, and temple work was established.[1] The biblical foundations for these beliefs are discussed in other chapters of this book.

What follows is a compilation of biblical parallels illustrating—if they do nothing else—that the life, work, and claims of Joseph were consistent with those of ancient prophets of the Bible; that his encounters with angels had many biblical precedents; and that his flaws, such as they were, were not unlike those of prophets before him.

BIBLICAL TEACHING

Visions and Miracles

The Bible foretells that prophecy, visions, and dreams will come to the children of men in the last days through the spirit of God (Acts 2:16–18). Joseph Smith, the latter-day prophets who came after him, and others have reported such prophecies, visions, and dreams.

The disciple Stephen saw Jesus Christ standing on the right hand of God (Acts 7:55–56); the prophet Joseph Smith saw God the Father and his Son, Jesus Christ (Joseph Smith—History 1:17). Angels have been sent by God to minister to men (Daniel 9:21–22); the angel Moroni visited the prophet Joseph many times (Joseph Smith—History 1:30–42, 44–46, 49, and 53–54). Angels have been called upon to perform physical tasks on earth (1 Chronicles 21:15–16); the angel

Moroni led the prophet Joseph to the gold plates containing the Book of Mormon and later retrieved them from Joseph (Joseph Smith—History 1:60).

The Bible teaches that the things of God are foolishness to the "natural man" and that the wisdom of the world will be made foolish and destroyed by the wisdom of God (1 Corinthians 2:14–16 and 1:19–21). When this lesson is taken, what men call "miraculous" becomes a comfortable expectation derived from faith.

Acts 2:16–18

> But this is that which was spoken by the prophet Joel; And it shall come to pass in the last days, saith God, I will pour out of my Spirit upon all flesh: and your sons and your daughters shall prophesy, and your young men shall see visions, and your old men shall dream dreams: And on my servants and on my handmaidens I will pour out in those days of my Spirit; and they shall prophesy. [*Prophets and prophecy are promised.*]

Acts 7:55–56

> But he, being full of the Holy Ghost, looked up stedfastly into heaven, and saw the glory of God, and Jesus standing on the right hand of God, And said, Behold, I see the heavens opened, and the Son of man standing on the right hand of God. [*Men seeing God is not without biblical precedent.*]

Daniel 9:21–22

> Yea, whiles I was speaking in prayer, even the man Gabriel, whom I had seen in the vision at the beginning, being caused to fly swiftly, touched me about the time of the evening oblation. And he informed me, and talked with me, and said, O Daniel, I am now come forth to give thee skill and understanding. [*It is not unusual for angels to minister to God's chosen servants.*]

1 Chronicles 21:15–16

> And God sent an angel unto Jerusalem to destroy it: and as he was destroying, the Lord beheld, and he repented him of the evil, and said to the angel that destroyed, It is enough, stay now thine hand. And the angel of the Lord stood by the threshingfloor of Ornan the Jebusite. And David lifted up his eyes, and saw the angel of the Lord stand between the earth and the heaven, having a drawn sword in his hand stretched out over Jerusalem. Then David and the elders of Israel, who were clothed in sackcloth, fell upon their faces. [*It is not*

unusual for angels to speak to men and to be seen by the men and to act upon men.]

1 Corinthians 2:14–16

But the natural man receiveth not the things of the Spirit of God: for they are foolishness unto him: neither can he know them, because they are spiritually discerned. But he that is spiritual judgeth all things, yet he himself is judged of no man. For who hath known the mind of the Lord, that he may instruct him? But we have the mind of Christ. [*It is not unusual for men to dismiss the miraculous.*]

1 Corinthians 1:19–21

For it is written, I will destroy the wisdom of the wise, and will bring to nothing the understanding of the prudent. Where is the wise? where is the scribe? where is the disputer of this world? hath not God made foolish the wisdom of this world? For after that in the wisdom of God the world by wisdom knew not God, it pleased God by the foolishness of preaching to save them that believe. [*It is not unusual for God to work through simple men, even flawed men.*]

Angels Appear and Speak

Joseph Smith reported being visited by angels and speaking with them. His experiences with angels were not unlike those recorded in the Bible.

Angels weave themselves in and out of the events of the Bible. Angels conversed freely with Manoah (Judges 13:13–16), Zechariah (Zechariah 1–5), Daniel (Daniel 9:21–22), a group of shepherds (Luke 2:9–10, 13, 15), Philip (Acts 8:26), and Cornelius (Acts 10:3, 7, 22), to name but a few. The angel Gabriel appeared to different people before the birth of Christ, including Zacharias (Luke 1:11, 13, 18–19); Mary (Luke 1:26, 30, 34, 38); and Mary's future husband, Joseph (Matthew 1:20).

Judges 13:13–16

And the angel of the Lord said unto Manoah, Of all that I said unto the woman let her beware. She may not eat of any thing that cometh of the vine, neither let her drink wine or strong drink, nor eat any unclean thing: all that I commanded her let her observe. And Manoah said unto the angel of the Lord, I pray thee, let us detain thee, until we shall have made ready a kid for thee. And the angel of the Lord said unto Manoah, Though thou detain me, I will not eat of thy bread: and if thou wilt offer a burnt offering, thou must offer it unto the Lord. For Manoah knew not that he was an angel of the Lord.

Zechariah, Chapter 1 to 5 (1:9–14 as an example)

Then said I, O my lord, what are these? And the angel that talked with me said unto me, I will shew thee what these be. And the man that stood among the myrtle trees answered and said, These are they whom the Lord hath sent to walk to and fro through the earth. And they answered the angel of the Lord that stood among the myrtle trees, and said, We have walked to and fro through the earth, and, behold, all the earth sitteth still, and is at rest. Then the angel of the Lord answered and said, O Lord of hosts, how long wilt thou not have mercy on Jerusalem and on the cities of Judah, against which thou hast had indignation these threescore and ten years? And the Lord answered the angel that talked with me with good words and comfortable words. So the angel that communed with me said unto me, Cry thou, saying, Thus saith the Lord of hosts; I am jealous for Jerusalem and for Zion with a great jealousy. [*Multiple mentions of angelic interactions with human beings.*]

Daniel 9:21–22

Yea, whiles I was speaking in prayer, even the man Gabriel, whom I had seen in the vision at the beginning, being caused to fly swiftly, touched me about the time of the evening oblation. And he informed me, and talked with me, and said, O Daniel, I am now come forth to give thee skill and understanding.

Luke 2:9–10, 13, 15

And, lo, the angel of the Lord came upon them, and the glory of the Lord shone round about them: and they were sore afraid. And the angel said unto them, Fear not: for, behold, I bring you good tidings of great joy, which shall be to all people. . . . And suddenly there was with the angel a multitude of the heavenly host praising God. . . . And it came to pass, as the angels were gone away from them into heaven, the shepherds said one to another, Let us now go even unto Bethlehem, and see this thing which is come to pass, which the Lord hath made known unto us.

Acts 8:26

And the angel of the Lord spake unto Philip, saying, Arise, and go toward the south unto the way that goeth down from Jerusalem unto Gaza, which is desert.

Acts 10:3, 7, 22

He saw in a vision evidently about the ninth hour of the day an angel of God coming in to him, and saying unto him, Cornelius. . . . And when the angel which spake unto Cornelius was departed, he called two of his household servants, and a devout soldier of them that waited on him continually. . . . And they said, Cornelius the centurion, a just man, and one that feareth God, and of good report among all the nation of the Jews, was warned from God by an holy angel to send for thee into his house, and to hear words of thee.

Luke 1:11, 13, 18–19

And there appeared unto him an angel of the Lord standing on the right side of the altar of incense. . . . But the angel said unto him, Fear not, Zacharias: for thy prayer is heard; and thy wife Elisabeth shall bear thee a son, and thou shalt call his name John. . . . And Zacharias said unto the angel, Whereby shall I know this? for I am an old man, and my wife well stricken in years. And the angel answering said unto him, I am Gabriel, that stand in the presence of God; and am sent to speak unto thee, and to shew thee these glad tidings.

Luke 1:26, 30, 34, 38

And in the sixth month the angel Gabriel was sent from God unto a city of Galilee, named Nazareth. . . . And the angel said unto her, Fear not, Mary: for thou hast found favour with God. . . . Then said Mary unto the angel, How shall this be, seeing I know not a man? . . . And Mary said, Behold the handmaid of the Lord; be it unto me according to thy word. And the angel departed from her.

Matthew 1:20

But while he thought on these things, behold, the angel of the Lord appeared unto him in a dream, saying, Joseph, thou son of David, fear not to take unto thee Mary thy wife: for that which is conceived in her is of the Holy Ghost.

Angels Take Action

Joseph Smith reported not only the visitation of angels but also their active work with him. His experiences were not unlike the interactions with angels recorded in the Bible.

Some angels in the Bible did not merely converse with men—they actively influenced events, sometimes with considerable violence. For example, the angel sent by the Lord to destroy Jerusalem wielded a sword (1 Chronicles 21:15–16). An angel did much destruction to the people of David (2 Samuel 24:16–17). An angel opened doors for the imprisoned apostles (Acts 5:19–20). An angel smote Peter in prison and helped him escape (Acts 12:7–11, 15), and an angel killed Herod for blasphemy (Acts 12:20–23). In the end times, several angels will carry out plagues upon the wicked (Revelation 16:1, 3–5, 8, 10, 12, 17).

1 Chronicles 21:15–16

And God sent an angel unto Jerusalem to destroy it: and as he was destroying, the Lord beheld, and he repented him of the evil, and said to the angel that destroyed, It is enough, stay now thine hand. And the angel of the Lord stood by the threshingfloor of Ornan the Jebusite. And David lifted up his eyes, and saw the angel of the Lord stand between the earth and the heaven, having a drawn sword in his hand stretched out over Jerusalem. Then David and the elders of Israel, who were clothed in sackcloth, fell upon their faces.

2 Samuel 24:16–17

And when the angel stretched out his hand upon Jerusalem to destroy it, the Lord repented him of the evil, and said to the angel that destroyed the people, It is enough: stay now thine hand. And the angel of the Lord was by the threshingplace of Araunah the Jebusite. And David spake unto the Lord when he saw the angel that smote the people, and said, Lo, I have sinned, and I have done wickedly: but these sheep, what have they done? let thine hand, I pray thee, be against me, and against my father's house.

Acts 5:19–20

But the angel of the Lord by night opened the prison doors, and brought them forth, and said, Go, stand and speak in the temple to the people all the words of this life.

Acts 12:7–11, 15

And, behold, the angel of the Lord came upon him, and a light shined in the prison: and he smote Peter on the side, and raised him up, saying, Arise up quickly. And his chains fell off from his hands. And the angel said unto him, Gird thyself, and bind on thy sandals. And so he did. And he saith unto him, Cast thy garment about thee, and follow me. And he went out, and followed him; and wist not that it was true which was done by the angel; but thought he saw a vision. When they were past the first and the second ward, they came unto the iron gate that leadeth unto the city; which opened to them of his own accord: and they went out, and passed on through one street; and forthwith the angel departed from him. And when Peter was come to himself, he said, Now I know of a surety, that the Lord hath sent his angel, and hath delivered me out of the hand of Herod, and from all the expectation of the people of the Jews. . . . And they said unto her, Thou art mad. But she constantly affirmed that it was even so. Then said they, It is his angel.

Acts 12:20–23

And Herod was highly displeased with them of Tyre and Sidon: but they came with one accord to him, and, having made Blastus the king's chamberlain their friend, desired peace; because their country was nourished by the king's country. And upon a set day Herod, arrayed in royal apparel, sat upon his throne, and made an oration unto them. And the people gave a shout, saying, It is the voice of a god, and not of a man. And immediately the angel of the Lord smote him, because he gave not God the glory: and he was eaten of worms, and gave up the ghost.

Revelation 16:1, 3–5, 8, 10, 12, 17

And I heard a great voice out of the temple saying to the seven angels, Go your ways, and pour out the vials of the wrath of God upon the earth. . . . And the second angel poured out his vial upon the sea; and it became as the blood of a dead man: and every living soul died in the sea. And the third angel poured out his vial upon the rivers and fountains of waters; and they became blood. And I heard the angel of the waters say, Thou art righteous, O Lord, which art, and wast, and shalt be, because thou hast judged thus. . . . And the fourth angel poured out his vial upon the sun; and power was given unto him to scorch men with fire. . . . And the fifth angel poured out his vial upon the seat of the beast; and his kingdom was full of darkness; and they gnawed their tongues for pain. . . . And the sixth angel poured out his vial upon the great river Euphrates; and the water thereof was dried up, that the way of the kings of the east might be prepared. . . . And the seventh angel poured out his vial into the air; and there came a great voice out of the temple of heaven, from the throne, saying, It is done.

Human and Imperfect

Like the prophets of old, Joseph Smith was human and imperfect. In nearly every way, he was unremarkable—like many of the prophets before him. It is the message and the mission of a prophet that makes him important. It was Joseph's message and mission that made him remarkable.

Before his calling as a prophet, Isaiah saw himself as man of "unclean lips." When he was called as a prophet, he was instantly made clean by the Lord (Isaiah 6:5–7). King David, a man after God's own heart, sent Uriah the Hittite to his death and was an adulterer with Bathsheba (2 Samuel 11:4, 15, 27), but was still permitted to author the Psalms and be a forefather of Christ. As the Lord later spoke to David's son Solomon, he praised David and made no mention of his grievous sins of the past (2 Chronicles 7:12–18; 1 Kings 15:4–5). Solomon had 700 wives, 300 concubines, and became an idol worshiper in his later years (1 Kings 11:3–6), yet he was permitted to author a portion of the Old Testament. The prophet Elisha cursed children who mocked him, causing two bears to kill the children, yet he was blessed in his ministry to the nation of Israel (2 Kings 2:23–24). Saul, before he became Paul, persecuted the Christians sending many men and women to their death (Acts 22:4, 20; 26:10–11; Galatians 1:13–14), yet he was given the privilege of being the premier author of the New Testament.

The Lord is never pleased with sin—he detests it and abhors the transgressions of men in all their wickedness. However, the Lord remembers his covenants with Abraham, Isaac, Jacob, and others and will use men, despite their sinfulness, to bring about his purposes (2 Kings 13:23).

Isaiah 6:5–7

> Then said I, Woe is me! for I am undone; because I am a man of unclean lips, and I dwell in the midst of a people of unclean lips: for mine eyes have seen the King, the Lord of hosts. Then flew one of the seraphims unto me, having a live coal in his hand, which he had taken with the tongs from off the altar: And he laid it upon my mouth, and said, Lo, this hath touched thy lips; and thine iniquity is taken away, and thy sin purged.

2 Samuel 11:4, 15, 27

> And David sent messengers, and took her; and she came in unto him, and he lay with her; for she was purified from her uncleanness: and she returned unto her house. . . . And he wrote in the letter, saying, Set ye Uriah in the forefront of the hottest battle, and retire ye from him, that he may be smitten, and die. . . . And when the

mourning was past, David sent and fetched her to his house, and she became his wife, and bare him a son. But the thing that David had done displeased the Lord.

2 Chronicles 7:12–18

And the Lord appeared to Solomon by night, and said unto him, I have heard thy prayer, and have chosen this place to myself for an house of sacrifice. If I shut up heaven that there be no rain, or if I command the locusts to devour the land, or if I send pestilence among my people; If my people, which are called by my name, shall humble themselves, and pray, and seek my face, and turn from their wicked ways; then will I hear from heaven, and will forgive their sin, and will heal their land. Now mine eyes shall be open, and mine ears attent unto the prayer that is made in this place. For now have I chosen and sanctified this house, that my name may be there for ever: and mine eyes and mine heart shall be there perpetually. And as for thee, if thou wilt walk before me, as David thy father walked, and do according to all that I have commanded thee, and shalt observe my statutes and my judgments; Then will I stablish the throne of thy kingdom, according as I have covenanted with David thy father, saying, There shall not fail thee a man to be ruler in Israel.

1 Kings 15:4–5

Nevertheless for David's sake did the Lord his God give him a lamp in Jerusalem, to set up his son after him, and to establish Jerusalem: Because David did that which was right in the eyes of the Lord, and turned not aside from any thing that he commanded him all the days of his life, save only in the matter of Uriah the Hittite.

1 Kings 11:3–6

And he [*Solomon*] had seven hundred wives, princesses, and three hundred concubines: and his wives turned away his heart. For it came to pass, when Solomon was old, that his wives turned away his heart after other gods: and his heart was not perfect with the Lord his God, as was the heart of David his father. For Solomon went after Ashtoreth the goddess of the Zidonians, and after Milcom the abomination of the Ammonites. And Solomon did evil in the sight of the Lord, and went not fully after the Lord, as did David his father.

2 Kings 2:23–24

And he [*Elisha*] went up from thence unto Beth-el: and as he was going up by the way, there came forth little children out of the city, and mocked him, and said unto him, Go up, thou bald head; go up, thou bald head. And he turned back, and looked on them, and cursed them in the name of the Lord. And there came forth two she bears out of the wood, and tare forty and two children of them.

Acts 22:4, 20, and Acts 26:10–11

And I persecuted this way unto the death, binding and delivering into prisons both men and women. . . . And when the blood of thy martyr Stephen was shed, I also was standing by, and consenting unto his death, and kept the raiment of them that slew him. . . .

Which thing I also did in Jerusalem: and many of the saints did I shut up in prison, having received authority from the chief priests; and when they were put to death, I gave my voice against them. And I punished them oft in every synagogue, and compelled them to blaspheme; and being exceedingly mad against them, I persecuted them even unto strange cities. [*Saul, before he became Paul, ruthlessly persecuted the saints.*]

Galatians 1:13–14

For ye have heard of my conversation in time past in the Jews' religion, how that beyond measure I persecuted the church of God, and wasted it: And profited in the Jews' religion above many my equals in mine own nation, being more exceedingly zealous of the traditions of my fathers. [*Saul, before his conversion, "wasted" the Church of God.*]

2 Kings 13:23

And the Lord was gracious unto them [*Israel*], and had compassion on them, and had respect unto them, because of his covenant with Abraham, Isaac, and Jacob, and would not destroy them, neither cast he them from his presence as yet. [*Despite the imperfection of his chosen servants, God honors his covenants with his children.*]

The Urim and Thummim

Joseph Smith used the Urim and Thummim.

The Urim and Thummim is described in the Old Testament as a combination of objects used for spiritual purposes by priests, prophets, and other men called of God.

The *Jewish Encyclopedia* provides this definition: "Objects connected with the breastplate of the high priest, and used as a kind of divine oracle. Since the days of the Alexandrian translators of the Old Testament it has been asserted to mean 'revelation and truth' . . . or 'lights and perfections.' "[2]

The Urim and Thummim first appears in Exodus 28:30 as part of Aaron's wardrobe in administering in the office of a priest. The Urim and Thummim then appears consecutively in the books of Leviticus, Numbers, and Deuteronomy (Leviticus 8:8; Numbers 27:21; Deuteronomy 33:8), and then again in the first book of Samuel, Ezra, and Nehemiah (1 Samuel 28:6; Ezra 2:63; and Nehemiah 7:65). In John's revelation of the last days, the Lord gives to the righteous (who repent and overcome evil) a "white stone" (Revelation 2:17).

Exodus 28:30

And thou shalt put in the breastplate of judgment the Urim and the Thummim; and they shall be upon Aaron's heart, when he goeth in before the Lord: and Aaron shall bear the judgment of the children of Israel upon his heart before the Lord continually.

Leviticus 8:8

And he put the breastplate upon him: also he put in the breastplate the Urim and the Thummim.

Numbers 27:21

And he shall stand before Eleazar the priest, who shall ask counsel for him after the judgment of Urim before the Lord: at his word shall they go out, and at his word they shall come in, both he, and all the children of Israel with him, even all the congregation.

Deuteronomy 33:8

And of Levi he said, Let thy Thummim and thy Urim be with thy holy one, whom thou didst prove at Massah, and with whom thou didst strive at the waters of Meribah.

1 Samuel 28:6

And when Saul enquired of the Lord, the Lord answered him not, neither by dreams, nor by Urim, nor by prophets.

Ezra 2:63

And the Tirshatha said unto them, that they should not eat of the most holy things, till there stood up a priest with Urim and with Thummim.

Nehemiah 7:65

And the Tirshatha said unto them, that they should not eat of the most holy things, till there stood up a priest with Urim and Thummim.

Revelation 2:17

> He that hath an ear, let him hear what the Spirit saith unto the churches; To him that overcometh will I give to eat of the hidden manna, and will give him a white stone, [*Interpreted to be some kind of Urim and Thummim*] and in the stone a new name written, which no man knoweth saving he that receiveth it.

Persecution and Martyrdom

Joseph Smith had a message. He talked like a prophet, acted like a prophet, wrote like a prophet, suffered like a prophet, and died like a prophet. His story is not unlike those of other prophets recorded in the Bible.

Prophets throughout the ages have been sent by God to deliver messages given to them by God. Rarely have these messages been welcomed, and the messengers frequently have been persecuted and killed. This is a pattern repeated throughout biblical history: kill the messenger.

The Lord encouraged Ezekiel to not to be afraid of the "imprudent and stiffhearted" people to whom he would preach (Ezekiel 2:4–7). Stephen reminded the Jewish leaders of this in his own time and was killed for his trouble (Acts 7:51–54). King Herod killed James the brother of John to appease the Jews, and then "proceeded further to take Peter also" (Acts 12:1–5). Peter endured prison and eventually death. Paul was stoned during his public ministry (Acts 14:19), persecuted and afflicted (2 Timothy 3:11–12), driven out of cities and regions (Acts 13:50), and eventually put to death—all because of the disapproval of the messages he was delivering from God.

Ezekiel 2:4–7

> For they [*the children of Israel*] are impudent children and stiffhearted. I do send thee [*Ezekiel*] unto them; and thou shalt say unto them, Thus saith the Lord God. And they, whether they will hear, or whether they will forbear, (for they are a rebellious house,) yet shall know that there hath been a prophet among them. And thou, son of man, be not afraid of them, neither be afraid of their words, though briers and thorns be with thee, and thou dost dwell among scorpions: be not afraid of their words, nor be dismayed at their looks, though they be a rebellious house. And thou shalt speak my words unto them, whether they will hear, or whether they will forbear: for they are most rebellious.

Acts 7:51–54

Ye stiffnecked and uncircumcised in heart and ears, ye do always resist the Holy Ghost: as your fathers did, so do ye. Which of the prophets have not your fathers persecuted? and they have slain them which shewed before of the coming of the Just One; of whom ye have been now the betrayers and murderers: Who have received the law by the disposition of angels, and have not kept it. When they heard these things, they were cut to the heart, and they gnashed on him with their teeth. [*Stephen's ministry and testimony angered the Pharisees who eventually stoned him to death.*]

Acts 12:1–5

Now about that time Herod the king stretched forth his hands to vex certain of the church. And he killed James the brother of John with the sword. And because he saw it pleased the Jews, he proceeded further to take Peter also. (Then were the days of unleavened bread.) And when he had apprehended him, he put him in prison, and delivered him to four quaternions of soldiers to keep him; intending after Easter to bring him forth to the people. Peter therefore was kept in prison: but prayer was made without ceasing of the church unto God for him. [*Joseph Smith was jailed several times by mobs who were angry at his ministry.*]

Acts 14:19

And there came thither certain Jews from Antioch and Iconium, who persuaded the people, and, having stoned Paul, drew him out of the city, supposing he had been dead. [*Joseph Smith was never stoned for his ministry, but he was tarred and feathered, beaten, and left for dead.*]

2 Timothy 3:11–12

Persecutions, afflictions, which came unto me at Antioch, at Iconium, at Lystra; what persecutions I endured: but out of them all the Lord delivered me. Yea, and all that will live godly in Christ Jesus shall suffer persecution. [*Joseph Smith endured years of persecution at the hands of those who opposed his ministry.*]

Acts 13:50

But the Jews stirred up the devout and honourable women, and the chief men of the city, and raised persecution against Paul and Barnabas, and expelled them out of their coasts. [*Not only was Joseph Smith expelled out of cities, but the entire Latter-day Saint population was expelled from places like Kirtland, Ohio, and Nauvoo, Illinois.*]

MORMON UNDERSTANDING

A Prophet of God

Joseph Smith—like Noah, Moses, Ezekiel, Isaiah, Peter, Paul, and others—was a prophet of God. Through him, on April 6, 1830, Jesus Christ restored his church to the earth:

> The rise of the Church of Christ in these last days, being one thousand eight hundred and thirty years since the coming of our Lord and Savior Jesus Christ in the flesh, it being regularly organized and established agreeable to the laws of our country, by the will and commandments of God, in the fourth month, and on the sixth day of the month which is called April—Which commandments were given to Joseph Smith, Jun., who was called of God, and ordained an apostle of Jesus Christ, to be the first elder of this church; And to Oliver Cowdery, who was also called of God, an apostle of Jesus Christ, to be the second elder of this church, and ordained under his hand; And this according to the grace of our Lord and Savior Jesus Christ, to whom be all glory, both now and forever. Amen. (D&C 20:1–4)

Thus Joseph became the first prophet of the Restoration and the first President of The Church of Jesus Christ of Latter-day Saints.

Visitations

In the spring of 1820, Heavenly Father and Jesus Christ appeared to Joseph, who was then a boy of fourteen. Joseph asked them which of the churches then competing for his devotion he should join. He was instructed to join none of them.

In 1829, John the Baptist appeared to Joseph and Oliver Cowdery and ordained them to the Aaronic Priesthood (D&C 13; 27:8). Later, Peter, James, and John appeared and ordained Joseph and Oliver to the Melchizedek Priesthood. Moses, Elias, Elijah, and others also appeared and gave further instructions and authority.

A Unique American

Joseph was a uniquely American religious leader. He was deeply influenced by and a formative agent of the nineteenth century forces of manifest destiny. Of him, Josiah Quincy, the distinguished former mayor of Boston and member of the Massachusetts State Legislature in 1837, wrote that Joseph Smith would be remembered for having a powerful influence in America:

It is by no means improbable that some future textbook, for the use of generations yet unborn, will contain a question something like this: What historical American of the nineteenth century has exerted the most powerful influence upon the destiny of his countrymen? And it is by no means impossible that the answer to that interrogatory may be thus written: Joseph Smith, the Mormon prophet. And the reply, absurd as it doubtless seems to most men now living, may be an obvious commonplace to their descendants.[3]

George Wharton James, lecturer, journalist, Methodist minister, and author of more than forty books and numerous articles on California and the American Southwest, wrote that Joseph Smith was one of the wonders of his time:

Let any one, even a literary genius, after forty years of life, try to write a companion volume to the Book of Mormon, and then almost daily for a number of years give out "revelations" by the score that internally harmonize one with another, at the same time formulate a system of doctrine for a new church, introduce many new principles, resuscitate extinct priesthoods, and formulate a system of church government which has no superior on earth.

Would he succeed in making the system coherent? Could he influence scores of intelligent, wise, thoughtful, educated, religiously trained men . . . besides attracting thousands to the fold of his church, as did Joseph Smith? Even if one were assured that the prophet was an impostor, that does not lessen the marvel. The mystery, the riddle, the problem, is even greater than before. Even if he be explained on the ground that he was a mystic gifted with superior psychic powers, the riddle still remains, the problem is still unsolved. . . . to deny such a man a wonderful power over the human heart and intellect is absurd. Only fanatical prejudice can ignore it. However he may be accounted for by the reasoning mind, Joseph Smith, the Mormon Prophet, was one of the wonders of his time.[4]

Harold Bloom, author of *The American Religion: The Emergence of the Post-Christian Nation*, had similar sentiments to that of Quincy and James. He wrote that it is impossible to doubt that Joseph Smith was an authentic prophet:

Whatever his lapses, Smith was an authentic religious genius, unique in our national history . . . I also do not find it possible to doubt that Joseph Smith was an authentic prophet. Where in all of

American history can we find his match? . . . In proportion to his importance and his complexity, [Joseph Smith] remains the least-studied personage, of an undiminished vitality, in our entire national saga. . . . If there is already in place any authentic version of the American Religion then, as Tolstoy surmised, it must be Mormonism, whose future as yet may prove decisive for the nation, and for more than this nation alone.[5]

Heikki Raisanen, a Finnish theologian, wrote: "Joseph's teachings provide solutions for most, if not all, of the genuine problems and contradictions of the Bible with which scholars have wrestled for generations."[6]

These non-Mormon observers took a correct measure of Joseph as a historical figure and religious leader.

Visions and Miracles

From the time of the First Vision at age fourteen to the time of his martyrdom at age thirty-eight, Joseph was rigorously engaged in the work assigned to him by Heavenly Father and Jesus Christ. This work included the mundane and the miraculous.

In any criticism of Mormonism, much turns on whether the observer believes Joseph was who he said he was and did what he said he did. To the observer who accepts Joseph's claim of prophetic calling, the miraculous events that Joseph described are as believable as any that are recorded in the Bible. To the observer who rejects this claim, Joseph was—indeed had to have been—a fraud.

Christian apologists have said that either Jesus was who he said he was or he was the biggest scoundrel in history. There is no middle ground. The same could be said of Joseph.

Human and Imperfect

Some who question the prophetic commission of Joseph point to certain negative testimonials of individuals close to him before, during, and after his call as a prophet. They say that his life was uncharacteristic of a holy man and that he was unfit to be an instrument in the hands of God. Joseph is charged with being a treasure seeker, dabbling in the occult, promoting polygamy to satisfy his own carnal desires, and engaging in other acts unbefitting a prophet of God.

Most of these stories are impossible to verify or are difficult to take seriously (incredulity works both ways). But even if some of them are true, Joseph still remains in the good company of flawed men like King David, Solomon, the prophet Isaiah, and the apostle Paul. The Lord must build his kingdom with imperfect men—or he could not build it at all.

Teachings

Some who question the prophetic commission of Joseph maintain that the divine communications which he claimed to have received were revelations of a spirit that was not of God and therefore was of the devil. Furthermore, some say Joseph preached a gospel that was not truly Christian.

Latter-day Saints are untroubled by these claims. It is well documented that Joseph testified that Jesus is the Christ, the only begotten son of the living God, who was born of a virgin, atoned for the sins of the world, died, was resurrected, and sits at the right hand of God. Joseph declared that all things "which pertain to our religion are only appendages" to the Atonement of Jesus Christ.[7]

Persecution and Martyrdom

Joseph, like the apostles and many other prophets described in the Bible, was slandered, persecuted, driven out, and finally murdered. On five separate occasions over a fourteen-year period, Joseph was arrested on ambiguous or unsubstantiated charges, none of which led to a court conviction.

In March of 1832, Joseph was taken from his home by an angry mob, beaten, tarred, and feathered. The mob's invasion of his home led to the death of one of his infant children.

On June 27, 1844, in Carthage, Hancock County, Illinois, the persecution of Joseph Smith ended with his martyrdom at the hands of a mob of armed men.

These anti-Mormon forces hoped that the Mormon Church would die with the Mormon prophet. But the Church did not die, nor did it fade away; indeed, it surged ahead with renewed vigor. This is a reminder of the counsel given by Gamaliel to the Jewish leaders to leave the Christian movement alone because "if it be of God, ye cannot overthrow it; lest haply ye be found even to fight against God" (Acts 5:34–39).

Latter-day Saints, then and now, take the persecution and martyrdom of the prophet Joseph and the persecution and murder of other

Church members over the years as powerful evidence for Joseph, not against him. Faithful Latter-day Saints are confident in their belief that Joseph was the prophet through whom Jesus Christ restored his church to the earth in these latter days.

Who He Was

Latter-day Saints do not believe Joseph Smith was a god. He was not a messiah. Nor was he a begotten son of God. They do not believe he was Christ come again or that he was an angel visiting the earth.

They do believe he was a prophet who, like Moses, had been appointed by the Lord to teach and to lead his people.

Joseph Smith was simply a man with a message from God. He delivered the message and was murdered for it. But the message was larger than the man. It lives on. Many other Latter-day Saint messengers have come and gone since the death of Joseph—all bearing the same message.

NOTES

1. *True to the Faith: A Gospel Reference*, 89.
2. Emil G. Hirsch et al. (1901–1906), 384, "Urim and Thummim." *The Jewish Encyclopedia*. Retrieved 10 February 2010 from http://www.jewishencyclopedia.com/view.jsp?artid=52&letter=U&search=urim).
3. Josiah Quincy, *Figures of the Past; From the Leaves of Old Journals* (Boston, MA: Roberts Brothers, 1896), 376.
4. George Wharton James, Utah, *The Land of Blossoming Valleys* (Boston, Massachusetts: The Page Company, 1922), 79–81.
5. Harold Bloom, *The American Religion: The Emergence of the Post-Christian Nation* (New York: Simon and Schuster, 1992), 82–97.
6. Edwin O. Haroldsen, " 'Good and Evil Spoken Of'," *Ensign*, Aug. 1995, 8.
7. Joseph Fielding Smith, comp., *Teachings of the Prophet Joseph Smith*, (American Fork, Utah: Covenant Communications, 2002), 122.

❧ 13 ❧

PRIESTHOOD

BIBLICAL TEACHING

The Priesthood

The priesthood is the power and authority of God. God has delegated this power and authority to certain men at certain times.

At the time of Abram (before he became Abraham), there was a priesthood that ministered in bread and wine, performed blessings, and managed tithing (Genesis 14:18–20). Later the Lord introduced the Levitical priesthood and referred to it as an "everlasting priesthood" (Exodus 40:13–15; Numbers 25:13).

Genesis 14:18–20

> And Melchizedek king of Salem brought forth bread and wine: and he was the priest of the most high God. And he blessed him, and said, Blessed be Abram of the most high God, possessor of heaven and earth: And blessed be the most high God, which hath delivered thine enemies into thy hand. And he gave him tithes of all.

Exodus 40:13–15

> [*The Lord speaking to Moses.*] And thou shalt put upon Aaron the holy garments, and anoint him, and sanctify him; that he may minister unto me in the priest's office. And thou shalt bring his sons, and clothe them with coats: And thou shalt anoint them, as thou didst anoint their father, that they may minister unto me in the priest's office: for their anointing shall surely be an everlasting priesthood throughout their generations.

Numbers 25:13

> [*The Lord speaking to Moses.*] And he [*Phinehas*] shall have it [*the priesthood*], and his seed after him, even the covenant of an everlasting priesthood; because he was zealous for his God, and made an atonement for the children of Israel.

The Priesthood and the Apostles

The priesthood was well established during the time of the apostles. Peter spoke of "a holy priesthood" (1 Peter 2:5) and "a royal priesthood" (1 Peter 2:9).

1 Peter 2:5

> Ye also, as lively stones, are built up a spiritual house, an holy priesthood, to offer up spiritual sacrifices, acceptable to God by Jesus Christ.

1 Peter 2:9

> But ye are a chosen generation, a royal priesthood, an holy nation, a peculiar people; that ye should shew forth the praises of him who hath called you out of darkness into his marvellous light.

The Levitical Priesthood—The Priesthood of Aaron

The Levitical Priesthood, also known as the Aaronic Priesthood (or the Priesthood of Aaron), was in place during the time of Christ; however, it was not possible for man to reach his spiritual potential (perfection in Christ) through the Levitical Priesthood alone. A greater priesthood, the Melchizedek Priesthood, was necessary (Hebrews 7:11–12).

Hebrews 7:11–12

> If therefore perfection were by the Levitical priesthood, (for under it the people received the law,) what further need was there that another priest should rise after the order of Melchisedec, and not be called after the order of Aaron? For the priesthood being changed [*changed, not done away with—the Levitical priesthood remains as the preparatory priesthood*], there is made of necessity a change also of the law.

Melchizedek

Melchizedek, or Melchisedec as the name is often spelled, is mentioned eleven times in the Bible. Melchizedek was the king of Salem and a "priest of the most high God" who was greatly revered by Abraham (Hebrews 7:1–3). References to Melchizedek have been found in the Dead Sea Scrolls and in the Nag Hammadi Library. He was an important biblical character.

Hebrews 7:1–3

> For this Melchisedec, king of Salem, priest of the most high God, who met Abraham returning from the slaughter of the kings, and blessed him; To whom also Abraham gave a tenth part of all; first being by interpretation King of righteousness, and after that also King of Salem, which is, King of peace; Without father, without mother, without descent, having neither beginning of days, nor end of life; but made like unto the Son of God; abideth a priest continually [*an everlasting priesthood in conjunction with the Aaronic Priesthood*].

The Melchizedek Priesthood and Christ

Jesus Christ is the great eternal priest after the order of Melchizedek (Psalm 110:4; Hebrews 7:15–17). The Savior is referred to in the New Testament as the "high priest" in the Melchizedek Priesthood (Hebrews 5:5–10; 6:20; 8:1)—the high priest of an "unchangeable priesthood" (Hebrews 7:24–26). He is a "merciful and faithful high priest" like unto his brethren (Hebrews 2:17). He set the ecclesiastical example for all men to be ordained to the Melchizedek Priesthood (Hebrews 5:1) as part of the "profession" of ministry in the Lord and Savior (Hebrews 3:1).

Psalm 110:4

> The Lord hath sworn, and will not repent, Thou art a priest for ever after the order of Melchizedek.

Hebrews 7:15–17

> And it is yet far more evident: for that after the similitude of Melchisedec there ariseth another priest, Who is made, not after the law of a carnal commandment, but after the power of an endless life. For he testifieth, Thou art a priest for ever after the order of Melchisedec.

Hebrews 5:5–10 (see also Hebrews 6:20 and 8:1)

> So also Christ glorified not himself to be made an high priest; but he that said unto him, Thou art my Son, to day have I begotten thee. As he saith also in another place, Thou art a priest for ever after

the order of Melchisedec. Who in the days of his flesh, when he had offered up prayers and supplications with strong crying and tears unto him that was able to save him from death, and was heard din that he feared; Though he were a Son, yet learned he obedience by the things which he suffered; And being made perfect, he became the author of eternal salvation unto all them that obey him; Called of God an high priest after the order of Melchisedec.

Hebrews 7:24–26

[*Speaking of Jesus*] But this man, because he continueth ever, hath an unchangeable priesthood. Wherefore he is able also to save them to the uttermost that come unto God by him, seeing he ever liveth to make intercession for them. For such an high priest became us, who is holy, harmless, undefiled, separate from sinners, and made higher than the heavens.

Hebrews 2:17

Wherefore in all things it behoved him to be made like unto his brethren, that he might be a merciful and faithful high priest in things pertaining to God, to make reconciliation for the sins of the people.

Hebrews 5:1

For every high priest taken from among men is ordained for men in things pertaining to God, that he may offer both gifts and sacrifices for sins.

Hebrews 3:1

Wherefore, holy brethren, partakers of the heavenly calling, consider the Apostle and High Priest of our profession, Christ Jesus.

Ordination and Setting Apart

It is an honor to hold the priesthood, and those who do so must be called of God and set apart, just as Aaron was set apart by the Lord through his servant Moses (Hebrews 5:4). The ordination and setting apart of a priesthood holder is accomplished by the laying on of hands by those in authority (Numbers 27:18–19). Christ and his apostles continued this method of ordination and setting apart.

Hebrews 5:4

And no man taketh this honour unto himself, but he that is called of God, as was Aaron.

Numbers 27:18–19

> And the Lord said unto Moses [*the man given authority by God*], Take thee Joshua the son of Nun, a man in whom is the spirit, and lay thine hand upon him [*ordaining by the laying on of hands*]; And set him before Eleazar the priest, and before all the congregation; and give him a charge in their sight. [*The people witness the calling of Joshua and sustain Joshua in his new office.*]

Priesthood Power and Authority

While God may grant anyone the opportunity to perform healings and other ministerial duties through the gifts of the spirit (1 Corinthians 12:28; 12:9), priesthood holders are set apart specifically to do so as part of their spiritual and ecclesiastical calling. Acting for the Lord on earth, priesthood holders cast out devils and lay hands upon the sick to heal (Mark 16:17–18), often using the ordinance of anointing with oil (James 5:14). Following the example of Jesus in ordaining his apostles, priesthood holders are given "power and authority" to minister in the name of the Lord (Luke 9:1–2).

1 Corinthians 12:28

> And God hath set some in the church, first apostles, secondarily prophets, thirdly teachers, after that miracles, then gifts of healings, helps, governments, diversities of tongues.

1 Corinthians 12:9

> To another faith by the same Spirit; to another the gifts of healing by the same Spirit.

Mark 16:17–18

> And these signs shall follow them that believe; In my name shall they cast out devils; they shall speak with new tongues; They shall take up serpents; and if they drink any deadly thing, it shall not hurt them: they shall lay hands on the sick, and they shall recover.

James 5:14

> Is any sick among you? let him call for the elders of the church; and let them pray over him, anointing him with oil in the name of the Lord.

Luke 9:1–2

> Then he called his twelve disciples together, and gave them power and authority over all devils, and to cure diseases. And he sent them to preach the kingdom of God, and to heal the sick.

Priesthood Qualifications

The Lord requires faith and worthiness in the men he calls to the priesthood. The Lord uses the foolish and weak things of the world to accomplish his work (1 Corinthians 1:27). There are instances in the scriptures where specific requirements have been given to hold an office in the priesthood. For example, Paul provided counsel to Titus about elders who are married ("elder" is an office in the Melchizedek Priesthood). Paul said that elders are to have only one wife and faithful children (Titus 1:5–6). Paul also gave specific counsel to Timothy on the requirements of a bishop (an office in the Aaronic Priesthood, but an office typically held by Melchizedek Priesthood holders as high priests), ensuring the individual was faithful and worthy to serve (1 Timothy 3:1–7).

1 Corinthians 1:27

> But God hath chosen the foolish things of the world to confound the wise; and God hath chosen the weak things of the world to confound the things which are mighty.

Titus 1:5–6

> For this cause left I thee in Crete, that thou shouldest set in order the things that are wanting, and ordain elders in every city, as I had appointed thee: If any be blameless, the husband of one wife, having faithful children not accused of riot or unruly.

1 Timothy 3:1–7

> This is a true saying, If a man desire the office of a bishop, he desireth a good work. A bishop then must be blameless, the husband of one wife, vigilant, sober, of good behaviour, given to hospitality, apt to teach; Not given to wine, no striker, not greedy of filthy lucre; but patient, not a brawler, not covetous; One that ruleth well his own house, having his children in subjection with all gravity; (For if a man know not how to rule his own house, how shall he take care of the church of God?) Not a novice, lest being lifted up with pride he fall into the condemnation of the devil. Moreover he must have a good report of them which are without; lest he fall into reproach and the snare of the devil.

MORMON UNDERSTANDING

Priesthood Power and Authority

By the power of the priesthood, God created the heavens and the earth and maintains the universe in its perfect order. Through the power of the priesthood, the Lord achieves his purpose, which is to bring to pass the immortality and eternal life of man. Priesthood authority is required to perform ordinances such as baptism, confirmation, blessing and passing the sacrament, administering to the sick, giving special blessings, and administering temple ordinances.

A Capacity, Not a Person

The priesthood is a capacity, not a person or group of people. It is "held" and "exercised" by men on whom it is properly conferred. Women share in the spiritual blessings of the priesthood but do not carry out the ecclesiastical duties of the priesthood. The efficacy of the priesthood in any given circumstance depends on the faith and worthiness of the priesthood holder, the recipient of priestly ministrations, and the will of the Lord.

Origins

There was a priesthood on the earth long before Christ came in the flesh. While modern scriptures teach of a priesthood during the time of Adam, the first biblical reference appears in Genesis 14:18, where Melchizedek, king of Salem, is identified as "the priest of the most high God."

The Levitical priesthood, also known as the priesthood of Aaron or the Aaronic Priesthood, was introduced shortly after the departure of the Israelites from Egypt (Exodus 28:1). The Levitical priesthood was passed on by lineage to members of the tribe of Levi. Moses and Aaron were members of this tribe and held this priesthood. Men who held this priesthood in the time of Moses were responsible for administrating the Mosaic law and the tabernacle sacrifice ceremonies.

Jesus and the Priesthood

The Levitical Priesthood was on the earth when Jesus was born. During his public ministry, Jesus ordained apostles to lead his church. He gave them the authority and power to perform miracles and act in his name (Mark 3:13–15; John 15:16). By this means and with his fulfillment of the Mosaic law, Christ established the Royal Priesthood, which came to be known as the Melchizedek Priesthood. The Levitical (Aaronic) priesthood remained but as a preparatory priesthood, a lesser included priesthood, leading to the Melchizedek Priesthood.

Priesthood in The Church of Jesus Christ of Latter-day Saints

Today the priesthood is divided into the Aaronic Priesthood (the lesser priesthood) and the Melchizedek Priesthood (the greater priesthood). The Aaronic Priesthood is sometimes referred to as the "preparatory priesthood" and is an appendage to the Melchizedek Priesthood.

A bishop presides over a ward, the basic congregational unit of the Church. If a congregation is too small to constitute a ward, it is called a branch and is presided over by a branch president. (With a few exceptions, references to wards in this book include branches, and references to bishops include branch presidents.)

The offices within the Aaronic Priesthood include deacon, teacher, priest, and bishop. The Aaronic Priesthood is organized into a deacons quorum (usually young men twelve and thirteen), a teachers quorum (usually young men fourteen and fifteen), and a priests quorum (usually young men sixteen and older). The bishop of the ward is also president of the priests quorum.

Offices within the Melchizedek Priesthood include elder, high priest, patriarch (evangelist), seventy, and apostle. The Melchizedek Priesthood within each ward is organized into an elders quorum and a high priest group. The high priest group is part of a stake-wide high priest quorum. The stake president is president of this quorum. An elders quorum president is called by the stake president to preside over the elders quorum in each ward. The bishop of each ward, as the local presiding high priest, supervises both the high priest group and the elders quorum at the ward level. All wards in a stake are presided over by the stake president.

The priesthood is available to all worthy male members of The Church of Jesus Christ of Latter-day Saints. The priesthood is passed from one priesthood holder to another by the laying on of hands by one having the authority to confer the priesthood. It is not passed on as a birthright or by lineage. There are no academic or professional requirements to hold the priesthood, nor are there any such requirements to hold any leadership position within the Church. Spiritual worthiness, however, remains the fundamental requirement.

⚮ 14 ⚮

CHURCH ORGANIZATION

BIBLICAL TEACHING

Priesthood Foundation

NOTE: The following is a summary. See the priesthood chapter for more details, including the cited biblical quotations.

The priesthood is the power and authority of God. God has delegated this power and authority to certain men at certain times, and it is the foundation of the church Christ established.

There was a priesthood that ministered in bread and wine, performed blessings, and managed tithing in the time of Abraham. Melchizedek, king of Salem, was revered by Abraham and called "the priest of the most high God" (Genesis 14:18–20).

Later the Lord introduced the Levitical Priesthood and called it an "everlasting priesthood" (Exodus 40:15; Numbers 25:13).

The Levitical Priesthood, also known as the Aaronic Priesthood, was in place during the time of Christ; however, men could not reach their full spiritual potential through the Levitical Priesthood alone. A greater priesthood, the Melchizedek Priesthood, was necessary (Hebrews 7:11–12). The early apostles of Christ held the priesthood. Peter wrote of a royal and holy priesthood during his public ministry (1 Peter 2:9; 2:5).

Jesus Christ is the great eternal priest after the order of Melchizedek

(Psalm 110:4; Hebrews 7:15–17). The Savior is called the "high priest" in the Melchizedek Priesthood (Hebrews 5:5–10; 6:20; 8:1)—the high priest of an "unchangeable priesthood" (Hebrews 7:24-26). Jesus was a "merciful and faithful high priest" like his brethren (Hebrews 2:17). He set the ecclesiastical example for all men to be ordained to the Melchizedek Priesthood (Hebrews 5:1) to conduct the ministry in the Lord and Savior (Hebrews 3:1).

To receive the priesthood, a man must be called of God and set apart, just as Aaron was set apart by the Lord through his servant Moses (Hebrews 5:4). The ordination and setting apart of a priesthood holder is accomplished by the laying on of hands by those in authority (Numbers 27:18–19).

Apostles and Prophets

NOTE: The following is a summary. See the chapter on revelation and prophets for more details.

Jesus ordained twelve apostles to be special witnesses of his gospel (Mark 3:14 and Luke 6:13–16) and to lead his church. It was important that there be twelve, so Matthias was called to replace Judas soon after the death of Judas (Acts 1:25–26). Paul wrote that the church is "built upon the foundation of the apostles and prophets," and he referred to apostles in several of his letters (Ephesians 2:19–22; 4:11; 1 Corinthians 12:28). The Lord reveals his mysteries (scriptural interpretation, doctrine, and so forth) to the apostles through the Holy Ghost (Ephesians 3:5).

Quorums of the Seventy

Jesus appointed a Quorum of the Seventy to go out among the people to preach, teach, and administer in the affairs of the church (Luke 10:1, 17). This quorum was subordinate to the Quorum of the Twelve Apostles and was responsible for the small geographical area where the Lord conducted his public ministry.

Luke 10:1, 17

> After these things the Lord appointed other seventy [*a quorum of seventy*] also, and sent them two and two before his face into every city and place, whither he himself would come. . . . And the seventy returned again with joy, saying, Lord, even the devils are subject unto us through thy name. [*Today there are multiple quorums of seventy to minister to the Saints around the world. The eighth such quorum was established in April 2005.*]

Bishops

Paul was acutely aware of the importance of bishops in the Church, and he gave Timothy comprehensive requirements for this position (1 Timothy 3:1–7).

1 Timothy 3:1–7

> This is a true saying, If a man desire the office of a bishop, he desireth a good work. A bishop then must be blameless, the husband of one wife, vigilant, sober, of good behaviour, given to hospitality, apt to teach; Not given to wine, no striker, not greedy of filthy lucre; but patient, not a brawler, not covetous; One that ruleth well his own house, having his children in subjection with all gravity; (For if a man know not how to rule his own house, how shall he take care of the church of God?) Not a novice, lest being lifted up with pride he fall into the condemnation of the devil. Moreover he must have a good report of them which are without; lest he fall into reproach and the snare of the devil.

Unpaid Clergy

From the very earliest biblical times, the Lord's ministers did not receive specified monetary compensation for their services. The priests of Levi were given food to support themselves and their families, but they were not given wages (see Deuteronomy 18). Jesus counseled his apostles not to take money with them in their ministry (see Luke 9:3), nor a purse for money (see Luke 10:4), as he likened those he sent forth as shepherds that are not hired for money (see John 10:12). Jesus expected his disciples to work without direct monetary compensation (see Matthew 10:8–10).

Paul, a missionary who had more reason than any other apostle to be paid for his labors, told the Thessalonians that he imparted to them freely and asked only for food to sustain his physical needs (see 1 Thessalonians 2:8–10; 2 Thessalonians 3:7–9). Paul did not seek money for his ministerial services (Acts 20:33–34), and he wrote to Titus that a bishop should not minister for money (Titus 1:7, 11). Peter said that ministers should work "willingly, not for filthy lucre [money]" (1 Peter 5:2).

Acts 20:33–34

> [*Paul speaking*] I have coveted no man's silver, or gold, or apparel. Yea, ye yourselves know, that these hands have ministered unto my necessities, and to them that were with me.

Titus 1:7, 11

> For a bishop must be blameless, as the steward of God; not self-willed, not soon angry, not given to wine, no striker, not given to filthy lucre. . . . Whose mouths must be stopped, who subvert whole houses, teaching things which they ought not, for filthy lucre's sake.

1 Peter 5:2

> Feed the flock of God which is among you, taking the oversight thereof, not by constraint, but willingly; not for filthy lucre, but of a ready mind.

MORMON UNDERSTANDING

The Restoration

The Church of Jesus Christ of Latter-day Saints is the restored church of Jesus Christ on earth. It is called "restored" because it is patterned after the church established by Jesus during his public ministry. After the Ascension of Christ and through the centuries that followed, men changed the ordinances and doctrines established by the Savior, including the organization of the Church.

The restoration of the Church of Jesus Christ included a full restoration of the organization of the early church, including restoration of the authority of the priesthood. In 1829, both the Aaronic and Melchizedek Priesthoods were restored to the earth, and on April 6, 1830, the restored Church of Jesus Christ was established.

The Church of Jesus Christ Restored

The Church was organized with the same offices as it had during the time of Christ's public ministry, including "apostles, prophets, seventies, evangelists (patriarchs), pastors (presiding officers), high priests, elders, bishops, priests, teachers, and deacons."[1] The commitment of the Church to restoring and maintaining the same ecclesiastical structure as that which existed during the time of Christ on earth is stated in the sixth article of faith:

> We believe in the same organization that existed in the Primitive Church, namely, apostles, prophets, pastors, teachers, evangelists, and so forth.

Jesus set up a hierarchical organization to avoid confusion and maintain doctrinal integrity. Today the prophet, the First Presidency, the apostles, and the Quorums of the Seventy are the presiding officers of the worldwide Church of Jesus Christ of Latter-day Saints.

At the local level, the Church is organized into stakes and wards (a stake is a group of wards), with priesthood leadership presiding over each. Each stake high council, consisting of twelve priesthood leaders answering to the stake president, provides a structure at the local level that echoes that of the Church as a whole, with its twelve apostles answering to the prophet.

Each ward is led by a bishop, who is called to this position by the stake president, and sustained by the ward membership. The bishop selects two counselors to serve with him; together, these three form the bishopric of the ward. All ward priesthood and auxiliary organizations serve under the bishopric.

The ward priesthood organization is divided into a high priest group and quorums of elders, priests, teachers, and deacons. The elders quorum is led by a president and his two counselors; the high priest group is presided over by a group leader and his two counselors. The elders quorum president and the high priest group leader report directly to the stake president; however, both serve under the bishop, who is the presiding high priest of the ward.

All worthy adult men eighteen and older belong to either the elders quorum or high priest group and are assigned as home teachers. Women, eighteen and older, are organized into the Relief Society, led by the Relief Society president and her two counselors. Similar organizations exist for youth and young children, and these are similarly led. There are also several functional organizations at the ward level.

Adaptations to Growth

The Church has grown from six members in 1830 to nearly 14 million members worldwide in 2010, and it continues to grow each year. The Church has adapted to this growth while maintaining essentially the same organizational structure as the early church. Such adaptation took place even in biblical times. For example, when the first apostles took up the matter of caring for widows, they directed that seven others be organized to carry out this particular duty so that the apostles could continue to focus on teaching, leading, and spreading the faith:

> Wherefore, brethren, look ye out among you seven men of honest report, full of the Holy Ghost and wisdom, whom we may appoint over this business. (Acts 6:3)

Such adaptation will continue in The Church of Jesus Christ of Latter-day Saints, but it will be done with great care and restraint to remain consistent with the forms established by Christ.

Names and Labels

On April 26, 1838, eight years after formal establishment of the Church, the Lord declared: "Thus shall my church be called in the last days, even The Church of Jesus Christ of Latter-day Saints" (D&C 115:4). The Church is named for its founder, Jesus Christ.

NOTE: There is a widespread misunderstanding that the Prophet Joseph Smith founded The Church of Jesus Christ of Latter-day Saints. He did not. He was the prophet of the restoration of Christ's church, not its founder.

The terms *Mormon* and *Mormonism* were first coined as pejoratives. Soon, however, these terms came into neutral and even friendly usage for the sake of brevity. The latter usages are common today.

The Church is often referred to as "the Mormon Church" or "the LDS (Latter-day Saint) Church." Both of these references are understandable: the proper name of the Church is lengthy. However, Church members are counseled to use the full name of the Church as much as possible to avoid confusion with other sects and to convey the fact that the Church is Christ-centered. "Latter-day Saint" is likewise formally preferred, but "Mormon" is commonly used today, even among members of the Church.

Unpaid Clergy

Christ and his apostles did not accept financial compensation for their ministry, and neither did their followers. This practice is carried forward in The Church of Jesus Christ of Latter-day Saints at the stake and ward levels and for missionaries worldwide. The grassroots ministry is unpaid.

The absence of financial compensation for anyone at the local level is considered an essential element of Church organization: It stimulates full participation of all Church members in all activities of the Church. Church members lead, teach, and assist one another—taking turns in various roles while seeking elsewhere for their livelihoods.

As of December 31, 2009, the Church consisted of 13,824,854 members in 2,865 stakes and 28,424 wards and branches. These stakes, wards, and branches were led by 31,289 lay ministers, all of whom were unpaid. These ministers perform ecclesiastical duties nearly identical to those of priests, pastors, and ministers in other Christian denominations.

At the same time, there were 51,736 full-time missionaries, all unpaid, serving across the globe.[2] Missionaries who cannot afford to fund their own missions may receive funds donated by individual Church members—the Church does not pay the living expenses of these missionaries out of tithes donated to the Church.

The global leadership of the Church consists of the three members of the First Presidency, the Quorum of the Twelve Apostles, and members of the eight Quorums of the Seventy—a total of 575 ministers. All qualify for a modest stipend for living expenses. Many decline this stipend because they have independent means. The 575 men who qualify for this stipend constitute 1.8 percent of the total ministry of the Church, excluding missionaries. If full-time missionaries are included in the above equation, the percentage of Church leaders who qualify for a stipend drops to 0.7 percent. If the hundreds of thousands of other men and women who serve without pay in auxiliary roles are added in, the percentage of leaders qualifying for a stipend shrinks to insignificance.

The Church employs and provides monetary compensation to a number of people in non-ecclesiastical roles such as non-ecclesiastical administration, building construction and maintenance, specialized teaching outside stakes and wards, and so forth. Even in these cases, however, unpaid service missionaries usually can be found working side-by-side with or under the direction of these employees.[2]

NOTE

1. *Gospel Principles,* 97–98.
2. "Statistical Report, 2009," The Church of Jesus Christ of Latter-day Saints, http://www.lds.org/conference/talk/display/0,5232,23-1-1207-10,00.html.

❦ 15 ❧

CHURCH
PRACTICES

Biblical Teaching

Pray Always

The Bible says to pray always, in all places and times, but particularly when alone (see Matthew 6:5–6). Pray to God the Father, praising him, petitioning him, and asking that his will be done (see Matthew 6:9–13). Pray spontaneously, without vain repetition (see Matthew 6:7). Pray with faith and confidence, knowing that God will grant to his children all that they need (see James 1:5–6).

Fasting—Old Testament

To fast is to abstain from food and drink for a specified purpose and usually for a specified time. Fasting can be an expression of repentance or lamentation (see Nehemiah 9:1; 1:4; Jonah 3:5; Zechariah 7:5; Joel 2:12, 15), an amplifier of prayers of thanksgiving (see Zechariah 8:19), or an expression of devotion to the Lord (see Joel 2:12, 15).

Fasting—New Testament

Jesus reinforced the principle of fasting as a means of gaining strength in the ministry (see Matthew 4:2; 7:21; Mark 9:29) and a way of gaining comfort from the Father in a time of reflection (see Matthew 9:15). The Savior counseled his followers to fast in good cheer without calling for attention to themselves (see Matthew 6:16–17).

The apostles fasted to gain spiritual strength and unity (see 1 Corinthians 7:5) and to receive direction from the Holy Ghost (see Acts 13:2–3). Through fasting, the children of God serve him more fully (see Luke 2:37).

The Sabbath—Old Testament

The blessing of the Sabbath began at the Creation (Genesis 2:3) and was taught as one of the Ten Commandments given to the Israelites (Exodus 23:12; 31:15–17). The urging of the Lord to keep the Sabbath holy continued through the early prophets (Ezekiel 20:19–21; Isaiah 58:13–14) as a means of showing reverence and keeping covenants.

Genesis 2:3

And God blessed the seventh day, and sanctified it: because that in it he had rested from all his work which God created and made.

Exodus 23:12 (see also Exodus 31:15–17)

Six days thou shalt do thy work, and on the seventh day thou shalt rest: that thine ox and thine ass may rest, and the son of thy handmaid, and the stranger, may be refreshed.

Ezekiel 20:19–21 (see also Isaiah 58:13–14)

I am the Lord your God; walk in my statutes, and keep my judgments, and do them; And hallow my sabbaths; and they shall be a sign between me and you, that ye may know that I am the Lord your God. Notwithstanding the children rebelled against me: they walked not in my statutes, neither kept my judgments to do them, which if a man do, he shall even live in them; they polluted my sabbaths: then I said, I would pour out my fury upon them, to accomplish my anger against them in the wilderness.

The Sabbath—New Testament

During his public ministry, the Savior declared himself to be Lord of the Sabbath (Matthew 12:8; Luke 6:5), admonishing the people to focus on the spirit of the Sabbath and less on the law of the Sabbath (Mark 2:27). The Sabbath was not done away with by Christ's fulfillment of the Mosaic Law; rather, Jesus said the Sabbath would last long after he ascended into heaven (Matthew 24:20). The apostles observed the Sabbath during their public ministry (Acts 13:44).

Matthew 12:8 (see also Luke 6:5)

For the Son of man is Lord even of the sabbath day.

Mark 2:27

And he said unto them, The sabbath was made for man, and not man for the Sabbath.

Matthew 24:20

But pray ye that your flight be not in the winter, neither on the sabbath day. [*Jesus speaks of the end times and his second coming—and refers to the Sabbath as a serious consideration, not as a cast-off ritual.*]

Acts 13:44

And the next Sabbath day came almost the whole city together to hear the word of God. [*After the Ascension of Jesus, the Sabbath day was observed by his followers.*]

Service

Jesus continually taught the importance of service. He said that to serve was a greater calling than to be served (see Luke 22:26–27; Matthew 20:26–28). The children of God are called and set apart by him to minister in specific capacities through the inspiration of the Holy Ghost (see Acts 13:2–3). Those called are given the gifts they need by the Father to minister effectively (see Exodus 31:1–6; 1 Timothy 4:14; 2 Timothy 1:6–7). Through service, the Savior is glorified (see 2 Thessalonians 1:11–12), the body of Christ is unified (see Ephesians 4:4), and pure religion is magnified (see James 1:27).

Physical Health

The Lord calls for temperance and in some cases abstinence in caring for the body. The early priests of Israel were admonished to refrain from drinking alcohol in order to keep themselves clean in the service of God (Leviticus 10:9–10). Daniel demonstrated how nutrition can affect one's countenance in the Lord (see Daniel 1:10–16). John the Baptist, a revered servant of the Lord, abstained from alcohol in order to keep his mind and spirit clear to receive revelation and to have the strength to carry out the ministry to which he was called (Luke 1:15). The calling of a bishop requires spiritual focus and energy, and therefore they are to be "not given to wine" (Titus 1:7). The early apostles warned against intemperance (1 Peter 4:3–4), urging the people to treat their body as the temple of God—both spiritually and physically (1 Corinthians 3:16–17).

Leviticus 10:9–10

    Do not drink wine nor strong drink, thou, nor thy sons with thee, when ye go into the tabernacle of the congregation, lest ye die: it shall be a statute for ever throughout your generations: And that ye may put difference between holy and unholy, and between unclean and clean.

Luke 1:15

    For he [*John the Baptist*] shall be great in the sight of the Lord, and shall drink neither wine nor strong drink; and he shall be filled with the Holy Ghost, even from his mother's womb.

Titus 1:7

    For a bishop must be blameless, as the steward of God; not self-willed, not soon angry, not given to wine, no striker, not given to filthy lucre.

1 Peter 4:3–4

    [*Peter speaking to followers of Christ*] For the time past of our life may suffice us to have wrought the will of the Gentiles, when we walked in lasciviousness, lusts, excess of wine, revellings, banquetings, and abominable idolatries: Wherein they think it strange that ye run not with them to the same excess of riot, speaking evil of you.

1 Corinthians 3:16–17

    Know ye not that ye are the temple of God, and that the Spirit of God dwelleth in you? If any man defile the temple of God, him shall God destroy; for the temple of God is holy, which temple ye are.

The Body Is a Temple

    The body is the Lord's temple and is therefore sacred. Modesty has been taught since the earliest times (Leviticus 18:16–17), urging the children of God not to allow inappropriate nakedness to corrupt them into sexual sin (Leviticus 18:24). Tattoos and piercings were forbidden among the Israelites (Leviticus 19:28) because they vandalized the body—a body which is created in the image of God.

Leviticus 18:16–17

    Thou shalt not uncover the nakedness of thy brother's wife: it is thy brother's nakedness. Thou shalt not uncover the nakedness of a woman and her daughter, neither shalt thou take her son's daughter, or her daughter's daughter, to uncover her nakedness; for they are her near kinswomen: it is wickedness.

Leviticus 18:24

Defile not ye yourselves in any of these things . . .

Leviticus 19:28

Ye shall not make any cuttings in your flesh for the dead, nor print any marks upon you: I am the Lord. [*Tattoos and body piercings are forbidden.*]

Profanity, Obscenity, Vulgarity

Jesus taught that what comes out of the mouth can defile the character, revealing the evil spirit within the speaker's heart (Mark 7:15; Matthew 15:11). James counsels that learning to control what one says is an integral part of being a religious person (James 1:26), while Paul urges believers to refrain from corrupt communication so that the ministry can glorify Jesus Christ (Ephesians 4:29).

Mark 7:15 (see also Matthew 15:11)

There is nothing from without a man, that entering into him can defile him: but the things which come out of him, those are they that defile the man.

James 1:26 (see also Ephesians 4:29)

If any man among you seem to be religious, and bridleth not his tongue, but deceiveth his own heart, this man's religion is vain.

Respect for Family

The Lord is the God of all of the families of Israel (Jeremiah 31:1), including those who have been adopted into the chosen family through faith in Christ. Beyond the earthly realm our Heavenly Father is the Father of the entire family of heaven and earth (Ephesians 3:14–15).

Jeremiah 31:1

At the same time, saith the Lord, will I be the God of all the families of Israel, and they shall be my people.

Ephesians 3:14–15

For this cause I bow my knees unto the Father of our Lord Jesus Christ, Of whom the whole family in heaven and earth is named,

Good Example

Jesus admonishes his disciples to let their example of faith shine before the entire world, glorifying their Father in Heaven (see Matthew 5:14–16; Luke 11:33) as people of righteousness (see 1 John 3:7). Christians are called to live the gospel (see 1 Corinthians 9:14) and be good examples in all things (see 1 Timothy 4:12). The ultimate example for the children of God to follow is Jesus Christ, who left for all mankind a model to emulate for all eternity (see 1 Peter 2:21; John 13:15).

Law of the Tithe

Giving to the Lord ten percent of one's time and substance is an eternal principle that is documented in the earliest scriptures (Genesis 14:20; Numbers 18:26). Abraham gave one-tenth of his increase as tithing (Hebrews 7:4, 9). Because God asks and deserves the very best, he commands that all of his children bring to him the finest they have to offer (2 Chronicles 31:5–6, 12; Deuteronomy 14:22–23, 28; Nehemiah 10:37–38). To withhold tithing from God is to rob God and to rob oneself, since God promises an abundance of blessings to all who love him and keep his commandments (Malachi 3:8–10). All of God's children are urged to give willingly and without complaint: God loves a "cheerful giver" (2 Corinthians 9:6–7).

Genesis 14:20

 And blessed be the most high God, which hath delivered thine enemies into thy hand. And he gave him tithes of all.

Numbers 18:26

 Thus speak unto the Levites, and say unto them, When ye take of the children of Israel the tithes which I have given you from them for your inheritance, then ye shall offer up an heave offering of it for the Lord, even a tenth part of the tithe.

Hebrews 7:4, 9

 Now consider how great this man was, unto whom even the patriarch Abraham gave the tenth of the spoils. . . . And as I may so say, Levi also, who receiveth tithes, payed tithes in Abraham.

2 Chronicles 31:5–6, 12 (see also Deuteronomy 14:22–23, 28)

 And as soon as the commandment came abroad, the children of Israel brought in abundance the firstfruits of corn, wine, and oil, and honey, and of all the increase of the field; and the tithe of all things brought they in abundantly. And concerning the children of Israel and Judah, that dwelt in the cities of Judah, they also brought in the tithe of oxen and sheep, and the tithe of holy things which were consecrated unto the Lord their God, and laid them by heaps. And brought in the offerings and the tithes and the dedicated things faithfully: over which Cononiah the Levite was ruler, and Shimei his brother was the next.

Nehemiah 10:37–38

And that we should bring the firstfruits of our dough, and our offerings, and the fruit of all manner of trees, of wine and of oil, unto the priests, to the chambers of the house of our God; and the tithes of our ground unto the Levites, that the same Levites might have the tithes in all the cities of our tillage. And the priest the son of Aaron shall be with the Levites, when the Levites take tithes: and the Levites shall bring up the tithe of the tithes unto the house of our God, to the chambers, into the treasure house.

Malachi 3:8–10

Will a man rob God? Yet ye have robbed me. But ye say, Wherein have we robbed thee? In tithes and offerings. Ye are cursed with a curse: for ye have robbed me, even this whole nation. Bring ye all the tithes into the storehouse, that there may be meat in mine house, and prove me now herewith, saith the Lord of hosts, if I will not open you the windows of heaven, and pour you out a blessing, that there shall not be room enough to receive it.

2 Corinthians 9:6–7

But this I say, He which soweth sparingly shall reap also sparingly; and he which soweth bountifully shall reap also bountifully. Every man according as he purposeth in his heart, so let him give; not grudgingly, or of necessity: for God loveth a cheerful giver.

Enduring Persecution

Jesus taught that persecutions would come to the believers just as they had come to him (see John 15:20), and that those who endure persecutions for following him would be blessed (see Luke 6:22; Matthew 5:10–12, 44). Familiar with persecution, Paul taught that the persecuted would not be forsaken by God (see 2 Corinthians 4:8–9) and that the persecuted for God's sake can enjoy spiritual blessings and joy (see 2 Corinthians 12:10; 2 Thessalonians 1:4–5). The righteous become familiar with the sufferings of Christ through persecution on earth, which in turn glorifies God (see 1 Peter 4:13–14; Mark 13:13).

A Peculiar People

The people of God will always appear to be a "peculiar people." The Israelites whom the Lord chose unto himself (Deuteronomy 14:2) and the early Christians whom Paul and Peter called "a peculiar people" (Titus 2:14; 1 Peter 2:9) suffered persecution and were sometimes called evil despite their righteousness (Isaiah 5:20).

Deuteronomy 14:2

> For thou [*the children of Israel*] art an holy people unto the Lord thy God, and the Lord hath chosen thee to be a peculiar people unto himself, above all the nations that are upon the earth.

1 Peter 2:9 (see also Titus 2:14)

> But ye are a chosen generation, a royal priesthood, an holy nation, a peculiar people; that ye should shew forth the praises of him who hath called you out of darkness into his marvellous light:

Isaiah 5:20

> Woe unto them that call evil good, and good evil; that put darkness for light, and light for darkness; that put bitter for sweet, and sweet for bitter!

By Their Fruits

The world will persecute, accuse, and fight against those who devote themselves to the teachings of God. A biblical test of favor in the Lord is whether the work of a man or a church bears good fruits (Acts 5:38–39). The Lord counseled, "Ye shall know them by their fruits" (see Matthew 7:16).

Acts 5:38–39

> And now I say unto you, Refrain from these men, and let them alone: for if this counsel or this work be of men, it will come to nought: But if it be of God, ye cannot overthrow it; lest haply ye be found even to fight against God.

Unity among Christians

God looks upon all men equally in the context of lineage, but he accepts unto himself only those who act in righteousness (Acts 10:34–35). The Lord seeks to have one church that will have the fulness of his gospel on earth to be a beacon of his divine commission to all mankind (Ephesians 4:5).

Acts 10:34–35

Then Peter opened his mouth, and said, Of a truth I perceive that God is no respecter of persons: But in every nation he that feareth him, and worketh righteousness, is accepted with him. [*Those who fear God and produce good fruits of faith are acceptable before him.*]

Ephesians 4:5

One Lord, one faith, one baptism.

MORMON UNDERSTANDING

Members of The Church of Jesus Christ of Latter-day Saints practice their faith in ways similar to most other Christian denominations. There are differences, however, and some of these are significant. Ten examples of Latter-day Saint religious practice are given here.

Prayer

Prayer is "sincere, heartfelt talk with our Heavenly Father,"[1] and it is one of the greatest blessings human beings enjoy during mortality. Prayer has been taught and practiced since the beginning of time, affects all manner of thoughts and actions, and will bring men and women close to God. Latter-day Saints accept the commandment to "pray always."

Latter-day Saints are instructed to pray with intent and a sincere heart. Formal prayers are directed to God the Father in the name of Jesus Christ and always contain expressions of gratitude. Latter-day Saints are counseled to pray at least morning and night and before meals and to have a prayer in their hearts at all times. Families pray together. All Church meetings and events begin and end with prayers.

Fasting

To fast is to abstain from food and drink for a given period of time and for a given purpose. Fasting magnifies petitions to God and is a formal way to demonstrate devotion and commitment. Latter-day Saints fast as a regular part of worship and prayer. On at least one Sunday of each month, the Saints fast (abstain from food and drink for two consecutive meals) and contribute to the needy the value of the uneaten meals. This fast usually occurs on the first Sunday of each month. In conjunction with this fast, members of the congregation bear their testimonies.

The Sabbath

Latter-day Saints observe the Sabbath on Sundays. The Sabbath day is given as a remembrance of God taking his rest after completing the Creation. It is a necessity to rest on the Sabbath, to lay aside the cares of the world in so far as possible, and to focus on spiritual concerns—not simply to rest from labor, but to worship, serve, attend thoughtfully to the "still small voice" of the Spirit, and give reverence to God. As in the early Christian church, the Sabbath today is also observed by Latter-day Saints as a remembrance of the Atonement of Christ. Because the Sabbath is given for these purposes, Latter-day Saints do not buy, sell, or labor for profit on this day.

Service

Jesus taught service, dedicating his life to helping and serving others—eventually giving his life to save mankind from the effects of sin.

Service to others is not contingent on age, financial ability, health, or societal status. Members of The Church of Jesus Christ of Latter-day Saints are taught to serve from the beginning of their lives to the end of their lives—and beyond. At age ninety-seven, President Gordon B. Hinckley served his last full day at his office on a Thursday and died the following Sunday.

Physical Health

The Church of Jesus Christ of Latter-day Saints teaches principles of good health. The Church emphasizes the mortal body as a temple of the Holy Ghost (see 1 Corinthians 6:19). As a temple of the Holy Ghost, mortal bodies of human beings are holy, and God desires that they be cared for and lived in with reverence. This does not mean that sickness and disease are a curse, nor does it mean that excesses in pursuit of physical health are warranted. It means that prudent care of the body is a necessity for service in mortality. It means that body and spirit are linked, that abuse of one is abuse of the other. Latter-day Saints are commanded to abuse neither.

Faithful Latter-day Saints live by certain covenants they take upon themselves. Among these is the promise not to consume alcoholic beverages, coffee, or caffeinated tea and not to use tobacco or illegal drugs. These promises are just a few of the many covenants that Latter-day Saints make with the Lord. However, these particular covenants are widely known outside the Church because it is not possible to keep them unobtrusively in certain settings. There are many other covenants that are kept without being so readily noticed. The emphasis is on making and keeping covenants, in this case out of respect for the gift of a body. The emphasis is not on spiritual or physical fads or fetishes.

Physical Appearance

Latter-day Saints show reverence to Heavenly Father by respecting their bodies on the outside as well as the inside. They covenant to dress modestly and not to deface their bodies with tattoos and excessive piercings. Modesty and avoidance of disfigurement demonstrate self-restraint, purity, and gratitude for the natural beauty of the temple of the Holy Ghost. Again, the emphasis is on making and keeping covenants, in this case out of respect for the gift of a body—not on spiritual or physical fads or fetishes.

Speech

Latter-day Saints avoid the use of colorful language that includes variations of the Lord's name, profanity, references to sexual acts, references to private parts of the body, and other forms of coarse or vulgar speech. Emphasis on this is strong in the Church because it is believed that as a man speaks, so he is—or soon becomes. All speech is representative, and the first thing represented is the speaker. All other representations are derivative of this first one.

Speaking, hearing, and seeing are linked, and similar moral principles apply to each. Latter-day Saints take a strong stand against pornography, lewd and hateful music, excessively violent and obscene entertainment, and similar literature.

One of the Ten Commandments is "[thou] shalt not take the name of the Lord thy God in vain; for the Lord will not hold him guiltless that taketh his name in vain" (Exodus 20:7). The violation of this commandment in Old Testament times carried with it serious consequences—even death. Today, it is still a serious sin to use the Lord's name in vain, although any social or legal consequences have all but vanished.

Family

Each man or woman who chooses to come to earth from the pre-mortal realm is born into a family. Families take many forms, but all have one thing in common: a mortal mother and father—it takes both to bring a child into the world. This form of the family may dissolve before or after a child's birth. The dissolution may be the result of death, abandonment, divorce, or some other form of separation, but all families nevertheless begin with a uniting of the essence of one man and one woman.

Some families are formed through adoption, and the Church, through the ordinance of sealing, recognizes such families as equal to those that may include only children born to the parents in the family. Single-parent families consist of a man or a woman as head. All other families consist of a man and a woman legally and lawfully married.

The family is a sacred entity in The Church of Jesus Christ of Latter-day Saints. In all its varieties, it is the basic organizational unit of in the Church and in the kingdom of God. A family can be exalted in heaven and endure forever in the eternities. The key purpose of the Church is to assist families in achieving this goal. The Church's organization, leadership, programs, and activities are all directed toward achieving this end.

Tithing

All faithful members of The Church of Jesus Christ of Latter-day Saints pay tithing.

God commanded his children, "Seek ye first the kingdom of God, and his righteousness; and all these things shall be added unto you" (Matthew 6:33). This commandment prepares men and women for life in the eternities through trust in the Lord, personal sacrifice, and gratitude. One way of expressing gratitude to the Lord is through the paying of tithes and offerings.

Endurance

Latter-day Saints believe in "enduring to the end."

Jesus warned his disciples that if they followed him in faith and righteousness, they would be persecuted by the world. Unrighteous persecution of the faithful has taken place throughout history, sometimes by the "faithful" of the faithful. Indeed, in times past, Christians fervently and violently persecuted one another and those of other faiths over differences of various description and sometimes little importance. Thankfully, the violence and ferocity of such persecution has declined significantly over the last few centuries. However, persecution of Christians from other religious and secular quarters is growing.

The gulf between what is called secular and what is called religious is growing ever wider, and a secular persecution is increasing. Christians are openly mocked, discriminated against, and harassed in some democratic countries today. They are sometimes banned or killed for their beliefs under other regimes.

None of this is a surprise to Latter-day Saints. From the foundation of The Church of Jesus Christ of Latter-day Saints in 1830, the Saints have endured the privations of violent anti-Mormon mobs, a government extermination order authorizing the killing of Mormons on sight, and a wide variety of legal and political efforts to destroy the Church. As with other new sects in earlier centuries, this persecution has abated with time, though it has by no means ended. It is today particularly prevalent on the Internet and in print and other media.

None of this should give rise to bitterness in any Christian. It is as promised. Christ gave an example for all Christians to follow when he said from the cross, "Father, forgive them, for they know not what they do" (Luke 23:34).

"Forgive and endure" is the rule of the Latter-day Saints.

NOTE
1. *Gospel Principles*, 41

∞ 16 ∞

MISSIONARY WORK

"To these we say in a spirit of love, bring with you all that you have of good and truth which you have received from whatever source, and come and let us see if we may add to it."

—*Gordon B. Hinckley*[1]

BIBLICAL TEACHING

Missionaries Two-by-Two

Jesus called and set apart his missionaries to go out two-by-two to harvest the souls of the ripened field and exercise dominion over unclean spirits (Luke 10:1–2; Mark 6:7). These missionaries were expected to discipline themselves in prayer and to dedicate themselves to the ministry (Acts 6:4–6).

Luke 10:1–2

> After these the Lord appointed other seventy also, and sent them two and two before his face into every city and place, whither he himself would come. Therefore said he unto them, The harvest truly is great, but the labourers are few: pray ye therefore the Lord of the harvest, that he would send forth labourers into his harvest.

Mark 6:7

> And he called unto him the twelve, and began to send them forth by two and two; and gave them power over unclean spirits.

Acts 6:4–6

> But we will give ourselves continually to prayer, and to the

ministry of the word. And the saying pleased the whole multitude: and they chose Stephen, a man full of faith and of the Holy Ghost, and Philip, and Prochorus, and Nicanor, and Timon, and Parmenas, and Nicolas a proselyte of Antioch: Whom they set before the apostles: and when they had prayed, they laid their hands on them.

All Are Missionaries

All followers of Christ are called to assist in the missionary effort. Just as he was sent by the Father, Jesus sends all his followers to teach and give service (John 20:21). Those who obey the call and are bold in accomplishing the task are blessed by God as they bring the good news to all who will listen (Romans 10:14–15).

John 20:21

> Then said Jesus to them again, Peace be unto you: as my Father hath sent me, even so send I you.

Romans 10:14–15

> How then shall they call on him in whom they have not believed? and how shall they believe in him of whom they have not heard? and how shall they hear without a preacher? And how shall they preach, except they be sent? as it is written, How beautiful are the feet of them that preach the gospel of peace, and bring glad tidings of good things!

Missionaries Preach the Gospel

The Savior sent his apostles as missionaries to teach and testify of the good news of the kingdom of God. They were to do this in humility and simplicity, yet with boldness of heart (Luke 9:1–6; Mark 16:15). Such preaching would be a witness unto the world of the divinity of Christ and a warning of his judgments (Matthew 24:14; Acts 10:42). The motivation to preach should be love—love of God, love of his son Jesus Christ, and love of one's neighbor as a brother and sister in Christ—not the glory of the world (John 21:17; 1 Corinthians 9:16). Missionary work is the work of men and angels and is not geographically limited (Revelation 14:6).

Luke 9:1–6 (see also Mark 16:15)

> Then he called his twelve disciples together, and gave them power and authority over all devils, and to cure diseases. And he sent them to preach the kingdom of God, and to heal the sick. And he

said unto them, Take nothing for your journey, neither staves, nor scrip, neither bread, neither money; neither have two coats apiece [*live a simple life*]. And whatsoever house ye enter into, there abide, and thence depart. And whosoever will not receive you, when ye go out of that city, shake off the very dust from your feet for a testimony against them [*be bold and do not waste time lamenting those who do not accept the gospel message*]. And they departed, and went through the towns, preaching the gospel, and healing everywhere.

Matthew 24:14

And this gospel of the kingdom shall be preached in all the world for a witness unto all nations; and then shall the end come.

Acts 10:42

And he commanded us to preach unto the people, and to testify that it is he which was ordained of God to be the Judge of quick and dead.

John 21:17

He saith unto him the third time, Simon, son of Jonas, lovest thou me? Peter was grieved because he said unto him the third time, Lovest thou me? And he said unto him, Lord, thou knowest all things; thou knowest that I love thee. Jesus saith unto him, Feed my sheep [*lead, guide, teach all mankind*].

1 Corinthians 9:16

For though I preach the gospel, I have nothing to glory of: for necessity is laid upon me; yea, woe is unto me, if I preach not the gospel!

Revelation 14:6

And I saw another angel fly in the midst of heaven, having the everlasting gospel to preach unto them that dwell on the earth, and to every nation, and kindred, and tongue, and people.

Missionaries Bring Souls to Christ

Jesus called his disciples to fish for men and to harvest souls (Matthew 4:19; John 4:35; Matthew 9:37–38). The metaphor of fishing and harvesting describes the process of conversion—spiritually engaging the children of men and helping them learn the truth, feel the Holy Ghost, and to be converted. Because of his infinite love, God sends his servants to teach, redeem, and where necessary chastise (Jeremiah 16:16).

Matthew 4:19
> And he saith unto them, Follow me, and I will make you fishers of men.

John 4:35 (see also Matthew 9:37–38)
> Say not ye, There are yet four months, and then cometh harvest? behold, I say unto you, Lift up your eyes, and look on the fields; for they are white already to harvest.

Jeremiah 16:16
> Behold, I will send for many fishers [*missionaries*], saith the Lord, and they shall fish them [*those who are lost or have fallen away*]; and after will I send for many hunters, and they shall hunt them from every mountain, and from every hill, and out of the holes of the rocks.

Missionaries Baptize the Repentant

Missionaries are commissioned to baptize the repentant "in the name of the Father, and of the Son, and of the Holy Ghost" (Acts 2:37–38; Matthew 28:19).

Acts 2:37–38
> Now when they [*men of Judea and Jerusalem*] heard this [*the words of Peter*], they were pricked in their heart, and said unto Peter and to the rest of the apostles, Men and brethren, what shall we do? Then Peter said unto them, Repent, and be baptized every one of you in the name of Jesus Christ for the remission of sins, and ye shall receive the gift of the Holy Ghost.

Matthew 28:19
> Go ye therefore, and teach all nations, baptizing them in the name of the Father, and of the Son, and of the Holy Ghost.

Missionaries are Blessed

Jesus told his disciples that missionaries will receive "wages" (blessings), will gather unto themselves "life eternal," and will rejoice together with the convert in the eternities (John 4:36).

John 4:36
> And he that reapeth receiveth wages, and gathereth fruit unto life eternal: that both he that soweth and he that reapeth may rejoice together.

MORMON UNDERSTANDING

Teach All Nations

Before Jesus ascended into heaven, he gave his disciples a bold commission: "Go ye therefore, and teach all nations, baptizing them in the name of the Father, and of the Son, and of the Holy Ghost: Teaching them to observe all things whatsoever I have commanded you" (Matthew 28:19–20).

The Apostle Paul

Paul took this commission seriously. He travelled widely in the Mediterranean region, and he endured many hardships. He faithfully obeyed the Lord's command. He taught and converted people in many countries. He organized Christian congregations and courageously addressed the spiritual and administrative needs of the growing Christian church. Paul risked his life and finally gave it in pursuing this work. He is the archetype of the Christian missionary. Latter-day Saint missionaries throughout the world seek to follow his example.

Prophets

All of the prophets were missionaries—called to preach to the children of God the good news of the gospel. Jesus ordained apostles and others during his public ministry. He commissioned them to preach the gospel to the Jews (Matthew 10:5–6) and, eventually, to the gentiles throughout the world. About 1,800 years later, the Prophet Joseph Smith was told by the Lord: "Proclaim my gospel from land to land, and from city to city. . . . Bear testimony in every place, unto every people."[2] Another revelation given in 1839 reaffirmed that "there are many yet on the earth among all sects, parties, and denominations . . . who are only kept from the truth because they know not where to find it."[3]

The First Mormon Missionary

Samuel Smith, brother of Joseph, was the first Mormon missionary. He was called to this work in 1830. Since then, more than one million Latter-day Saint missionaries have been sent into the world to preach the good news of the gospel of Jesus Christ, to proclaim the message of the restoration of his Church, and to baptize in the name of the Father, and of the Son, and of the Holy Ghost. This is in fulfillment of the prophecy of Isaiah, reiterated by Paul, that "every knee shall bow to me, and every tongue shall confess to God" (Romans 14:11; Isaiah 45:23).

Every Member a Missionary

"Every member a missionary" is a common admonition in the Church. The main proselyting missionary effort is carried out by two cooperating groups of people:

- Full-time missionaries who serve for eighteen to twenty-four months in places typically far away from where they live and
- Church members in local communities who prepare family and friends to receive the full-time missionaries.

Working together, the full-time missionaries and local Church members work in the same structured and methodical way as written about in the New Testament.

Full-Time Missionaries

Full-time missionaries are paired up in the same way Jesus paired his own disciples—two by two. This pairing of missionaries allows for mutual support of one another both spiritually and temporally, complies with the law of two witnesses, and enables missionaries to "team teach" according to the spirit.

Full-time missionaries are called and set apart by the laying on of hands to be obedient to a strict set of mission rules and to maintain a tight focus on the ministry of Jesus Christ. Missionaries spend much of their time proselyting door-to-door or in public venues, but their primary role is to teach people the gospel of Jesus Christ. While most missionaries are called on proselyting missions, others may be called on humanitarian missions where preaching of the gospel is secondary to providing a vitally needed service.

Conversion

Through missionary work carried out by the inspiration of the Holy Ghost, the disciples of Christ are called to convert people to his gospel. Conversion in its simplest religious sense means to change from one set of beliefs to another, perhaps even changing from one religion to another. This change may be as radical as converting from Hinduism to Christianity, for example, or it may be as simple as converting from one set of Christian beliefs to another.

At their best Latter-day Saints simply preach the restored gospel and give service where it is needed. No man or woman is compelled or manipulated into the Church. All must choose freely. This is the will of the Lord. The principle of religious liberty is precious to the Latter-day Saints, and the methods they use in bringing souls to Christ respect this principle.

According to the *World Christian Encyclopedia*, there are approximately 33,820 Christian denominations throughout the world.[4] This proliferation of Christian sects can be confusing. Many questions arise, and many answers are offered. Some believe strongly that they have the true answers; others believe there is no one true answer or collection of true answers. The Mormon missionaries seek to penetrate this confusion and provide a few clear and simple answers.

The Work

When Jesus told his disciples that the fields were white and ready to harvest, he meant that there was work to do. He told them he would make them fishers of men and that there was work to do. But ultimately the great work must be done in the minds and hearts of seekers after the truth under the inspiration of the Holy Ghost. It is those considering conversion who must do the final work. It is they, not the missionaries, who must decide whether to take upon themselves the name of Christ and the profound covenants that Christ requires of his followers.

When the gospel is preached and people are converted, the process of repentance, baptism, and confirmation begins. This is beautifully illustrated in the New Testament story of Pentecost, when Peter and the apostles were teaching the people and they were converted (Acts 2:37–38).

Missionary work is more than just preaching, teaching, and converting; the fruits of missionary work are repentance, rebirth in baptism, and the gift of the Holy Ghost. Through baptism, the children of God are born again and come into the fold of Christ. For many, baptism in the Church is the formal initiation of their personal relationship with Christ. For others, baptism in the Church is an affirmation of an existing personal relationship with Jesus. In either case, this rebirth is preceded by repentance and followed by receiving the gift of the Holy Ghost.

Blessings

The Lord has promised great blessings from missionary work. Speaking through the prophet Joseph, the Lord told a group of returned missionaries, "Ye are blessed, for the testimony which ye have borne is recorded in heaven for the angels to look upon; and they rejoice over you."[5] This same blessing is promised to all who perform missionary labors:

> If it so be that you should labor all your days in crying repentance unto this people, and bring, save it be one soul unto me, how great shall be your joy with him in the kingdom of my Father! And now, if your joy will be great with one soul that you have brought unto me into the kingdom of my Father, how great will be your joy if you should bring many souls unto me![6]

Members of Other Churches

The missionary spirit of The Church of Jesus Christ of Latter-day Saints was expressed beautifully by the late prophet, Gordon B. Hinckley:

> There are many good people in other churches. There is much of good in them. Your family and your prior religious traditions may have taught you many good things and established many good habits. . . . Bring the good things with you, keep them, and use them in the Lord's service.[7]

> We recognize the good in all churches. We recognize the value of religion generally. We say to everyone: live the teachings which you have received from your church. We invite you to come and learn from us, to see if we can add to those teachings and enhance your life and your understanding of things sacred and divine.[8]

NOTES

1. Gordon B. Hinckley, "The Marvelous Foundation of Our Faith," Ensign, Nov. 2002, 78)
2. Doctrine and Covenants 66:5, 7.
3. Doctrine and Covenants 123:12.
4. David B. Barrett, *World Christian Encyclopedia* (New York, NY: Oxford University Press, 2001), 10.
5. Doctrine and Covenants 62:3
6. Doctrine and Covenants 18:15–16.
7. Gordon B. Hinckley, "A Perfect Brightness of Hope—to New Members of the Church," *Ensign*, Oct. 2006, 2–5.
8. Gordon B. Hinckley, "Excerpts from Recent Addresses of President Gordon B. Hinckley," *Ensign*, Aug. 1996, 60–61.

❧ 17 ❧

ORDINANCES AND COVENANTS

---

*I*n its broadest meaning, an ordinance is simply a law. In Mormonism, an ordinance is a formal ritualistic act, often including a covenant, performed by the authority of the priesthood. There is a similarity between ordinances in The Church of Jesus Christ of Latter-day Saints and sacraments in other Christian churches.

In its broadest meaning, a covenant is a formal promise to do or not to do something. In Judaism and Christianity, covenants are made with God and are binding aspects of an alliance with God.

BIBLICAL TEACHING

Ordinances—Old Testament

The Old Testament details many ordinances—all given to prepare God's chosen people for the coming of the Savior and to discipline them in keeping the commandments of the Lord. Ordinances are meant to be understood (Job 38:33) and kept (Leviticus 18:4; Malachi 3:7; Isaiah 58:2; Psalm 99:7; Psalm 119:91). The Lord expects those who love him to act upon the ordinances received (Ezekiel 43:11) and to teach them to others so they too may walk in the ways of the Lord (Exodus 18:20). Ordinances are eternal and have no end (Exodus 12:14, 43; Jeremiah 31:36).

Job 38:33

    Knowest thou the ordinances of heaven? canst thou set the dominion thereof in the earth?

Leviticus 18:4

    Ye shall do my judgments, and keep mine ordinances, to walk therein: I am the Lord your God.

Malachi 3:7

    Even from the days of your fathers ye are gone away from mine ordinances, and have not kept them. Return unto me, and I will return unto you, saith the Lord of hosts. But ye said, Wherein shall we return?

Isaiah 58:2

    Yet they seek me daily, and delight to know my ways, as a nation that did righteousness, and forsook not the ordinance of their God: they ask of me the ordinances of justice; they take delight in approaching to God.

Psalm 99:7 (see also Psalm 119:91)

    He spake unto them in the cloudy pillar: they kept his testimonies, and the ordinance that he gave them.

Ezekiel 43:11

    And if they be ashamed of all that they have done, shew them the form of the house, and the fashion thereof, and the goings out thereof, and the comings in thereof, and all the forms thereof, and all the ordinances thereof, and all the forms thereof, and all the laws thereof: and write it in their sight, that they may keep the whole form thereof, and all the ordinances thereof, and do them.

Exodus 18:20

    And thou [*Moses*] shalt teach them [the children of Israel] ordinances and laws, and shalt shew them the way wherein they must walk, and the work that they must do.

Exodus 12:14, 43 (see also Jeremiah 31:36)

    And this day shall be unto you for a memorial; and ye shall keep it a feast to the Lord throughout your generations; ye shall keep it a feast by an ordinance for ever [*the ordinance is forever and continued in Jesus Christ*]. . . . And the Lord said unto Moses and Aaron, This is the ordinance of the passover: There shall no stranger eat thereof.

Covenants Associated with Ordinances

Ordinances are given by God as part of his laws, decrees, and commandments to the children of men. Joshua as a servant of the Lord made a covenant with the people as a similitude of an ordinance given in the land of Shechem (Joshua 24:25). The Lord spoke to Jeremiah of his covenants and ordinances (Jeremiah 33:25). The prophet Isaiah chastised the people for distorting the Lord's ordinances and their associated covenants (Isaiah 24:5). The relationship of ordinances and covenants extends far beyond the Old Testament times as Paul wrote to the Hebrews about the importance of certain ordinances as prefigurings of the ministry of Jesus (Hebrews 9:1).

Joshua 24:25

So Joshua made a covenant with the people that day, and set them a statute and an ordinance in Shechem.

Jeremiah 33:25–26

Thus saith the Lord; If my covenant be not with day and night, and if I have not appointed the ordinances of heaven and earth; Then will I cast away the seed of Jacob, and David my servant, so that I will not take any of his seed to be rulers over the seed of Abraham, Isaac, and Jacob: for I will cause their captivity to return, and have mercy on them.

Isaiah 24:5

The earth also is defiled under the inhabitants thereof; because they have transgressed the laws, changed the ordinance, broken the everlasting covenant.

Hebrews 9:1

Then verily the first covenant had also ordinances of divine service, and a worldly sanctuary.

Why Ordinances and Covenants

The Lord warned Moses that the Jews had to keep his covenants to be a treasure unto him and to obtain the blessings of being his chosen (Exodus 19:5–6). The Lord gave the prophet Ezekiel a similar warning when he said that as the people keep the Lord's statutes and ordinances, they become his people (Ezekiel 11:20). The Lord takes sacred covenants (or vows) so seriously that he teaches it is better not to make a covenant than to make a covenant and break it (Ecclesiastes 5:4–5). Jesus told his disciples that unless they were "born of water" (born again through the ordinance of baptism), they could not enter into the kingdom of God (John 3:5). When the children of God participate in sacred ordinances and keep their associated covenants, they are protected from Satan and are exalted as the people of God.

Exodus 19:5–6

> Now therefore, if ye will obey my voice indeed, and keep my covenant, then ye shall be a peculiar treasure unto me above all people: for all the earth is mine: And ye shall be unto me a kingdom of priests, and an holy nation. These are the words which thou shalt speak unto the children of Israel.

Ezekiel 11:20

> That they may walk in my statutes, and keep mine ordinances, and do them: and they shall be my people, and I will be their God.

Ecclesiastes 5:4–5

> When thou vowest a vow unto God [*a vow is a covenant*], defer not to pay it; for he hath no pleasure in fools: pay that which thou hast vowed. Better is it that thou shouldest not vow, than that thou shouldest vow and not pay. [*It is better not to make a covenant, then to make and break a covenant.*]

John 3:5

> Jesus answered, Verily, verily, I say unto thee, Except a man be born of water and of the Spirit, he cannot enter into the kingdom of God.

Baptism

The words *baptize* and *baptism* do not appear in the Old Testament. However, these words appear dozens of times in the New Testament, and Paul assures the faithful that the spirit of the ordinance of baptism was alive and well in Old Testament times. He taught that the children of Israel were baptized "in the cloud and in the sea" (1 Corinthians 10:1–2). Paul was so inspired by his own baptism (Acts 9:18), that he feverishly urged his followers to repent and be baptized (Acts 19:3–5). The Savior was intent on his own baptism, not for the remission of sins, but to "fulfil all righteousness" (Matthew 3:13–17; Mark 1:9–11; Luke 3:21–22).

1 Corinthians 10:1–2

Moreover, brethren, I would not that ye should be ignorant, how that all our fathers were under the cloud, and all passed through the sea; And were all baptized unto Moses in the cloud and in the sea.

Acts 9:18

And immediately there fell from his eyes as it had been scales: and he received sight forthwith, and arose, and was baptized. [*Saul became Paul—a new person—after his baptism.*]

Acts 19:3–5

And he said unto them, Unto what then were ye baptized? And they said, Unto John's baptism. Then said Paul, John verily baptized with the baptism of repentance [*repentance—arguably requiring that the baptized person has reached the age of reason*], saying unto the people, that they should believe on him which should come after him, that is, on Christ Jesus. When they heard this, they were baptized in the name of the Lord Jesus. [*John had the authority to baptize as a preparation for the coming of Christ; however, baptism in the name of Jesus Christ was so essential that those baptized by John were again baptized in the name of Jesus Christ.*]

Matthew 3:13–17 (see also Mark 1:9–11 and Luke 3:21–22)

Then cometh Jesus from Galilee to Jordan unto John, to be baptized of him. But John forbad him, saying, I have need to be baptized of thee, and comest thou to me? And Jesus answering said unto him, Suffer it to be so now: for thus it becometh us to fulfil all righteousness. Then he suffered him. And Jesus, when he was baptized, went up straightway out of the water: and, lo, the heavens were opened unto him, and he saw the Spirit of God descending like a dove, and lighting upon him: And lo a voice from heaven, saying, This is my beloved Son, in whom I am well pleased.

Confirmation

Peter invited the faithful to repent and be baptized and thereafter receive the gift of the Holy Ghost (Acts 2:38). Thus, confirmation, receiving the gift of the Holy Ghost, follows baptism. A confirmation is carried out through the laying on of hands (Acts 8:17; 9:17) by those in authority holding the Melchizedek Priesthood (Acts 8:18–20). Paul referred to the human body as the temple of the Holy Ghost (1 Corinthians 6:19).

Acts 2:38

> Then Peter said unto them, Repent, and be baptized every one of you in the name of Jesus Christ for the remission of sins, and ye shall receive the gift of the Holy Ghost.

Acts 8:17 (see also Acts 9:17)

> Then laid they their hands on them, and they received the Holy Ghost.

Acts 8:18–20

> And when Simon saw that through laying on of the apostles' hands the Holy Ghost was given, he offered them money, Saying, Give me also this power, that on whomsoever I lay hands, he may receive the Holy Ghost. But Peter said unto him, Thy money perish with thee, because thou hast thought that the gift of God may be purchased with money. [*Confirmation and granting of the gift of the Holy Ghost can only be done by those in authority.*]

1 Corinthians 6:19

> What? know ye not that your body is the temple of the Holy Ghost which is in you, which ye have of God, and ye are not your own?

The Sacrament

During the Last Supper, Jesus instituted the ordinance of the sacrament whereby emblems of his body and blood were given in remembrance of his atoning sacrifice (Matthew 26:26–28). As a precursor to introducing this sacred ordinance, Jesus broke bread among his disciples (Mark 8:6), saying to them that he was the "bread of life" (John 6:35). Paul reaffirms the importance of the sacrament in his letter to the Corinthians, emphasizing the word *remembrance*. This is the word Jesus spoke to his disciples in reference to his infinite Atonement for all mankind and how it would be "remembered" throughout eternity in the form of an ordinance (1 Corinthians 11:23–25).

Matthew 26:26–28

> And as they were eating, Jesus took bread, and blessed it, and brake it, and gave it to the disciples, and said, Take, eat; this is my body. And he took the cup, and gave thanks, and gave it to them, saying, Drink ye all of it; For this is my blood of the new testament, which is shed for many for the remission of sins.

Mark 8:6

And he commanded the people to sit down on the ground: and
he took the seven loaves, and gave thanks, and brake, and gave to his
disciples to set before them; and they did set them before the people.

John 6:35

And Jesus said unto them, I am the bread of life: he that cometh
to me shall never hunger; and he that believeth on me shall never
thirst.

1 Corinthians 11:23–25

For I have received of the Lord that which also I delivered unto
you, That the Lord Jesus the same night in which he was betrayed
took bread: And when he had given thanks, he brake it, and said,
Take, eat: this is my body, which is broken for you: this do in remembrance of me. After the same manner also he took the cup, when he
had supped, saying, This cup is the new testament in my blood: this
do ye, as oft as ye drink it, in remembrance of me.

Healing the Sick and Afflicted

Jesus often demonstrated the ordinance of the healing of the sick,
typically by the laying on of hands (Luke 13:12–13; Mark 6:5; Luke
4:40). Jesus gave the authority of the priesthood to his apostles who then
went forth to perform the ordinance of the healing of the sick (Matthew 10:8; Mark 6:13; Acts 28:8). The apostles passed on the authority
to perform this ordinance, each time by the laying on of hands (Mark
16:15–18). Sometimes the ordinance of healing was performed with the
anointing of oil and an accompanying prayer (James 5:14).

Luke 13:12–13 (see also Mark 6:5 and Luke 4:40)

And when Jesus saw her, he called her to him, and said unto her,
Woman, thou art loosed from thine infirmity. And he laid his hands
on her: and immediately she was made straight, and glorified God.

Matthew 10:8 (see also Mark 6:13)

[*Jesus talking to his disciples*] Heal the sick, cleanse the lepers,
raise the dead, cast out devils: freely ye have received, freely give.

Acts 28:8

And it came to pass, that the father of Publius lay sick of a fever
and of a bloody flux: to whom Paul entered in, and prayed, and laid
his hands on him, and healed him.

Mark 16:15–18

And he [*Jesus after his resurrection*] said unto them [*the disciples*], Go ye into all the world, and preach the gospel to every creature. He that believeth and is baptized shall be saved; but he that believeth not shall be damned. And these signs shall follow them that believe; In my name shall they cast out devils; they shall speak with new tongues; They shall take up serpents; and if they drink any deadly thing, it shall not hurt them; they shall lay hands on the sick, and they shall recover.

James 5:14

Is any sick among you? let him call for the elders of the church; and let them pray over him, anointing him with oil in the name of the Lord.

Blessing Children

Jesus loved children and instituted the ordinance of blessing them. He took them into his arms to administer this blessing (Mark 10:16; Matthew 19:13).

Mark 10:16

And he took them up in his arms, put his hands upon them, and blessed them.

Matthew 19:13

Then were there brought unto him little children, that he should put his hands on them, and pray.

Priesthood Ordination

The priesthood is the power and authority of God on earth. Moses laid hands upon Joshua to ordain him to the Aaronic Priesthood (Deuteronomy 34:9). Priesthood ordination comes as a calling from the Lord (Luke 9:1; Mark 6:7) and is carried out by those in authority through the ritual laying on of hands (Acts 6:5–6).

Deuteronomy 34:9

And Joshua the son of Nun was full of the spirit of wisdom; for Moses had laid his hands upon him: and the children of Israel hearkened unto him, and did as the Lord commanded Moses.

Luke 9:1

Then he called his twelve disciples together, and gave them power [*ordained them*] and authority over all devils, and to cure diseases.

Mark 6:7

And he called unto him the twelve, and began to send them forth by two and two; and gave them power over unclean spirits.

Acts 6:5–6

And the saying pleased the whole multitude: and they chose Stephen, a man full of faith and of the Holy Ghost, and Philip, and Prochorus, and Nicanor, and Timon, and Parmenas, and Nicolas a proselyte of Antioch: Whom they set before the apostles: and when they had prayed, they laid their hands on them.

Baptisms for the Dead

Paul refers to baptism for the dead in his dissertation to the Corinthians (1 Corinthians 15:29).

1 Corinthians 15:21–24, 29

For since by man [*Adam*] came death [*mortality*], by man [*Jesus*] came also the resurrection of the dead. For as in Adam all die, even so in Christ shall all be made alive. But every man [*is resurrected*] in his own order: Christ the firstfruits; afterward they that are Christ's at his [*second*] coming. Then cometh the end, when he [*Jesus*] shall have delivered up the kingdom to God, even the Father; when he shall have put down all rule and all authority and power. . . . Else what shall they do which are baptized for the dead [*why bother to baptize for the dead*], if the dead rise [*are resurrected*] not at all? why are they then baptized for the dead?

Washing and Anointing

The ordinances of washing and anointing (or purification) are introduced in the Old Testament (Exodus 29:4; 40:12), and continued in the New Testament both before and after the Ascension of Jesus (John 13:5; Acts 21:26; 24:17–18).

Exodus 29:4 (see also Exodus 40:12)

And Aaron and his sons thou shalt bring unto the door of the tabernacle of the congregation, and shalt wash them with water.

John 13:5

After that he poureth water into a bason, and began to wash the disciples' feet, and to wipe them with the towel wherewith he was girded.

Acts 21:26 (see also Acts 24:17–18)

> Then Paul took the men, and the next day purifying himself with them entered into the temple, to signify the accomplishment of the days of purification, until that an offering should be offered for every one of them.

Endowment

The act of being endowed with power from on high is an ordinance introduced as a similitude of the Savior being taken up into heaven (Luke 24:49–53).

Luke 24:49–53

> And, behold, I send the promise of my Father upon you: but tarry ye in the city of Jerusalem, until ye be endowed with power from on high. And he led them out as far as to Bethany, and he lifted up his hands, and blessed them. And it came to pass, while he blessed them, he was parted from them, and carried up into heaven. And they worshipped him, and returned to Jerusalem with great joy: And were continually in the temple, praising and blessing God. Amen.

Sealing

The crowning ordinance of the sealing of families comes through the power of the priesthood to bind on earth and in heaven as given by Christ to Peter and his successors (Matthew 16:19).

Matthew 16:19

> And I will give unto thee [*Peter*] the keys of the kingdom of heaven [*priesthood authority*]: and whatsoever thou shalt bind [*seal*] on earth shall be bound in heaven: and whatsoever thou shalt loose on earth shall be loosed in heaven.

MORMON UNDERSTANDING

Ordinances

In The Church of Jesus Christ of Latter-day Saints, an ordinance is a formal sacred act performed under the authority of the priesthood. Several ordinances performed in the Church today are frequently mentioned in the Bible. These include baptism, confirmation, the sacrament, and the healing of the sick. Other ordinances include priesthood blessings, ordinations, and temple ordinances. The lack of biblical detail on some ordinances is explained in a prophecy from Isaiah: "The earth also is defiled under the inhabitants thereof; because they have transgressed the laws, changed the ordinance, broken the everlasting covenant" (Isaiah 24:5). Because of this falling away, some ordinances were lost or distorted. Modern revelation has restored these ordinances.

Covenants

In both the Old and New Testaments, the Lord instituted ordinances as a means of spiritually committing his chosen people to making and keeping covenants. Ordinances are gateways to covenants. Covenants are sacred contracts—two-way promises with the Lord. The combination of ordinances and covenants helps the children of God remember who they are, where they come from, and where they are going.

Salvation

The Church of Jesus Christ of Latter-day Saints accepts the biblical teaching that saving ordinances are required for exaltation (entry into the Kingdom of God). Baptism is such an ordinance. However, an ordinance alone does not save or exalt. It is exercising faith and keeping the covenant associated with the ordinance that have saving power. When a person acts upon faith, makes a covenant with God, and participates in the ordinance, the doorway to the heavens is opened. However, the covenant must be kept and faith in Christ maintained for the full measure of blessings to be received.

Baptism

Baptism is primary among the saving ordinances. Not only was Jesus himself baptized to "fulfil all righteousness" (Matthew 3:15), but he boldly proclaimed that unless an individual was baptized, he could not enter into the kingdom of God (John 3:5). The ordinance of baptism symbolizes death (buried under the water) and rebirth in the resurrection (coming out of the water)—thus the ritual importance of full immersion. The covenant made at baptism is that the baptized person will take upon himself the name of Jesus Christ as Savior and Redeemer, always remember him, and keep his commandments.

Confirmation

An extension of the ordinance and covenant of baptism is the ordinance of confirmation, through which the baptized person is confirmed a member of the Church of Jesus Christ and granted the gift of the Holy Ghost. This ordinance is performed by the authority of the priesthood with the laying on of hands. The gift of the Holy Ghost is the Lord's promise of the constant companionship of the Holy Ghost as long as the confirmed person remains worthy of this companionship. In this state of constant companionship, the confirmed person's body is the temple of the Holy Ghost (1 Corinthians 6:19).

The Sacrament

Receiving the ordinance of the sacrament, consuming bread and the water as emblems of the body and blood of Jesus Christ, is spiritually integrated with the ordinance and covenant of baptism. According to the example set by the Savior, the sacrament is usually received each week. The sacrament is a reminder of the Atonement of Christ, an invitation to renew covenants made at baptism, and a prompting to repent through the redeeming sacrifice of Jesus Christ. The sacrament includes an examination of conscience and a humble petition for forgiveness.

Healing the Sick and Afflicted

Healing of the sick is an ordinance performed by Jesus, carried on by the apostles, and continued to this day. Healing of the sick is performed typically by priesthood authority and may include a preliminary anointing with sacred oil. Latter-day Saints believe that this ordinance and others like it have the plain and simple purpose suggested in the title—in this case, healing the sick. Jesus taught that those who had faith in him would do even greater works (John 14:12), laying the foundation for the healing ordinances and other miraculous events in modern times.

Blessing Children

A traditional ordinance in The Church of Jesus Christ of Latter-day Saints is the blessing of children (usually infants). Shortly after a baby's birth, parents present their child to the congregation, announce the name by which the child will be known in the records of The Church of Jesus Christ of Latter-day Saints, and give the child a blessing through the authority of the priesthood and in the name of Jesus Christ. This ordinance follows the example of Jesus blessing the children during his public ministry. Latter-day Saint children must wait until age eight to be baptized. At that age, they are considered capable of repentance and of making a free and informed choice to be baptized.

Priesthood Ordination

Priesthood ordination is another ordinance that has its roots in the Old Testament, was carried over to the New Testament, and is continued in these latter days. All worthy Latter-day Saint men, young and old, are eligible to hold the priesthood, either Aaronic or Melchizedek. A man is ordained to a particular office in the priesthood. The offices of the Aaronic Priesthood are deacon, teacher, priest, and bishop. Bishop is the highest office in the Aaronic Priesthood; bishops also hold the Melchizedek Priesthood and are called as high priests so they can preside over the entire ward. The offices of the Melchizedek Priesthood are apostle, seventy, patriarch, high priest, and elder. (See priesthood chapter for further.)

Temple Ordinances

Among the most sacred and important of all ordinances are those administered in the temples of The Church of Jesus Christ of Latter-day Saints. Some of these ordinances are performed for the person attending the temple. These include washing and anointing, the endowment, and the sealing of families for eternity. The endowment, which literally means "gift," includes making covenants associated with sacrifice, consecration, and love and loyalty to spouse. These ordinances are also performed vicariously for the dead. In this case, the ordinances have no efficacy unless and until they are freely accepted by the deceased person in the spirit world. No ordinance is forced on anyone, living or dead. Some of these temple ordinances were introduced in the Bible; all were brought forth in completion during the restoration.

❧ 18 ❧

FAITH, GRACE, WORKS

*F*aith, grace, and works are key principles in Christian theology. The relationship between these principles has long been the subject of debate in Christendom. "Saved by grace," "saved by faith," and "faith without works is dead" are catch phrases in a maze of possibilities and potential contradictions that have pitted Christian against Christian for centuries.

BIBLICAL TEACHING

The Divine Combination

The pattern of grace through faith followed by works is revealed clearly in the Bible, and the interconnectivity of these spiritual principles is addressed repeatedly. King David, author of Psalms, urged all men to trust (have faith) in the Lord, to "do good" (work), and then reap the benefits of combining the two principles (Psalm 37:3). Paul, the New Testament's primary commentator on grace, said in his writings to the Ephesians that it is grace, accessed through faith, that brings salvation to the souls of men (Ephesians 2:8–10). He went on to teach that grace is followed by good works, that is, men and women under the influence of grace are guided unfailingly to do good works (2 Corinthians 9:8; Titus 3:7–8; 2 Thessalonians 2:16–17). James wrote that faith is made perfect through works (James 2:22, 24).

Psalm 37:3

Trust in [*have faith in*] the Lord, and do good [*produce good works*]; so shalt thou dwell in the land, and verily thou shalt be fed.

Ephesians 2:8–10

For by grace are ye saved through faith; and that not of your-selves: it is the gift of God: Not of works [*vain accomplishments*], lest any man should boast. For we are his workmanship [*we are God's spirit offspring*], created in Christ Jesus unto good works [*created to do good works by grace*], which God hath before ordained [*ordered or decreed, not predestined*] that we should walk in them [*good works*].

2 Corinthians 9:8 (see also Titus 3:7–8)

And God is able to make all grace abound toward you; that ye, always having all sufficiency in all things, may abound to every good work: [*by grace men and women are led to good works*].

2 Thessalonians 2:16–17

Now our Lord Jesus Christ himself, and God, even our Father, which hath loved us, and hath given us everlasting consolation and good hope through grace, Comfort your hearts, and stablish you in every good word and work. [*Love, consolation, good hope, grace, and comfort are facilitators of good works.*]

James 2:22, 24

Seest thou how faith wrought with his works, and by works was faith made perfect? . . . Ye see then how that by works a man is justi-fied, and not by faith only.

Faith without Works

While Paul wrote extensively on the unity of grace and faith, James wrote extensively on the unity of faith and works. Indeed, James put a sharp point on this unity, saying three times in the same chapter that faith without works is dead (James 2:14–17, 18–20, 26). Likewise, Paul in his letter to Titus described the useless condition of one who professes to know God, but in his works does not demonstrate such knowledge (Titus 1:15–16). Paul calls such a person "abominable."

James 2:14–17

What doth it profit, my brethren, though a man say he hath faith, and have not works? can faith save him? If a brother or sister be naked, and destitute of daily food, And one of you say unto them,

Depart in peace, be ye warmed and filled; notwithstanding ye give them not those things which are needful to the body; what doth it profit? Even so faith, if it hath not works, is dead, being alone.

James 2:18–20 (see also James 2:26)

Yea, a man may say, Thou hast faith, and I have works: shew me thy faith without thy works, and I will shew thee my faith by my works. [*The claim of faith requires verification by works.*] Thou believest that there is one God; thou doest well: the devils also believe [*believing alone does not distinguish the righteous from the wicked*], and tremble. But wilt thou know, O vain man, that faith without works is dead? [*Belief alone is not enough; the essential manifestation of faith is works.*]

Titus 1:15–16

Unto the pure all things are pure: but unto them that are defiled and unbelieving is nothing pure; but even their mind and conscience is defiled. They profess that they know God; but in works they deny him, being abominable, and disobedient, and unto every good work reprobate. [*Talk is cheap; faith is a mere concept, empty words, without expression in works.*]

Salvation

In teaching the interconnectivity of faith, grace, and works, the Lord proclaimed through Paul that a man must work out his own salvation with "fear and trembling" (Philippians 2:12–13). By exercising faith through works, men and women are saved through the Atonement of Christ and can then have a significant impact on the salvation of others (1 Timothy 4:16). Jesus told his disciples that the only way a man could save himself was to lose himself, to expend himself, and to work in the cause of Christ (Mark 8:35; Matthew 16:24–25; Luke 9:24; 17:33).

Philippians 2:12–13

Wherefore, my beloved, as ye have always obeyed, not as in my presence only, but now much more in my absence, work out your own salvation with fear and trembling. For it is God which worketh in you both to will and to do of his good pleasure.

1 Timothy 4:16

Take heed unto thyself, and unto the doctrine; continue in them: for in doing this thou shalt both save thyself, and them that hear thee.

Mark 8:35

> For whosoever will save his life shall lose it; but whosoever shall lose his life for my sake and the gospel's, the same shall save it.

Matthew 16:24–25 (see also Luke 9:23–24 and Luke 17:33)

> Then said Jesus unto his disciples, If any man will come after me, let him deny himself, and take up his cross, and follow me. For whosoever will save his life shall lose it: and whosoever will lose his life for my sake shall find it.

Love without Action

The Savior said the two great commandments were to love God and to love one another (Matthew 22:36–40, Mark 12:30–31; Luke 10:25–28). He taught that love of the Lord is more than a simple emotion or profession of devotion: Indeed, love without loving action is an empty abstraction or an emotional self-indulgence. Jesus said, "If ye love me, keep my commandments" (John 14:15). Those who keep (do works in compliance with) his commandments will abide in his love just as he abides in his Father's love (John 15:10). John sternly wrote that anyone who claims to know Christ but does not keep his commandments "is a liar" (1 John 2:4).

Matthew 22:36–40 (see also Mark 12:30–31)

> Master, which is the great commandment in the law? Jesus said unto him, Thou shalt love [*here "love" is used as a verb denoting an action that is taken, a work that is performed*] the Lord thy God with all thy heart, and with all thy soul, and with all thy mind. This is the first and great commandment. And the second is like unto it, Thou shalt love thy neighbour as thyself. On these two commandments hang all the law and the prophets.

Luke 10:25–28

> And, behold, a certain lawyer stood up, and tempted him, saying, Master, what shall I do to inherit eternal life? He said unto him, What is written in the law? how readest thou? And he answering said, Thou shalt love the Lord thy God with all thy heart, and with all thy soul, and with all thy strength, and with all thy mind; and thy neighbour as thyself. And he said unto him, Thou hast answered right: this do, and thou shalt live. [*Jesus gives not the slightest hint that mere belief is sufficient. He demands love and pointedly commands, "This do." Love is something done. It is work, or it is nothing.*]

John 15:10 (see also John 14:15)

If ye keep [*act in compliance with*] my commandments, ye shall abide in my love; even as I have kept my Father's commandments, and [*therefore*] abide in his love.

1 John 2:4

He that saith, I know him, and keepeth not his commandments, is a liar, and the truth is not in him. [*The claim of faith is a lie without fulfillment in works.*]

Doers of the Word

God gives words to live by, and he requires obedience to those words (Micah 6:8). God commands all men and women to be "doers of the word, and not hearers only" (James 1:22–25). During his public ministry Jesus relentlessly taught the principle of "doing" (Luke 3:11–14 and Mark 10:21). He said that those who "heareth these sayings of mine, and doeth them" are wise, and those who do not do them are foolish (Matthew 7:21–27). On Judgment Day, the Lord will separate the sheep (doers of the word) from the goats (hearers only). He proclaimed that a man or woman who serves others serves the Lord (Matthew 25:34–40).

Micah 6:8

He hath shewed thee, O man, what is good; and what doth the Lord require of thee, but to do [*take action, work*] justly, and to love mercy, and to walk humbly with thy God?

James 1:22–25

But be ye doers of the word, and not hearers only, deceiving your own selves. For if any be a hearer of the word, and not a doer, he is like unto a man beholding his natural face in a glass: For he beholdeth himself, and goeth his way, and straightway forgetteth what manner of man he was. But whoso looketh into the perfect law of liberty, and continueth therein, he being not a forgetful hearer, but a doer of the work, this man shall be blessed in his deed.

Luke 3:11–14

He [*Jesus*] answereth and saith unto them, He that hath two coats, let him impart [*give, hand over*] to him that hath none; and he that hath meat, let him do likewise. Then came also publicans to be baptized, and said unto him, Master, what shall we do [*how shall we act, what works shall we perform*]? And he said unto them, Exact no more than that which is appointed you. And the soldiers likewise demanded of him, saying, And what shall we do? And he said unto them, Do violence to no man, neither accuse any falsely; and be content with your wages. [*In all cases, Jesus told his disciples to "do" something, not merely know, believe, or have faith in something. Jesus issued a call to action, not a call to feeling.*]

Mark 10:21

Then Jesus beholding him loved him, and said unto him, One thing thou lackest: go thy way, sell whatsoever thou hast [*work*], and give to the poor [*work*], and thou shalt have treasure in heaven: and come, take up the cross [*work*], and follow me [*work*]. [*It is not enough to love Jesus as an object of affection. Work is required, and Jesus lists the tasks.*]

Matthew 7:21–27

Not every one that saith unto me, Lord, Lord, [*professes faith in me*] shall enter into the kingdom of heaven; but he that doeth [*takes action consistent with*] the will of my Father which is in heaven. Many will say to me in that day, Lord, Lord, have we not prophesied in thy name? and in thy name have cast out devils? and in thy name done many wonderful works? And then will I profess unto them, I never knew you: depart from me, ye that work iniquity. [*Jesus rejects those who go through the religious motions, who profess great faith, who make a great show but fail to do the simple work of love.*] Therefore whosoever heareth these sayings of mine, and doeth them, I will liken him unto a wise man, which built his house upon a rock: And the rain descended, and the floods came, and the winds blew, and beat upon that house; and it fell not: for it was founded upon a rock. And every one that heareth these sayings of mine, and doeth them not, shall be likened unto a foolish man, which built his house upon the sand: And the rain descended, and the floods came, and the winds blew, and beat upon that house; and it fell: and great was the fall of it.

Matthew 25:34–40

Then shall the King say unto them on his right hand, Come, ye blessed of my Father, inherit the kingdom prepared for you from the foundation of the world: For I was an hungred, and ye gave me meat [*you did the work that was needed*]: I was thirsty, and ye gave me drink: I was a stranger, and ye took me in: Naked, and ye clothed me: I was sick, and ye visited me: I was in prison, and ye came unto me. Then shall the righteous answer him, saying, Lord, when saw we thee an hungred, and fed thee? or thirsty, and gave thee drink? When saw we thee a stranger, and took thee in? or naked, and clothed thee? Or when saw we thee sick, or in prison, and came unto thee? And the King shall answer and say unto them, Verily I say unto you, Inasmuch as ye have done it unto one of the least of these my brethren, ye have done it unto me.

Sacrifice as Works

To sacrifice is to deny one's self in service of others, to lose one's life in order to find it, to enlarge the self by including others in it (Mark 8:34–36; Luke 9:24; Matthew 16:25; and Luke 17:33). Peter encouraged the early Christians to "offer up spiritual sacrifices acceptable to God by Jesus Christ" (1 Peter 2:5).

Mark 8:34–36

And when he had called the people unto him with his disciples also, he said unto them, Whosoever will come after me, let him deny himself [*deny sin, devotion to physical comfort and sensual pleasure, the praise of men, materialism, and all worldly enticements*], and take up his cross [*do the difficult work that needs to be done*], and follow me [*take the higher path, the one leading to eternal life*]. For whosoever will save his life [*the worldly life of pleasure and comfort*] shall lose it [*injury, disease, and death will intervene; sorrow and disappointment will intrude*]; but whosoever shall lose his life [*give up attachment to things of this world*] for my sake and the gospel's, the same shall save it [*save his or her better self, the soul that has no end*]. For what shall it profit a man, if he shall gain the whole world, and lose his own soul?"

Luke 9:24 (see also Matthew 16:25 and Luke 17:33)

For whosoever will save his [*worldly*] life shall lose it: but whosoever will lose his [*worldly*] life for my sake, the same shall save it [*eternal life*].

1 Peter 2:5

Ye also, as lively stones, are built up a spiritual house, an holy priesthood, to offer up spiritual sacrifices, acceptable to God by Jesus Christ.

Charity as Works

Charity marked by selfless service given through the pure love of Christ is greater than prophecy, understanding, and faith

(1 Corinthians 13:2, 13). Paul proclaimed that those who are without charity are "nothing." James defined pure religion as service given to those who are in greatest need (James 1:27).

1 Corinthians 13:2, 13

> And though I have the gift of prophecy, and understand all mysteries, and all knowledge; and though I have all faith, so that I could remove mountains, and have not charity, I am nothing . . . And now bideth faith, hope, charity, these three; but the greatest of these is charity.

James 1:27

> Pure religion and undefiled before God and the Father is this, To visit the fatherless and widows in their affliction, and to keep himself unspotted from the world.

Humility as Works

Humility is essential for spiritual progress. Peter taught the disciples to be "clothed with humility" (1 Peter 5:5). James said that with humility comes wisdom (James 3:13). Humility (or meekness) is so important that those who possess it will not only inherit the earth (Psalm 37:11; Matthew 5:5), but will also be exalted (1 Peter 5:6; Matthew 23:12).

1 Peter 5:5

> Likewise, ye younger, submit yourselves unto the elder. Yea, all of you be subject one to another, and be clothed with humility: for God resisteth the proud, and giveth grace to the humble.

James 3:13

> Who is a wise man and endued with knowledge among you? let him shew out of a good conversation his works with meekness of wisdom.

Psalm 37:11 (see also Matthew 5:5)

> But the meek shall inherit the earth; and shall delight themselves in the abundance of peace.

1 Peter 5:6 (see also Matthew 23:12)

> Humble yourselves therefore under the mighty hand of God, that he may exalt you in due time:

Endurance as Works

Endurance is the willing acceptance of afflictions and persecutions. Jesus warned his followers against being like the man who "dureth for a while: for when tribulation or persecution ariseth because of the word, by and by he is offended" and is without fruits (Matthew 13:18–23). Jesus urged his disciples to endure to the end (Matthew 24:13; Mark 13:13) despite persecution (John 15:20). Enduring to the end brings great blessings (Matthew 5:10–12, 44; Luke 6:22). The persecuted are promised they will not be forsaken (2 Corinthians 4:8–9), and are encouraged to rejoice and take pleasure in being persecuted for their faith in Jesus Christ (2 Corinthians 12:10; 1 Peter 4:13–14). The reward of endurance in the eternities is beyond measure, including a "crown of righteousness" (2 Timothy 4:5–8), "life everlasting" (1 Timothy 1:16), and "to be counted worthy of the kingdom of God" (2 Thessalonians 1:4–5).

Matthew 13:18–23

> [*Jesus speaking to the multitudes who had gathered to hear him*] Hear ye therefore the parable of the sower. When any one heareth the word of the kingdom, and understandeth it not, then cometh the wicked one [*Satan*], and catcheth away that which was sown in his heart. This is he which received seed by the way side. But he that received the seed into stony places, the same is he that heareth the word, and anon with joy [*great emotion*] receiveth it; Yet hath he not root in himself, but dureth for a while: for when tribulation or persecution ariseth because of the word, by and by he is offended [*fallen away*]. He also that received seed among the thorns is he that heareth the word; and the care of this world, and the deceitfulness of riches, choke the word, and he becometh unfruitful [*produces no works*]. But he that received seed into the good ground is he that heareth the word, and understandeth it; which also beareth fruit [*does good works*], and bringeth forth, some an hundredfold, some sixty, some thirty [*works by degrees*].

Matthew 24:13 (see also Mark 13:13)

> But he that shall endure unto the end, the same shall be saved.

John 15:20

> Remember the word that I said unto you, The servant is not greater than his lord. If they have persecuted me, they will also persecute you; if they have kept my saying, they will keep yours also.

Matthew 5:10–12 (see also Luke 6:22)

    Blessed are they which are persecuted for righteousness' sake: for theirs is the kingdom of heaven. Blessed are ye, when men shall revile you, and persecute you, and shall say all manner of evil against you falsely, for my sake. Rejoice, and be exceeding glad: for great is your reward in heaven: for so persecuted they the prophets which were before you.

2 Corinthians 4:8–9

    We are troubled on every side, yet not distressed; we are perplexed, but not in despair; Persecuted, but not forsaken; cast down, but not destroyed;

2 Corinthians 12:10 (see also 1 Peter 4:13–14)

    Therefore I take pleasure in infirmities, in reproaches, in necessities, in persecutions, in distresses for Christ's sake: for when I am weak, then am I strong.

2 Timothy 4:5–8

    But watch thou in all things, endure afflictions, do the work of an evangelist, make full proof of thy ministry. For I am now ready to be offered, and the time of my departure is at hand. I have fought a good fight, I have finished my course, I have kept the faith: Henceforth there is laid up for me a crown of righteousness, which the Lord, the righteous judge, shall give me at that day: and not to me only, but unto all them also that love his appearing.

1 Timothy 1:16

    Howbeit for this cause I obtained mercy, that in me first Jesus Christ might shew forth all longsuffering, for a pattern to them which should hereafter believe on him to life everlasting.

2 Thessalonians 1:4–5

    So that we ourselves glory in you in the churches of God for your patience and faith in all your persecutions and tribulations that ye endure: Which is a manifest token of the righteous judgment of God, that ye may be counted worthy of the kingdom of God, for which ye also suffer.

Works as Examples

The Savior exhorted his disciples to let their good works shine before men to glorify God (Matthew 5:16). Peter taught that good works when seen by men will "glorify God in the day of visitation" (1 Peter 2:12).

Matthew 5:16

Let your light so shine before men, that they may see your good works, and glorify your Father which is in heaven.

1 Peter 2:12

Having your conversation honest among the Gentiles: that, whereas they speak against you as evildoers, they may by your good works, which they shall behold, glorify God in the day of visitation.

Works in the Afterlife

Works follow the worker into the afterlife (Revelation 14:13).

Revelation 14:13

And I heard a voice from heaven saying unto me, Write, Blessed are the dead which die in the Lord from henceforth: Yea, saith the Spirit, that they may rest from their labours; and their works do follow them.

Works and the Final Judgment

The children of God are judged on earth and in the afterlife for their works in mortality. While salvation (immortality) is assured through acceptance of the Atonement of Christ, the Lord records works in the "book of life," upon which he will judge all mankind (Revelation 20:12–13). Paul wrote that judgments will be made according to what each person has done (2 Corinthians 5:10).

Revelation 20:12–13

And I saw the dead, small and great, stand before God; and the books were opened: and another book was opened, which is the book of life: and the dead were judged out of those things which were written in the books, according to their works. And the sea gave up the dead which were in it; and death and hell delivered up the dead which were in them: and they were judged every man according to their works. [*Both the righteous and the unrighteous will be judged according to their works.*]

2 Corinthians 5:10

For we must all appear before the judgment seat of Christ; that every one may receive the things done in his body, according to that he hath done, whether it be good or bad.

Works and Rewards

Men and women who do good works lay up "in store for themselves" a solid foundation for eternal life (1 Timothy 6:18–19). Rewards are determined according to works (Matthew 16:27; Psalm 62:12; Revelation 22:12; 1 Peter 1:17). Those who live in and propagate righteousness will earn a great reward (Proverbs 11:18; Psalm 18:20–21; 37:29), while those who render evil will be given a far lesser, though just, reward (2 Timothy 4:14). Because good works flow from faith and faith flows from diligently seeking the Lord, the Lord will reward those who "diligently seek him" (Hebrews 11:6). The rewards that flow from rendering good works in the glory of God include receiving a crown of life (James 1:12), sharing in the Lord's throne (Revelation 3:21), and becoming a "ruler over many things" (Matthew 25:21).

1 Timothy 6:18–19

That they do good, that they be rich in good works, ready to distribute, willing to communicate; Laying up in store for themselves a good foundation against the time to come, that they may lay hold on eternal life.

Matthew 16:27 (see also Psalm 62:12)

For the Son of man shall come in the glory of his Father with his angels; and then he shall reward every man according to his works.

Revelation 22:12

And, behold, I come quickly; and my reward is with me, to give every man according as his work shall be.

1 Peter 1:17

And if ye call on the Father, who without respect of persons judgeth according to every man's work, pass the time of your sojourning here in fear.

Proverbs 11:18

The wicked worketh a deceitful work: but to him that soweth righteousness shall be a sure reward.

Psalm 18:20–21 (see also Psalm 37:29)

The Lord rewarded me according to my righteousness; according to the cleanness of my hands hath he recompensed me. For I have kept the ways of the Lord, and have not wickedly departed from my God.

2 Timothy 4:14

Alexander the coppersmith did me much evil: the Lord reward him according to his works.

Hebrews 11:6

But without faith it is impossible to please him: for he that cometh to God must believe that he is, and that he is a rewarder of them that diligently seek him.

James 1:12

Blessed is the man that endureth temptation: for when he is tried, he shall receive the crown of life, which the Lord hath promised to them that love him.

Revelation 3:21

To him that overcometh will I grant to sit with me in my throne, even as I also overcame, and am set down with my Father in his throne.

Matthew 25:21

His lord said unto him, Well done, thou good and faithful servant: thou hast been faithful over a few things, I will make thee ruler over many things: enter thou into the joy of thy lord.

MORMON UNDERSTANDING

The Divine Combination

Faith, works, and grace are the three legs of a spiritual platform that must be put in place to fully praise and experience God. The platform collapses if any of these legs is taken away. Faith is necessary for works to have meaning, and grace is necessary for works to have efficacy.

The Great Debate

There is a centuries-old debate about the matrix of faith, works, and grace. Some see an insurmountable contradiction: "If it is by undeserved grace that man is saved, how can faith or works also be a necessity of salvation?" Latter-day Saints disentangle from this either-or construct and embrace faith, works, and grace as a perfect unity. In this unity, a new life in Christ becomes possible, and fear of damnation is replaced with the joy of divine labor under the protection of grace.

Progression

Line upon line, precept upon precept, here a little, and there a little faith grows, works proliferate, and the purposes of God are fulfilled. As faith and works combine, human understanding deepens. This deepening can in time and by the grace of God culminate in pure knowledge.

Faith and Works

The Bible places enormous emphasis on faith and works together. According to a metaphor by C. S. Lewis, they operate like the blades of a pair of scissors. This is why James boldly proclaimed that "faith, if it hath not works, is dead" (James 2:17).

Jesus said,

> Verily, verily, I say unto you, He that believeth on me, the works that I do shall he do also; and greater works than these shall he do; because I go unto my Father. And whatsoever ye shall ask in my name, that will I do, that the Father may be glorified in the Son. If ye shall ask any thing in my name, I will do it. *If ye love me, keep my commandments* (1 John 14:12-17, emphasis added).

Jesus preached love as an action verb. To love is to do. Love and action are inseparable in Christ's message. Paul said, "Without faith it is impossible to please him: for he that cometh to God must believe that he is . . . he is a rewarder of them that diligently seek him" (Hebrews 11:6).

Paul does not invite men to simply bask in their saved condition. He preached seeking. Latter-day Saints are seekers. They have faith, do good works, and trust that the grace of God through the Atonement of Jesus Christ will erase whatever deficit may remain.

❦ 19 ❧

TEMPLES

BIBLICAL TEACHING

The Last Days

Isaiah and Micah both prophesied that in the last days, "the mountain of the Lord's house" would be established and that nations would "flow unto it" to learn of the Lord (Isaiah 2:2–3; Micah 4:1–2). In a complementary scripture, Obadiah spoke of saviours coming to "mount Zion" (Obadiah 1:21).

Isaiah 2:2–3 (see also Micah 4:1–2)

> And it shall come to pass in the last days, that the mountain of the Lord's house shall be established in the top of the mountains, and shall be exalted above the hills; and all nations shall flow unto it. And many people shall go and say, Come ye, and let us go up to the mountain of the Lord, to the house of the God of Jacob; and he will teach us of his ways, and we will walk in his paths: for out of Zion shall go forth the law, and the word of the Lord from Jerusalem.

Obadiah 1:21

> And saviours shall come up on mount Zion to judge the mount of Esau; and the kingdom shall be the Lord's.

Houses of the Lord

Before the public ministry of Jesus, temples were built as houses of worship and dwelling places of the Lord (Zechariah 6:12–14; Zechariah 8:8–9; Haggai 1:2, 8), each one dedicated to the "Lord my God"

(1 Kings 5:5). These same temples were defended and cleansed by Jesus (Mark 11:15–17; Matthew 21:12–13) and preached in by his apostles following his Ascension (Acts 2:46–47). Temples are simple yet beautiful, divinely crafted in all manner of workmanship (Exodus 25–27; 2 Chronicles 3–4). Temples possess a variety of spiritual symbols such as the twelve oxen to represent the twelve tribes of Israel (2 Chronicles 4:2–4) and the engraving "Holiness to the Lord" on the outside of its walls (Exodus 28:36; 39:30).

Zechariah 6:12–14 (see also Zechariah 8:8–9)

And speak unto him, saying, Thus speaketh the Lord of hosts, saying, Behold the man whose name is The Branch; and he shall grow up out of his place, and he shall build the temple of the Lord: Even he shall build the temple of the Lord; and he shall bear the glory, and shall sit and rule upon his throne; and he shall be a priest upon his throne: and the counsel of peace shall be between them both. And the crowns shall be to Helem, and to Tobijah, and to Jedaiah, and to Hen the son of Zephaniah, for a memorial in the temple of the Lord.

Haggai 1:2, 8

Thus speaketh the Lord of hosts, saying, This people say, The time is not come, the time that the Lord's house should be built. . . . Go up to the mountain, and bring wood, and build the house [*the temple*]; and I will take pleasure in it, and I will be glorified, saith the Lord.

1 Kings 5:5

And, behold, I purpose to build an house unto the name of the Lord my God, as the Lord spake unto David my father, saying, Thy son, whom I will set upon thy throne in thy room, he shall build an house unto my name.

Mark 11:15–17 (see also Matthew 21:12–13)

And they come to Jerusalem: and Jesus went into the temple, and began to cast out them that sold and bought in the temple, and overthrew the tables of the moneychangers, and the seats of them that sold doves; And would not suffer that any man should carry any vessel through the temple. And he taught, saying unto them, Is it not written, My house shall be called of all nations the house of prayer? but ye have made it a den of thieves. [*The temple was exceedingly important to Jesus. He called the temple "his house" and in one of the few instances where he manifested anger and used violence, he cleansed it.]*

Acts 2:46–47

And they, continuing daily with one accord in the temple, [*the apostles visited the temple daily after the Ascension of Christ*] and breaking bread from house to house, did eat their meat with gladness and singleness of heart, Praising God, and having favour with all the people. And the Lord added to the church daily such as should be saved.

Exodus 25, 26, and 27; 2 Chronicles 3 and 4

NOTE: These chapters give exquisite detail on how the tabernacle was to be built as a house of the Lord. Only the finest materials and workmanship were tolerated. The same care and craftsmanship went into building the temple during the time of Solomon. The same is true for the construction of temples today.

2 Chronicles 4:2–4

Also he made a molten sea of ten cubits from brim to brim, round in compass, and five cubits the height thereof; and a line of thirty cubits did compass it round about. And under it was the similitude of oxen, which did compass it round about: ten in a cubit, compassing the sea round about. Two rows of oxen were cast, when it was cast. It stood upon twelve oxen [*the baptismal founts in temples today sit on top of twelve oxen*], three looking toward the north, and three looking toward the west, and three looking toward the south, and three looking toward the east: and the sea was set above upon them, and all their hinder parts were inward.

Exodus 28:36 (see also Exodus 39:30)

And thou shalt make a plate of pure gold, and grave upon it, like the engravings of a signet, Holiness to the Lord. [*Inscribed outside of each temple today are the words "Holiness to the Lord."*]

Love by Proxy

The Atonement of Christ was the ultimate act of love by proxy. Christ suffered the sins of all mankind because men and women were unable to do this for themselves (Romans 5:6–11).

Romans 5:6–11

For when we were yet without strength, in due time Christ died for the ungodly. For scarcely for a righteous man will one die: yet peradventure for a good man some would even dare to die. But God commendeth his love toward us, in that, while we were yet sinners, Christ died for us. [*Christ did for us what we could not do for ourselves*]. Much more then, being now justified by his blood, we shall be saved from wrath through him. For if, when we were enemies, we were reconciled to God by the death of his Son, much more, being reconciled, we shall be saved by his life. And not only so, but we also joy in God through our Lord Jesus Christ, by whom we have now received the atonement. [*Christ set the perfect example of ordinances by proxy by which one can take the place of another.*]

Work for the Dead

Jesus commenced the preaching of the gospel to the dead (1 Peter 4:6) in the hope that those who accepted it could have their earthly ordinances performed by men in the flesh. For example, because baptism is required to "enter into the kingdom of God" (John 3:5), the Lord made a way for those who are dead to be baptized by proxy (1 Corinthians 15:29). This pattern of surrogacy is part of God's plan. The faithful perform work on behalf of others, helping them progress in their journey to perfection (Hebrews 11:40).

1 Peter 4:6

For this cause was the gospel preached also to them that are dead, that they might be judged according to men in the flesh, but live according to God in the spirit. [*If the dead do not have any opportunity for salvation, why then would the gospel be preached to them?*]

John 3:5

Jesus answered, Verily, verily, I say unto thee, Except a man be born of water and of the Spirit, he cannot enter into the kingdom of God. [*Baptism is an essential ordinance to enter into the kingdom of God.*]

1 Corinthians 15:29

Else what shall they do which are baptized for the dead, if the dead rise not at all? why are they then baptized for the dead?

Hebrews 11:40

God having provided some better thing for us, that they without us should not be made perfect. [*The living can step in and help those who have passed on and help them in their eternal progression to perfection in Christ.*]

Everlasting Covenants

The Lord has the power and authority to make "everlasting cov-enants," covenants that last for all eternity and are accessible to the people of God for "evermore" (Ezekiel 37:26).

Ezekiel 37:26

> Moreover I will make a covenant of peace with them; it shall be an everlasting covenant with them [*there are some covenants that are everlasting*]: and I will place them, and multiply them, and will set my sanctuary in the midst of them for evermore.

New Names

Unannounced and without warning, the Lord spoke to Abram and Jacob and gave each one a new name—Abraham and Israel respectively (Genesis 17:5; 32:28)—signifying a covenant. Isaiah had a similar expe-rience with the Lord, and the people were given a new name (Isaiah 62:2). In the last days "in the temple of my God," there will be a new name given (Revelation 3:12).

Genesis 17:5

> Neither shall thy name any more be called Abram, but thy name shall be Abraham; for a father of many nations have I made thee. [*God gave Abram a new name.*]

Genesis 32:28

> And he said, Thy name shall be called no more Jacob, but Israel: for as a prince hast thou power with God and with men, and hast prevailed. [*God gave Jacob a new name.*]

Isaiah 62:2

> And the Gentiles shall see thy righteousness, and all kings thy glory: and thou shalt be called by a new name, which the mouth of the Lord shall name.

Revelation 3:12

> Him that overcometh will I make a pillar in the temple of my God, and he shall go no more out: and I will write upon him the name of my God, and the name of the city of my God, which is new Jerusalem, which cometh down out of heaven from my God: and I will write upon him my new name.

Sealing

Jesus gave his disciples the power to bind on earth and in heaven (Matthew 18:18). There is no giving or taking of marriage in heaven (Matthew 22:30–32), but rather all such matters relating to marriage are performed upon the earth. Husband and wife are to become one flesh joined together by God (Matthew 19:5–6; 1 Corinthians 11:3, 11).

Matthew 18:18

Verily I say unto you, Whatsoever ye shall bind on earth shall be bound in heaven: and whatsoever ye shall loose on earth shall be loosed in heaven. [*Through the authority of the priesthood, husbands, wives, and families can be bound (or sealed) together on earth and in heaven.*]

Matthew 22:30–32

For in the resurrection they neither marry, nor are given in marriage, but are as the angels of God in heaven. But as touching the resurrection of the dead, have ye not read that which was spoken unto you by God, saying, I am the God of Abraham, and the God of Isaac, and the God of Jacob? God is not the God of the dead, but of the living.

Matthew 19:5–6

And said, For this cause shall a man leave father and mother, and shall cleave to his wife: and they twain shall be one flesh? Wherefore they are no more twain, but one flesh. What therefore God hath joined together, let not man put asunder.

1 Corinthians 11:3, 11

But I would have you know, that the head of every man is Christ; and the head of the woman is the man; and the head of Christ is God . . . Nevertheless neither is the man without the woman, neither the woman without the man, in the Lord.

Ordinances

Ordinances are associated with temples. See the chapter on ordinances for more details.

Genealogy

Nehemiah was told by God to gather the genealogies of the people (Nehemiah 7:5). Matthew took the time to painstakingly write out in detail the genealogy of Jesus Christ (Matthew 1:1–17), as did many others in the Old Testament. It is in part by the keeping of genealogies that the hearts of the children can be turned to their fathers in fulfillment of the prophecy of Malachi (Malachi 4:5–6).

Nehemiah 7:5 (see also Matthew 1:1–17)

And my God put into mine heart to gather together the nobles, and the rulers, and the people, that they might be reckoned by genealogy. And I found a register of the genealogy of them which came up at the first, and found written therein. [*The keeping of genealogies is a deeply rooted tradition that provides both a spiritual and temporal record for families and nations.*]

Malachi 4:5–6

Behold, I will send you Elijah the prophet before the coming of the great and dreadful day of the Lord: And he shall turn the heart of the fathers to the children, and the heart of the children to their fathers, [*this is accomplished in part through genealogy*] lest I come and smite the earth with a curse.

Temple Worthiness

It is only those with clean hands and a pure heart that can "ascend into the hill of the Lord" (Psalm 24:3–4). In ancient times there were porters at the gates of the temple to check the worthiness of patrons before they entered (2 Chronicles 23:19). The followers of Jesus Christ are called to be holy, clean, and worthy in their temporal and spiritual lives in order to be taught from on high and enter into the temple of the Lord (1 Thessalonians 4:7; Acts 21:24–26).

Psalm 24:3–4

Who shall ascend into the hill of the Lord? or who shall stand in his holy place? He that hath clean hands, and a pure heart; who hath not lifted up his soul unto vanity, nor sworn deceitfully.

2 Chronicles 23:19

And he set the porters at the gates of the house of the Lord, that none which was unclean in any thing should enter in.

1 Thessalonians 4:7

For God hath not called us unto uncleanness, but unto holiness.

Acts 21:24–26

Them take, and purify thyself with them, and be at charges with them, that they may shave their heads: and all may know that those things, whereof they were informed concerning thee, are nothing; but that thou thyself also walkest orderly, and keepest the law. As touching the Gentiles which believe, we have written and concluded that they observe no such thing, save only that they keep themselves from things offered to idols, and from blood, and from strangled, and from fornication. Then Paul took the men, and the next day purifying himself with them entered into the temple, to signify the accomplishment of the days of purification, until that an offering should be offered for every one of them. [*Paul, long after the Ascension of Christ, participated in purification ceremonies to enter into the temple.*]

Garments

Clothing can have both real and symbolic importance, especially in relation to ecclesiastical duties. In the days of Moses, the priests were given specific garments to wear, each piece of which had a symbolic meaning associated with ecclesiastical duties (Exodus 28:2–4, 41–42). Isaiah mentioned "the garment of praise" (Isaiah 61:3), and Paul, the "armour of God" (Ephesians 6:13). John the Revelator mentioned robes in the temple of God (Revelation 7:13–15) and the blessings that come from keeping one's garments (Revelation 16:15). Whether it is symbolic or physical, garments play a role in the affairs of the Lord in matters of spirituality.

Exodus 28:2–4, 41–42
    And thou shalt make holy garments for Aaron thy brother for glory and for beauty. And thou shalt speak unto all that are wise hearted, whom I have filled with the spirit of wisdom, that they may make Aaron's garments to consecrate him, that he may minister unto me in the priest's office. And these are the garments which they shall make; a breastplate, and an ephod, and a robe, and a broidered coat, a mitre, and a girdle: and they shall make holy garments for Aaron thy brother, and his sons, that he may minister unto me in the priest's office . . . And thou shalt put them upon Aaron thy brother, and his sons with him; and shalt anoint them, and consecrate them, and sanctify them, that they may minister unto me in the priest's office. And thou shalt make them linen breeches to cover their nakedness; from the loins even unto the thighs they shall reach. [*Garments worn for special spiritual ceremonies, or those worn on a regular basis, do not make people holy, but are worn symbolically as a sign of faith and as a reminder of covenants.*]

Isaiah 61:3

> To appoint unto them that mourn in Zion, to give unto them beauty for ashes, the oil of joy for mourning, the garment of praise for the spirit of heaviness; that they might be called trees of righteousness, the planting of the Lord, that he might be glorified.

Ephesians 6:13

> Wherefore take unto you the whole armour of God, that ye may be able to withstand in the evil day, and having done all, to stand. [*Armor can be both spiritual and physical—in the case of a garment of the priesthood, it can be both.*]

Revelation 7:13–15

> And one of the elders answered, saying unto me, What are these which are arrayed in white robes? and whence came they? And I said unto him, Sir, thou knowest. And he said to me, These are they which came out of great tribulation, and have washed their robes, and made them white in the blood of the Lamb. Therefore are they before the throne of God, and serve him day and night in his temple: and he that sitteth on the throne shall dwell among them. [*The clothing worn in the temple, including robes, are symbolic of the purity of Christ and his holiness.*]

Revelation 16:15

> Behold, I come as a thief. Blessed is he that watcheth, and keepeth his garments, lest he walk naked, and they see his shame.

Temples in the Millennium

During the millennial reign of Christ, temples upon the earth will be filled day and night for the glory of God (Revelation 7:15; 11:1; 15:8).

Revelation 7:15

> Therefore are they before the throne of God, and serve him day and night in his temple: and he that sitteth on the throne shall dwell among them.

Revelation 11:1

> And there was given me a reed like unto a rod: and the angel stood, saying, Rise, and measure the temple of God, and the altar, and them that worship therein.

Revelation 15:8

> And the temple was filled with smoke from the glory of God, and from his power; and no man was able to enter into the temple, till the seven plagues of the seven angels were fulfilled.

MORMON UNDERSTANDING

History and Prophecy

The Old Testament prophets Isaiah and Micah spoke of the house of the Lord being built in the "last days" and being "established in the top of the mountains, and shall be exalted above the hills." These prophecies foretell of many nations and people coming to the house of the Lord to be taught, to be strengthened, and to covenant with the Lord. Latter-day Saints believe that each of their temples is a house of the Lord, and they seek to build them throughout the world. This work has been continuous since construction of the first Latter-day Saint temple in Kirtland, Ohio, in 1836.

The tabernacle during the time of Moses and the temple during the time of Solomon were built to accommodate the presence of the Lord. Jesus showed clearly his reverence for the Jewish temple when he said, "My house shall be called of all nations the house of prayer." Latter-day Saint temples are built today with the same perspective and purpose.

Latter-day Saint Temples

Latter-day Saints are a temple-building people.

> In the temples, members of the Church who make themselves eligible can participate in the most exalted of the redeeming ordinances that have been revealed to mankind. There, in a sacred ceremony, an individual may be washed and anointed and instructed and endowed and sealed. And when we have received these blessings for ourselves, we may officiate for those who have died without having had the same opportunity. In the temples sacred ordinances are performed for the living and for the dead alike.[1]

Temples are perpetual houses of the Lord. They are places for spiritual learning and sacred work. There is no provision for casual visits.

In the temples, worthy members of the Church learn about and participate in the sacred ordinances that will enable them to return to Heavenly Father and live with him throughout the eternities.

Latter-day Saint temples are elegant and beautiful, yet divinely simple. Each temple bears the prominent inscription, "Holiness to the Lord." Temples are not shrines erected in honor of the Church or any of its leaders; they are monuments to the Lord. A person not knowing this might remark, "Oh, there is a Mormon temple." A Latter-day Saint overhearing this might rightly think, "No, there is a house of the Lord."

Ordinances for the Living and the Dead

The ordinances performed in the temple include baptisms, confirmations, initiatories, priesthood ordinations, endowments, and sealings. Temple baptisms and confirmations are always done for the dead, while initiatories, ordinations, endowments, and sealings are done for those in attendance at the temple as well as for the dead.

Baptism and Confirmation

Temple baptisms and confirmations are performed for ancestors of Church members and, with appropriate permission, others who while on the earth were either not baptized at all or not baptized by proper authority.

Jesus taught that baptism was essential for a person to enter into the kingdom of God. In his infinite mercy, the Lord has therefore prepared a way for those who died without having been baptized to be baptized and confirmed by proxy in the temple. Church members can go to the temple and "act for and in behalf of" those who are deceased. Because moral agency is an eternal principle, the deceased are completely free in the spirit world to accept or reject a baptism, confirmation, or any other temple ordinance performed on their behalf.

The Initiatory

The initiatory is an ordinance similar to biblical washing and anointing. This ordinance is performed in preparation for the endowment. For men, it includes bestowing of the Melchizedek Priesthood. After completing an initiatory for one's self, an individual can complete by proxy initiatories for those who are deceased.

The Endowment

The endowment is an ordinance in which the participant learns about the Creation, Heavenly Father's plan of salvation, and the sacred covenants necessary to fulfill this plan. Part of the endowment is the making of these covenants with the Lord and being endowed with power from on high.

Celestial Marriage and Sealing

In the ordinance of celestial marriage, a man and woman make sacred marriage covenants and are sealed to one another in marriage for time and all eternity. If they have children (alive or deceased), those children are sealed to their sealed parents. Children born after the marriage sealing are "born under the covenant" and thus sealed at birth. It is through this sealing ordinance that families can be together forever. This is possible because Jesus gave certain bearers of the priesthood the authority to perform ordinances that are binding on earth and in heaven.

Family History

Work done for deceased individuals begins with genealogical investigations outside the temple. Church members are encouraged to conduct family history searches and genealogical work to identify ancestors. This can also be done by individuals who are not Latter-day Saints. These genealogical records are then prepared by the Church and made available for temple work. Through the linking of genealogies and temple ordinances, families can be sealed together through the holy ordinances of the temple under the authority of the priesthood. As with all ordinances done on their behalf, the deceased can accept or reject any ordinance.

Worthiness

Consistent with the sacredness of the temple and the work done there, only Church members who hold temple recommends may enter the temple. A temple recommend is a certification of worthiness. This certification is required for youth as well as adults. Worthiness is determined through two brief interviews: one with a member of the bishopric of the ward or the president of a branch and a second with a member of the stake presidency or the mission president. These interviews are not interrogations. Members are asked simple questions about basic moral conduct, obedience to the commandments, and adherence to their covenants. If there are no major transgressions, a temple recommend is granted. A temple recommend lasts two years for adults and one year for youth if worthiness is sustained.

For youth ages twelve to eighteen and adults who have been Church members for less than one year, a temporary recommend may be granted to participate in baptism and confirmation ordinances. The questions asked are similar to those asked for a two-year recommend.

Garments

Endowed members of the Church covenant to wear a special temple garment night and day for the rest of their lives. These garments are in the form of comfortable underclothing that bears simple symbols of the covenants made in the endowment. The temple garment is a constant reminder of these covenants, a protection against the temptations of the adversary, and a discrete outward expression of a member's inward commitment to follow Jesus and keep his commandments.

With a few exceptions, white outer garments are worn by all those who are within the ordinance areas of the temple. Temple staff also wear white. This adds to the peace and tranquility of the temple and is a symbol of the purity of thought and action that prevails there.

Sacred Silence

The details of the ordinances performed in the temple and the personal experiences had in the temple are not matters for discussion outside the temple.

This absence of discussion is a source of skepticism for some who are not members of the Church. They ask, "Why the secrets? If what you are doing there is not wrong, why not discuss it openly?" The short reply given by some Latter-day Saints is that temple ordinances "are not secret; they are sacred."

Those familiar with the cloister in the Catholic monastic tradition might more easily understand the silence that attends the temple experience. Much is gained in silence; much is lost in conversation.

The ancient Jews were forbidden to speak the name of God. In the same way and for the same reason, temple experiences are not up for discussion.

The Millennium

Several passages in the book of Revelation make clear that temples will be operating and will play a significant role before, during, and after the Second Coming of Jesus Christ. In fulfillment of these scriptural prophecies, The Church of Jesus Christ of Latter-day Saints continues to build temples throughout the world.

NOTE

1.   Boyd K. Packer, "The Holy Temple," *Ensign*, Feb. 1995, 32.

20

THE AFTERLIFE

BIBLICAL TEACHING

The Partial Judgment

Because the Final Judgment does not take place until after the Resurrection, which occurs at the Second Coming of Christ, a partial judgment takes place first. The results of this partial judgment determine where spirits of the dead reside as they await the Resurrection, the Second Coming, and the Final Judgment.

Spirits of the dead wait for their resurrection before the Final Judgment, and some are punished while waiting (2 Peter 2:9; Luke 12:47–48). Man's body was formed from the dust of ground (Genesis 2:7) and will return to the dust of the ground after death (Genesis 3:19), but his spirit lives on (Ecclesiastes 12:7).

2 Peter 2:9

The Lord knoweth how to deliver the godly out of temptations, and to reserve the unjust unto the day of judgment to be punished. [*Those who are good will be protected and those who are not will be punished.*]

Luke 12:47–48

And that servant, which knew his lord's will, and prepared not himself, neither did according to his will, shall be beaten with many stripes. [*Those who know the gospel and do not live it will be punished.*] But he that knew not, and did commit things worthy of stripes, shall be beaten with few stripes. [*Those who do not know the gospel, and do wickedly, will be punished, but not as severely as those who knew better*]

For unto whomsoever much is given, of him shall be much required: and to whom men have committed much, of him they will ask the more.

Genesis 2:7 and 3:19

And the Lord God formed man of the dust of the ground, and breathed into his nostrils the breath of life; and man became a living soul. . . .

In the sweat of thy face shalt thou eat bread, till thou return unto the ground; for out of it wast thou taken: for dust thou art, and unto dust shalt thou return.

Ecclesiastes 12:7

Then shall the dust return to the earth as it was: and the spirit shall return unto God who gave it. [*The spirit lives on after death, on a path, if chosen, leading back to the Father*]

The Spirit World

After physical death, the spirit of a man or woman remains in the same character in which it left the earth (Revelation 22:11–12). When Saul sought the help of a sorceress, it was revealed through a visitation by Samuel that those who have passed into the spirit world are in adult form and dwell (as spirits) upon the earth (1 Samuel 28:13–15).

Revelation 22:11–12

He that is unjust, let him be unjust still: and he which is filthy, let him be filthy still: and he that is righteous, let him be righteous still: and he that is holy, let him be holy still. And, behold, I come quickly; and my reward is with me, to give every man according as his work shall be. [*In death the body separates from the spirit; however, the character remains with the spirit. If a person is just, he will be just still; if he is unjust, he will be unjust still. Repentance, however, is still possible.*]

1 Samuel 28:13–15

And the king said unto her, Be not afraid: for what sawest thou? And the woman said unto Saul, I saw gods ascending out of the earth. And he said unto her, What form is he of? And she said, An old man cometh up; and he is covered with a mantle. And Saul perceived that it was Samuel, and he stooped with his face to the ground, and bowed himself. And Samuel said to Saul, Why hast thou disquieted me, to bring me up?

Paradise in the Spirit World

Jesus Christ and Paul called the most glorious level of the spirit world "paradise" (Luke 23:43; 2 Corinthians 12:3–4), a place of rest for those who have died in the Lord (Daniel 12:13; Isaiah 57:2; Revelation 14:13).

Luke 23:43

And Jesus said unto him, Verily I say unto thee, To day shalt thou be with me in paradise.

2 Corinthians 12:3–4

And I knew such a man, (whether in the body, or out of the body, I cannot tell: God knoweth;) How that he was caught up into paradise, and heard unspeakable words, which it is not lawful for a man to utter.

Daniel 12:13

But go thou thy way till the end be: for thou shalt rest, and stand in thy lot at the end of the days.

Isaiah 57:2

He shall enter into peace: they shall rest in their beds, each one walking in his uprightness.

Revelation 14:13

And I heard a voice from heaven saying unto me, Write, Blessed are the dead which die in the Lord from henceforth: Yea, saith the Spirit, that they may rest from their labours; and their works do follow them.

Spirit Prison in the Spirit World

Isaiah and Peter called the more perilous level of the spirit world a "prison," where both punishments for the wicked and preaching to the open-hearted take place (Isaiah 24:21–22; 1 Peter 3:19–20).

Jesus prophesied of the opening of the spirit prison (John 5:25) where the dead would hear the gospel and by proxy have the opportunity to be redeemed in Christ (1 Peter 4:6). Jesus revealed that there is a great gulf between those in paradise and those in spirit prison (Luke 16:19–26).

Peter spoke of the temporary "hell" that exists in the spirit prison where souls are left only for a time and have the opportunity for life in the eternities (Acts 2:25–31). Such souls in this hell will be delivered up at the Final Judgment (Revelation 20:13–14).

Isaiah 24:21–22

And it shall come to pass in that day, that the Lord shall punish the host of the high ones that are on high, and the kings of the earth upon the earth. And they shall be gathered together, as prisoners are gathered in the pit, and shall be shut up in the prison, and after many days shall they be visited.

1 Peter 3:19–20

By which also he went and preached unto the spirits in prison; Which sometime were disobedient, when once the longsuffering of God waited in the days of Noah, while the ark was a preparing, wherein few, that is, eight souls were saved by water.

John 5:25

Verily, verily, I say unto you, The hour is coming, and now is, when the dead shall hear the voice of the Son of God: and they that hear shall live. [*Jesus commenced the preaching of the gospel to the spirits of the dead.*]

1 Peter 4:6

For this cause was the gospel preached also to them that are dead, that they might be judged according to men in the flesh, but live according to God in the spirit.

Luke 16:19–26

There was a certain rich man, which was clothed in purple and fine linen, and fared sumptuously every day: And there was a certain beggar named Lazarus, which was laid at his gate, full of sores, And desiring to be fed with the crumbs which fell from the rich man's table: moreover the dogs came and licked his sores. And it came to pass, that the beggar died, and was carried by the angels into Abraham's bosom [*to paradise in the spirit world*]: the rich man also died, and was buried; And in hell [*temporary hell in the spirit world*] he lift up his eyes, being in torments, and seeth Abraham afar off, and Lazarus in his bosom. And he cried and said, Father Abraham, have mercy on me, and send Lazarus, that he may dip the tip of his finger in water, and cool my tongue; for I am tormented in this flame. But Abraham said, Son, remember that thou in thy lifetime receivedst thy good things, and likewise Lazarus evil things: but now he is comforted, and thou art tormented. And beside all this, between us and you there is a great gulf fixed [*the separation between the righteous and the wicked in the spirit world*]: so that they which would pass from hence to you cannot; neither can they pass to us, that would come from thence.

Acts 2:25–31

For David speaketh concerning him, I foresaw the Lord always before my face, for he is on my right hand, that I should not be moved: Therefore did my heart rejoice, and my tongue was glad; moreover also my flesh shall rest in hope: Because thou wilt not leave my soul in hell, neither wilt thou suffer thine Holy One to see corruption. Thou hast made known to me the ways of life; thou shalt make me full of joy with thy countenance. Men and brethren, let me freely speak unto you of the patriarch David, that he is both dead and buried, and his sepulchre is with us unto this day. Therefore being a prophet, and knowing that God had sworn with an oath to him, that of the fruit of his loins, according to the flesh, he would raise up Christ to sit on his throne; He seeing this before spake of the resurrection of Christ, that his soul was not left in hell, neither his flesh did see corruption.

Revelation 20:13–14

And the sea gave up the dead which were in it; and death and hell [*temporary hell*] delivered up the dead which were in them: and they were judged every man according to their works. And death and hell were cast into the lake of fire. This is the second death.

The Second Coming

Job was given a vision of the Second Coming in which the redeemer, Jesus Christ, "[stood] at the latter day upon the earth" (Job 19:25). Isaiah was given a similar vision and prophesied of the peace that would exist during the Second Coming of the Savior (Isaiah 2:4; 11:6–9).

Jesus described his Second Coming as a glorious event (Matthew 25:31). John wrote that a thousand years would pass between the Second Coming and the final conflict (Revelation 20:2–4; 20:7). Isaiah and Ezekiel describe the earth as becoming like the Garden of Eden during this thousand-year period (Isaiah 51:3; Ezekiel 36:35).

Job 19:25

For I know that my redeemer liveth, and that he shall stand at the latter day upon the earth

Isaiah 2:4 (see also Isaiah 11:6–9)

> And they shall beat their swords into plowshares, and their spears into pruninghooks: nation shall not lift up sword against nation, neither shall they learn war any more.

Matthew 25:31

> When the Son of man shall come in his glory, and all the holy angels with him, then shall he sit upon the throne of his glory.

Revelation 20:2–4 (see also Revelation 20:7)

> And he laid hold on the dragon, that old serpent, which is the Devil, and Satan, and bound him a thousand years [*the Millennium*], And cast him into the bottomless pit, and shut him up, and set a seal upon him, that he should deceive the nations no more, till the thousand years should be fulfilled: and after that he must be loosed a little season. And I saw thrones, and they sat upon them, and judgment was given unto them: and I saw the souls of them that were beheaded for the witness of Jesus, and for the word of God, and which had not worshipped the beast, neither his image, neither had received his mark upon their foreheads, or in their hands; and they lived and reigned with Christ a thousand years. [*Those who come forth in the first resurrection will be with Jesus Christ during the Millennium.*]

Isaiah 51:3

> For the Lord shall comfort Zion: he will comfort all her waste places; and he will make her wilderness like Eden, and her desert like the garden of the Lord; joy and gladness shall be found therein, thanksgiving, and the voice of melody.

Ezekiel 36:35

> And they shall say, This land that was desolate is become like the garden of Eden; and the waste and desolate and ruined cities are become fenced, and are inhabited.

Resurrection

Jesus prophesied of his resurrection to his disciples. He told them that he would die a physical death, but that in three days he would take on a new life, and because of this, all mankind would live (John 14:18–19). Interestingly, the New Testament describes other people being resurrected in and around the holy city directly after Christ's resurrection (Matthew 27:52–53), and Paul later wrote how man's resurrection was made possible by Christ's resurrection (1 Corinthians 15:21–22; 15:13–14; 15:54–55).

There will be a first resurrection at the commencement of the Millennium (the Second Coming). There will be a second resurrection immediately before the Final Judgment. The first resurrection will be of "everlasting life," the second will be of "everlasting contempt" (Daniel 12:2; John 5:29; Revelation 20:5–6).

John 14:18–19

I will not leave you comfortless: I will come to you. Yet a little while, and the world seeth me no more; but ye see me: because I live, ye shall live also. [*We live in Christ. His resurrection is assurance of our own.*]

Matthew 27:52–53

And the graves were opened; and many bodies of the saints which slept arose, And came out of the graves after his resurrection, and went into the holy city, and appeared unto many.

1 Corinthians 15:21–22 (see also 1 Corinthians 15:13–14, 54–55)

For since by man came death, by man came also the resurrection of the dead. For as in Adam all die, even so in Christ shall all be made alive.

Daniel 12:2

And many of them that asleep in the dust of the earth shall awake, some to everlasting life, and some to shame and everlasting contempt. [*There are two resurrections.*]

John 5:29

And shall come forth; they that have done good, unto the resurrection of life [*the first resurrection*]; and they that have done evil, unto the resurrection of damnation [*the second resurrection*].

Revelation 20:5–6

But the rest of the dead lived not again [*were not resurrected*] until the thousand years were finished. [*They will, however, come up in the second resurrection, before the Final Judgment.*] This is the first resurrection. Blessed and holy is he that hath part in the first resurrection [*the resurrection that takes place at the commencement of the Millennium, the Second Coming*]: on such the second death hath no power, but they shall be priests of God and of Christ, and shall reign with him a thousand years. [*The righteous who participate in the first resurrection will reign with Christ throughout the Millennium.*]

Final conflict

After the Millennium and before the Final Judgment, there will be a final conflict as Satan is loosed (see Revelation 20:2–3, 7–8). Despite the uprising Satan will be defeated (see Revelation 20:9–10).

The Final Judgment

In the Final Judgment, men and women will be judged upon their works (Revelation 20:12–13; 1 Corinthians 3:13–14; Matthew 16:27), their words (Matthew 12:36–37), the thoughts and feelings within their hearts (Romans 2:15–16; 2 Corinthians 3:1–3; Romans 10:9), and their diligence in seeking after the Lord Jesus Christ (Hebrews 11:6).

Jesus Christ will preside over the Final Judgment (John 5:22) and will appoint his apostles and others to render righteous judgments upon the twelve tribes of Israel (Matthew 19:28; Luke 22:29–30)—that is, all mankind.

Revelation 20:12–13

> And I saw the dead, small and great, stand before God; and the books were opened: and another book was opened, which is the book of life: and the dead were judged out of those things which were written in the books, according to their works. And the sea gave up the dead which were in it; and death and hell delivered up the dead which were in them: and they were judged every man according to their works.

1 Corinthians 3:13–14

> Every man's work shall be made manifest: for the day shall declare it, because it shall be revealed by fire; and the fire shall try every man's work of what sort it is. If any man's work abide which he hath built thereupon, he shall receive a reward.

Matthew 16:27

> For the Son of man shall come in the glory of his Father with his angels; and then he shall reward every man according to his works.

Matthew 12:36–37

> But I say unto you, That every idle word that men shall speak, they shall give account thereof in the day of judgment. For by thy words thou shalt be justified, and by thy words thou shalt be condemned.

Romans 2:15–16 (see also 2 Corinthians 3:1–3)

Which shew the work of the law written in their hearts, their conscience also bearing witness, and their thoughts the mean while accusing or else excusing one another; In the day when God shall judge the secrets of men [*thoughts, all that has been hidden*] by Jesus Christ according to my gospel.

Romans 10:9

That if thou shalt confess with thy mouth the Lord Jesus, and shalt believe in thine heart that God hath raised him from the dead, thou shalt be saved. [*Faith can save. It does not alone reward.*]

Hebrews 11:6

But without faith it is impossible to please him: for he that cometh to God must believe that he is, and that he is a rewarder of them that diligently seek him. [*Faith, works, rewards.*]

John 5:22

For the Father judgeth no man, but hath committed all judgment unto the Son. [*Jesus Christ will preside over the Final Judgment.*]

Matthew 19:28 (see also Luke 22:29–30)

And Jesus said unto them, Verily I say unto you, That ye which have followed me, in the regeneration when the Son of man shall sit in the throne of his glory, ye also shall sit upon twelve thrones, judging the twelve tribes of Israel. [*The Twelve Apostles will judge on behalf of Jesus Christ.*]

Heaven

Finally, the earth will be completely renewed (Revelation 21:1). There will be three kingdoms (2 Corinthians 12:2). The highest kingdom (celestial) is likened to the sun, being the brightest of all of the kingdoms. The second highest kingdom (terrestrial) is likened to the moon, being the second brightest of the kingdoms. The lowest kingdom is likened to the stars being the least bright among the heavenly bodies (1 Corinthians 15:40–42.)

Revelation 21:1

And I saw a new heaven and a new earth: for the first heaven and the first earth were passed away; and there was no more sea.

2 Corinthians 12:2

I knew a man in Christ above fourteen years ago, (whether in the body, I cannot tell; or whether out of the body, I cannot tell: God knoweth;) such an one caught up to the third heaven.

1 Corinthians 15:40–42

There are also celestial bodies, and bodies terrestrial: but the glory of the celestial is one, and the glory of the terrestrial is another. There is one glory of the sun, [*the celestial glory, the highest heaven*] and another glory of the moon, [*the terrestrial glory, the next highest heaven*] and another glory of the stars [*the telestial glory, the lowest heaven*]: for one star differeth from another star in glory. So also is the resurrection of the dead. It is sown in corruption; it is raised in incorruption.

Heavenly Beings

Those worthy of heaven will shine like celestial bodies (Daniel 12:3), and they will occupy many "mansions" in heaven (John 14:2). It will be those, even a few, who will journey the narrow path (Matthew 7:14) to take their place as the greatest (in the greatest place, the celestial space) in the kingdom of heaven (Matthew 18:4). Jesus said there will be some who will become "as the angels which are in heaven" (Mark 12:25).

Daniel 12:3

And they that be wise shall shine as the brightness of the firmament; and they that turn many to righteousness as the stars for ever and ever. [*Different degrees of glory.*]

John 14:2

In my Father's house are many mansions [*levels of heaven and places between*]: if it were not so, I would have told you. I go to prepare a place for you.

Matthew 7:14

Because strait is the gate, and narrow is the way, which leadeth unto life, and few there be that find it. [*Few will achieve the highest level of heaven, the celestial.*]

Matthew 18:4

Whosoever therefore shall humble himself as this little child, the same is greatest in the kingdom of heaven. [*Those who humble themselves shall occupy the highest kingdom in heaven, the celestial.*]

Mark 12:25

> For when they shall rise from the dead, they neither marry, nor are given in marriage [*no weddings in heaven*]; but are as the angels which are in heaven.

Exaltation

Exaltation, or becoming exalted, comes to those who keep the Lord's way (Psalm 37:34). Jesus taught that those who humble themselves will be exalted (Luke 14:11; Matthew 23:12). The Apostle Peter reiterated this in his first epistle (1 Peter 5:6).

Psalm 37:34

> Wait on the Lord, and keep his way, and he shall exalt thee to inherit the land: when the wicked are cut off, thou shalt see it.

Luke 14:11 (see also Matthew 23:12)

> For whosoever exalteth himself shall be abased; and he that humbleth himself shall be exalted.

1 Peter 5:6

> Humble yourselves therefore under the mighty hand of God, that he may exalt you in due time

Perfection

Perfection is not attainable in mortality or any time soon thereafter, but it is a journey taken by the children of God in Christ (Hebrews 6:1). The Lord calls all men on the journey to perfection. He told Abraham, "Be thou perfect" (Genesis 17:1). This same call was issued by Jesus to all his disciples: He told them to be meek and pure in heart as part of the process of perfection (Matthew 5:5, 8, 48). Paul urged the Colossians to put on charity as part of the course towards perfection (Colossians 3:14). He urged good works on the journey of perfection (2 Timothy 3:17). James encouraged patience as part of the eternal road to the perfecting of one's spirit (James 1:4).

Hebrews 6:1

> Therefore leaving the principles of the doctrine of Christ, let us go on unto perfection; not laying again the foundation of repentance from dead works, and of faith toward God.

Genesis 17:1

> And when Abram was ninety years old and nine, the Lord

appeared to Abram, and said unto him, I am the Almighty God; walk before me, and be thou perfect.

Matthew 5:5, 8, 48

Blessed are the meek: for they shall inherit the earth. . . . Blessed are the pure in heart: for they shall see God. . . . Be ye therefore perfect, even as your Father which is in heaven is perfect.

Colossians 3:14

And above all these things put on charity, which is the bond of perfectness.

2 Timothy 3:17

That the man of God may be perfect, thoroughly furnished unto all good works.

James 1:4

But let patience have her perfect work, that ye may be perfect and entire, wanting nothing.

Godliness

All of the children of men who act in righteousness can attain godliness (Psalm 32:6; 2 Peter 1:6–7). Although godliness is a mystery to the human intellect (1 Timothy 3:16), when attained by the righteous it will lead to the strength to be delivered from temptation (2 Peter 2:9). It will also lead to persecution (2 Timothy 3:12).

Psalm 32:6

For this shall every one that is godly pray unto thee in a time when thou mayest be found: surely in the floods of great waters they shall not come nigh unto him.

2 Peter 1:6–7

And to knowledge temperance; and to temperance patience; and to patience godliness; And to godliness brotherly kindness; and to brotherly kindness charity.

1 Timothy 3:16

And without controversy great is the mystery of godliness: God was manifest in the flesh, justified in the Spirit, seen of angels, preached unto the Gentiles, believed on in the world, received up into glory.

2 Peter 2:9

> The Lord knoweth how to deliver the godly out of temptations, and to reserve the unjust unto the day of judgment to be punished.

2 Timothy 3:12

> Yea, and all that will live godly in Christ Jesus shall suffer persecution.

Rewards

A crown is reserved for a king. Peter prophesied that at the Second Coming of Christ, there will be some who will "receive a crown of glory" that will last forever (1 Peter 5:4). James gave a similar promise to those who endure to the end and love the Savior—they will receive a "crown of life" (James 1:12). Paul said there will be a "crown of righteousness" for all of the faithful in Christ (2 Timothy 4:7–8). Those who earn these crowns from the Lord will reign forever and ever (Revelation 22:5) and be made rulers "over many things" (Matthew 25:21).

1 Peter 5:4

> And when the chief Shepherd shall appear, ye shall receive a crown of glory that fadeth not away.

James 1:12

> Blessed is the man that endureth temptation: for when he is tried, he shall receive the crown of life, which the Lord hath promised to them that love him.

2 Timothy 4:7–8

> I have fought a good fight, I have finished my course, I have kept the faith: Henceforth there is laid up for me a crown of righteousness, which the Lord, the righteous judge, shall give me at that day: and not to me only, but unto all them also that love his appearing.

Revelation 22:5

> And there shall be no night there; and they need no candle, neither light of the sun; for the Lord God giveth them light: and they shall reign for ever and ever.

Matthew 25:21

> His lord said unto him, Well done, thou good and faithful servant: thou hast been faithful over a few things, I will make thee ruler over many things: enter thou into the joy of thy lord.

Becoming Christlike

Being "like Christ," or like a god, was introduced early in the Old Testament. The Lord God said of Adam, "The man is become as one of us" (Genesis 3:22). Speaking of Jesus, John taught that "we shall be like him" when he appears (1 John 3:2). Paul taught that we can be with him (Christ) "in glory" (Colossians 3:2–4; 2 Thessalonians 2:14).

Paul wrote to the Galatians that man is a son of God, "an heir of God through Christ" (Galatians 4:6–7), adding to the Romans and to Timothy that to be glorified with Christ will require suffering on the part of the individual being glorified (Romans 8:16–18; 2 Timothy 2:11–12). In the book of Revelation, the Lord proclaims that those who overcome will be granted the privilege to sit with him on his throne (Revelation 3:21).

Genesis 3:22

And the Lord God said, Behold, the man is become as one of us, to know good and evil: and now, lest he put forth his hand, and take also of the tree of life, and eat, and live for ever.

1 John 3:2

Beloved, now are we the sons of God, and it doth not yet appear what we shall be: but we know that, when he shall appear, we shall be like him; for we shall see him as he is.

Colossians 3:2–4

Set your affection on things above, not on things on the earth. For ye are dead, and your life is hid with Christ in God. When Christ, who is our life, shall appear, then shall ye also appear with him in glory.

2 Thessalonians 2:14

Whereunto he called you by our gospel, to the obtaining of the glory of our Lord Jesus Christ.

Galatians 4:6–7

And because ye are sons, God hath sent forth the Spirit of his Son into your hearts, crying, Abba, Father. Wherefore thou art no more a servant, but a son; and if a son, then an heir of God through Christ.

Romans 8:16–18

The Spirit itself beareth witness with our spirit, that we are the children of God: And if children, then heirs; heirs of God, and joint-heirs with Christ; if so be that we suffer with him, that we may be also glorified together. For I reckon that the sufferings of this present time are not worthy to be compared with the glory which shall be revealed in us.

2 Timothy 2:11–12

It is a faithful saying: For if we be dead with him, we shall also live with him: If we suffer, we shall also reign with him: if we deny him, he also will deny us.

Revelation 3:21

To him that overcometh will I grant to sit with me in my throne, even as I also overcame, and am set down with my Father in his throne.

Gods and Sons of Gods

While the Bible makes clear that there is one God the Father, one God the Son, and one Holy Ghost, it tells of other "gods" on earth or in heaven (1 Corinthians 8:5–6) and says the sons of God (plural) are many in the kingdom of heaven (Job 1:6; 2:1).

1 Corinthians 8:5–6

For though there be that are called gods, whether in heaven or in earth, (as there be gods many, and lords many,) But to us there is but one God, the Father, of whom are all things, and we in him; and one Lord Jesus Christ, by whom are all things, and we by him.

Job 1:6 and 2:1

Now there was a day when the sons of God came to present themselves before the Lord, and Satan came also among them. . . .

Again there was a day when the sons of God came to present themselves before the Lord, and Satan came also among them to present himself before the Lord.

Outer Darkness

The one-third of the host of heaven who joined Satan in rebellion against God kept not their first estate (rejected their life with the Father in the premortal realm) and were cast to the earth. They, with Satan, will be condemned to everlasting darkness after the Final Judgment (Jude 1:6). These sons of perdition are lost (John 17:12), along with those who turn away to crucify Christ a second time (Hebrews 6:4–6) and commit blasphemy against the Holy Ghost (Matthew 12:31–32).

Jude 1:6

And the angels which kept not their first estate, but left their own habitation, he hath reserved in everlasting chains under darkness unto the judgment of the great day.

John 17:12

While I was with them in the world, I kept them in thy name: those that thou gavest me I have kept, and none of them is lost, but [*except*] the son of perdition [*Judas Iscariot*]; that the scripture might be fulfilled.

Hebrews 6:4–6

For it is impossible for those who were once enlightened, and have tasted of the heavenly gift, and were made partakers of the Holy Ghost, And have tasted the good word of God, and the powers of the world to come, If they shall fall away, to renew them again unto repentance; seeing they crucify to themselves the Son of God afresh, and put him to an open shame.

Matthew 12:31–32

Wherefore I say unto you, All manner of sin and blasphemy shall be forgiven unto men: but the blasphemy against the Holy Ghost shall not be forgiven unto men. And whosoever speaketh a word against the Son of man, it shall be forgiven him: but whosoever speaketh against the Holy Ghost, it shall not be forgiven him, neither in this world, neither in the world to come.

MORMON UNDERSTANDING

Entry into the Afterlife

As mortality is a distinguishable extension of premortal existence, so the afterlife is a distinguishable extension of mortality. Eternity is not divisible; however, distinguishable states and places do exist, and changes do occur within and between these states. The state, place, and change that appears at the conclusion of mortality is called the afterlife. There is no space between life and afterlife. To die is simply to walk from one room (mortality) into the next (afterlife).

Certain work can only be accomplished in mortality. Other work can only be accomplished in the afterlife. If a person is alive, then his or her work in mortality is not finished. When the work is finished, the portal of death will appear and the work of the afterlife will commence.

Human beings do not travel from life to death. They travel from life to life, from one form of work to another, from one state of being to another. Death is merely the connecting doorway.

Events and Places

It is understood through revelation that the afterlife includes the following events and places. Names are assigned to these events and places largely by convention. Definitions follow.

- Partial Judgment
- Spirit World
- Paradise
- Spirit Prison
- Temporary Hell
- First Resurrection
- Second Coming of Christ (Millennium)
- Second Resurrection
- Final Conflict
- Final Judgment and Assignment
- Celestial Kingdom
- Terrestrial Kingdom
- Telestial Kingdom
- Outer Darkness (Eternal Hell)

The Partial Judgment

Each person who dies before the Second Coming of Christ takes on the form of a spirit and goes through a partial judgment. The spirit of each person is then assigned to a temporary place in the spirit world: either a place in paradise or a place in spirit prison. Assignments are made according to the person's faith and works in mortality. In one of these two places, all the dead await their resurrection (reunification of their spirits with their perfected bodies).

The Spirit World

Paradise is the term used to denote the higher place in the spirit world. Paradise is not heaven. Heaven is a permanent state outside the spirit world; paradise is a temporary state within the spirit world.

Spirit prison is the term used to denote the lower place in the spirit world. Spirit prison is not hell. Hell is a permanent state outside the spirit world; spirit prison is a temporary state within the spirit world. Therefore, spirit prison can be considered a temporary hell. The spirits in temporary hell are separated from all other spirits in the spirit world.

All the spirits in paradise and the spirits in spirit prison who are not confined to temporary hell learn and work to prepare for the first resurrection. The first resurrection will occur at the moment of the Second Coming of Christ. The spirits in temporary hell must suffer and await the second resurrection. The second resurrection will occur at the end of the Millennium.

The spirits of the dead retain attitudes, thought patterns, desires, and appetites similar to those they had on earth: it could be said that the mortal personality is continued in spiritual form in the afterlife. For example, if a person dies with a certain attitude about righteousness or wickedness, his spirit will have a similar attitude in the afterlife. Spiritual refinement is still possible, however.

The spirit world occupies the same "space" spiritually that the earth occupies physically. Satan and his minions also occupy this spiritual space on earth.

The Second Coming and the First Resurrection

The Church of Jesus Christ of Latter-day Saints teaches that the Second Coming of Christ will usher in a period known as the Millennium. Taken from the Latin word *mille* (a thousand) and *annum* (year), the millennial reign of Christ will be on earth, which will be converted to a terrestrial degree of glory, and there will be one thousand years of peace, joy, and love.

With the Second Coming of Christ, the spirits in paradise will be resurrected (the first resurrection) and will live and work throughout the Millennium. In the "morning" of the first resurrection will come up those assigned celestial bodies. In the "afternoon" of the first resurrection will come up those assigned terrestrial bodies.

These resurrected men and women will be righteous people who in mortality lived lives worthy of this opportunity or were able to find conversion in the spirit world.

These resurrected beings and mortal members of Christ's church will do missionary and temple work throughout the Millennium. Missionary work will include teaching Heavenly Father's plan of salvation to those on earth who have not received this teaching or did not fully understand it. Temple work will include ordinances of salvation and exaltation, including baptisms, endowments, marriages, and sealings.

There will be no suffering, disease, or fear of death during the Millennium. Satan will be bound. He will be unable to use his evil powers of persuasion or to do any harm whatsoever. There will be universal peace. All livings things will live together without violence. Mortal and immortal beings will mingle and work in harmony. The entire earth will be in a state of terrestrial glory.

The Second Resurrection

The second resurrection will come at the end of the Millennium, about one thousand years after the first resurrection. The second resurrection is sometimes called the resurrection of the damned, since this resurrection includes spirits out of Spirit Prison and the sons of perdition. These are they who made a free and fully informed choice to refuse Christ, to refuse repentance, and to refuse participation in Heavenly Father's plan of salvation. The most vile and wicked will come forth in this resurrection, including the worst of these, the sons of perdition.

The Final Conflict

After the second resurrection, Satan and his host will be loosed for the final conflict. This conflict will engulf the entire earth. Satan will gather his armies, and Michael the Archangel will gather his. They will engage in one final battle for the souls of men. Some will choose Satan; others will choose the Lord.

The Final Judgment

The Final Judgment will occur at the conclusion of the final conflict, and Satan and his followers will be cast out of the earth and consigned forever to outer darkness. The three kingdoms of heaven— telestial, terrestrial, and celestial—will be established, and the earth will be advanced from a terrestrial state to a celestial state. The loyal spirit children of God will be consigned to one of the three kingdoms of heaven.

The Final Judgment is the last in a succession of judgments that began in premortal life and continued through mortal life and life in the spirit world.

The works of mankind are written in the books referred to in Revelation 20:12. However, Paul taught about being judged out of different records, those written in the hearts of men. These records will be made known during the Final Judgment and also used to render the final verdict upon all beings.

Men and women will be judged not only by Christ, but by those to whom Christ delegates the power and authority to judge. God the Father will not judge anyone directly but will delegate that power and authority to Christ.

Based on the Final Judgment, all men and women will inherit a place in the kingdom for which they are prepared: the celestial kingdom (the highest degree of glory), the terrestrial kingdom (the second degree), or the telestial kingdom (the lowest degree).[1]

Heaven

The Latter-day Saint doctrine of heaven is founded on several key scriptures in the Bible and modern revelation. The Bible gives little detail on the particulars of heaven. Modern revelation gives more detail.

For example, biblical scriptures introduce and outline the existence of three levels of heaven, while the revelations given in the Doctrine and Covenants describe in detail the various glories in heaven.

Jesus spoke of "many mansions" in heaven and of "preparing" a place in the house of his father for all of his followers. In concert with these preparations, men and women in mortality prepare themselves for the heavenly kingdom into which they choose to enter. Their works and faith in Christ, exercised in the choices they make on earth, will decide which kingdom (place or state) they are prepared to live in following the Final Judgment. The pervasive doctrine of moral agency (free will) is evident in this process as in all others. Heaven is a choice leading to a just reward.

The Celestial Kingdom

The celestial kingdom is the highest level of heaven (the "third heaven" spoken of by Paul). This is the kingdom Paul described as being the "glory of the sun," in which Jesus Christ and Heavenly Father will dwell. The happiness of those who will enter the celestial kingdom and the beauty and glory of the surroundings are unimaginable.

Those who will enter the celestial kingdom are those who love and have chosen to obey Jesus Christ and Heavenly Father. These individuals will have repented of their sins, committed their lives to Jesus Christ as their savior, entered the waters of baptism, received the gift of the Holy Ghost, and exercised faith sufficient to triumph over the world through the mediating Atonement of Jesus Christ.

Individuals who choose and then are blessed to dwell in the celestial kingdom will eventually become like Jesus and Heavenly Father and receive by inheritance all that Heavenly Father has and is. Jesus alluded to this great blessing in the parable of the talents when he said, "Well done, thou good and faithful servant; thou hast been faithful over a few things, I will make thee ruler over many things: enter thou into the joy of thy lord" (Matthew 25:23).

The Terrestrial Kingdom

The terrestrial kingdom is the second highest level of heaven. This is the kingdom Paul described as being the "glory of the moon." Jesus will dwell here on a frequent basis. Those who will enter into the terrestrial kingdom are those who rejected the gospel of Jesus Christ on earth but received it in the spirit world. Although not close to the happiness of those who will dwell in the celestial kingdom, the happiness of the terrestrial kingdom will match the happiness that beings assigned there will be prepared and willing to receive. As in all things, agency is paramount.

The Telestial Kingdom

The telestial kingdom is the lowest level of heaven. This is the kingdom Paul described as being the "glory of the stars," in which the influence of the Holy Ghost will reside and angels will minister. Those who will enter into the telestial kingdom are those who made a free and fully informed choice on earth and in the spirit world to reject Heavenly Father's plan of salvation and the Atonement of Jesus Christ but whose rejection and evil deeds and intentions do not warrant consignment to outer darkness. Although not close to the happiness of those who will dwell in the celestial or terrestrial kingdom, the happiness of the telestial kingdom will match the happiness that beings assigned there will be prepared and willing to receive. Again, agency is paramount. There will be many who will be consigned to the telestial kingdom following the Final Judgment.

Outer Darkness

Outer darkness is a term used synonymously with hell—not the temporary hell of the spirit world, but the permanent hell in which the devil and his loyal followers are confined for all eternity. "Perdition" is a term denoting Satan or eternal hell. The sons of perdition are those who received the Holy Ghost and knew God but later denied both; those who in mortality chose without reservation to rebel against God and follow Satan; and those premortal spirits who joined with Satan in rebelling against God in the premortal realm. The sons of perdition will dwell in outer darkness and have no hope of forgiveness. They are eternally separated from God. They are made fully aware of this separation, and this awareness causes them great suffering.

NOTE

1. *Gospel Principles*, 271.

❦ 21 ❧

PLURAL MARRIAGE

Biblical Teaching

Biblical History

The Bible recognizes plural marriage and regulates it, but neither encourages nor discourages it. For example, the Old Testament specifies that a man who takes an additional wife is responsible for her temporal needs (see Exodus 21:10). If a man who has two wives, one beloved and the other hated, he must acknowledge the rights of the firstborn son without regard to the wife who bears him (see Deuteronomy 21:15–17). The men of the tribe of Benjamin took multiple wives to replenish their dwindling numbers (see Judges 21:23). King David, a man after God's own heart (see Acts 13:22–23), was admonished for his sin of adultery and murder, but not for taking multiple wives (see 2 Samuel 5:13; 12:7–8).

Scriptural References to Polygamists

Abdon (Judges 12:14)	David (2 Samuel 5:13)
Abijah (2 Chronicles 13:21)	Eliphaz (Genesis 36:11–12)
Abraham (Genesis 16:3; 25:1)	Elkanah (1 Samuel 1:2)
Ahab (1 Kings 20:3)	Esau (Genesis 26:34)
Ahasuerus (Esther 1:9)	Ezra (1 Chronicles 4:17–18)
Ashur (1 Chronicles 4:5)	Gideon (Judges 8:30)
Belshazzar (Daniel 5:2)	Heman (1 Chronicles 25:4)
Benhadad (1 Kings 20:3)	Hosea (Hosea 1:3; 3:1)
Caleb (1 Chronicles 2:18–19)	Ibzan (Judges 12:9)

Issachar (1 Chronicles 7:4; Numbers 1:29)

Jacob (Genesis 30:4–9)

Jair (Judges 10:4),

Jehoiachin (2 Kings 24:15)

Jehoram (2 Chronicles 21:14)

Jerahmeel (1 Chronicles 2:26)

Jehoiada (2 Chronicles 24:3)

Lamech (Genesis 4:19)

Machir (1 Chronicles 7:15–16)

Manasseh (1 Chronicles 7:14)

Mered (1 Chronicles 4:17–19)

Moses (Numbers 12:1)

Nahor (Genesis 22:20–24)

Rehoboam (2 Chronicles 11:18–23)

Saul (2 Samuel 3:7)

Shaharaim (1 Chronicles 8:8)

Shimei (1 Chronicles 4:27)

Simeon (Exodus 6:15)

Solomon (1 Kings 11:3)

Zedekiah (Jeremiah 38:23)

Ziba (2 Samuel 9:10)

Biblical Commentary on Plural Marriage

Jesus quoted and Paul reiterated the scripture from Genesis about a man and woman becoming one flesh (see Genesis 2:24; Matthew 19:4–6; Ephesians 5:31). No mention is made of plural wives. Paul in his counsel to the Romans on the laws of marriage appeared to address only monogamous marriage (see Romans 7:2–3). When Jesus taught his disciples about divorce, he did not address plural marriage (see Matthew 19:8–9). King Solomon, who practiced plural marriage on a grand scale, was said to have allowed "many strange women" to come into his life, leading him away from the Lord (see 1 Kings 11:1–4).

The Millennium

Speaking of the time in or around the millennial reign of Christ, the prophet Isaiah wrote of seven women who will "take hold of one man." The seven women will do this to be called by the one man's name that some form of reproach be taken from them (see Isaiah 4:1).

MORMON UNDERSTANDING

Among the Latter-day Saints

The practice of plural marriage nearly destroyed The Church of Jesus Christ of Latter-day Saints.

This near-destruction was more a sociopolitical phenomenon, not a moral or religious one. Enemies of the Church were far more concerned with economics and voting blocks and the mass production of fighting-age males who could determine the course of nineteenth century American expansionism than with the protection of Mormon women and children.

Plural marriage was officially banned by The Church of Jesus Christ of Latter-day Saints on October 6, 1890. From April 4, 1904, to the present, Church members found to be practicing plural marriage have been systematically excommunicated. Yet even to this day, plural marriage remains a topic of great interest. Indeed, the first chapter that many readers of this book will turn to is this one. The fascination with plural marriage seems boundless.

Biblical History

At various times throughout biblical history, the Lord looked favorably on men and women who were living in plural marriages. Theologians debate whether the Lord sanctioned or merely tolerated polygamy, but the fact that it was practiced openly and unapologetically is undisputed. Many, if not most, judges, prophets, and kings of the Old Testament were polygamists.

Revered biblical figures, such as Abraham, Jacob, David, and others, had multiple wives. Wicked individuals, such as Ahab, Jeroboam, Rehoboam, and others, had multiple wives. The Old Testament does not condemn the many men who married multiple wives. In fact, the polygamist David was said to be a man after God's own heart; was given the privilege of authoring Psalms; and was given the honor by lineage of fathering Jesus (son of David). While God clearly stated his displeasure with some of David's actions, he did not condemn David for having multiple wives.

The books of Exodus and Deuteronomy mention without condemnation men taking additional wives. The practice was had for good and for evil. For good, it led to many righteous offspring in strong families. For evil, it did in some cases enforce the social and political subordination of women and their use to simply satisfy the lusts of powerful men.

Solomon was told by the Lord, "Behold, I have done according to thy words: lo, I have given thee a wise and an understanding heart; so that there was none like thee before thee, neither after thee shall any arise like unto thee" (1 Kings 3:12). Although Solomon may have been the wisest man who ever lived, it may have been unwise for him to take on seven hundred wives and three hundred concubines. Because

Solomon chose to marry "strange" women of various cultures and faiths, he was eventually led away to idolatry.

Origins

In the early years of the Church, there were long periods of hardship, and Latter-day Saint women frequently outnumbered men by a substantial margin. At the same time, the Lord revealed his desire to build his Church with righteous souls raised in strong families. One way of addressing both of these dynamics was to call specific individuals to plural marriage.

The revelation establishing eternal marriage and the plurality of wives was given in 1843. Historical records suggest that the doctrines and principles appearing in this revelation were known to the Prophet Joseph as far back as 1831. It is said that Joseph was greatly troubled by the principle of plural marriage and spent a great deal of time praying and pondering the principle in the hope of greater understanding. Public announcement of plural marriage was not made until 1852.

Mormon History

The Lord commanded a select few in the Church to practice plural marriage. The Prophet Joseph and those closest to him, including Brigham Young and Heber C. Kimball, were troubled by this command, but they obeyed it. Church leaders regulated the practice. Those entering into plural marriage had to be authorized to do so, and the marriages had to be performed through the sealing power of the priesthood.

Less than five percent of Mormon men were allowed to enter into plural marriage. In 1862 Abraham Lincoln signed the Morrill Anti-Bigamy Law; however, it was not until 1874 that prosecution of polygamists was possible. In 1882 the Edmunds Act was passed by the Senate. It was ratified by the House in 1887. This act made it illegal for anyone practicing or suspected of practicing polygamy to vote.

This was a difficult time for the Saints. The twelfth article of faith, written in 1842, states, "We believe in being subject to kings, presidents, rulers, and magistrates, in obeying, honoring, and sustaining the law." With the passage of federal laws targeting polygamy, there arose a clear conflict between the laws of the land and the laws of God.

While torn on this issue, Latter-day Saints continued practicing polygamy and were sorely persecuted by surrounding communities and the federal government. Men and women who were law-abiding citizens were suddenly faced with the prospect of breaking up their families or preserving them by going into hiding. Many chose family and what they firmly believed was a commandment of the Lord and went into hiding. Included among these were the prophet John Taylor and his first counselor, George Q. Cannon.

During this period, leaders of The Church of Jesus Christ of Latter-day Saints were seeking statehood for the Utah Territory. There were important economic and political reasons for this, not the least of which was the hope that statehood would end the continuing persecution of the Church. It was in the context of this struggle for statehood and an end of persecution that the president of the Church, Wilford Woodruff, finally issued the manifesto ending plural marriage. The year was 1890. Utah became a state in 1896.

Triumph and Tragedy

This is a story of triumph and tragedy. Utah became a state, and the Church began a new chapter in its long struggle for acceptance and the safety of its members. For these benefits, plural families paid a heavy price. They were broken up. The emotional suffering was intense. Some left the Church to continue their families elsewhere. But the faithful Saints obeyed. The greater good for the greater number was achieved in compliance with the will of the Lord as spoken through his prophet.

In 1998, President Gordon B. Hinckley made the following statement about polygamy: "This Church has nothing whatever to do with those practicing polygamy. They are not members of this Church. . . . If any of our members are found to be practicing plural marriage, they are excommunicated, the most serious penalty the Church can impose. Not only are those so involved in direct violation of the civil law, they are in violation of the law of this Church."[1]

Plural Marriage Today

Although The Church of Jesus Christ of Latter-day Saints ended the practice of plural marriage more than a century ago, some people still see the Church in the reflected light of this abandoned practice. Perhaps this is because they imagine plural marriage to be the hedonistic aberration of a cult. The historical record does not support this notion.

There are heretic sects today that practice polygamy inside and outside of the United States, but these sects have no relationship with The Church of Jesus Christ of Latter-day Saints.

Living the Law

In times past, some Latter-day Saints lived the law of monogamy while others lived the law of polygamy—some were directed to one marital arrangement, others to the other marital arrangement.

Today Latter-day Saints live the law of monogamy exclusively and have done so continuously for more than one hundred years.

NOTE

1. Gordon B. Hinckley, "What Are People Asking about Us?" *Ensign*, Nov 1998, 70.

❧ 22 ❧

SPECIAL CONCERNS

ABORTION

BIBLICAL TEACHING

The Bible refers to the human embryo as a person. The Lord communicates with, teaches, ministers to, sanctifies, and even ordains living persons within a woman's womb (Psalm 139:13–16; Jeremiah 1:4–5). The Bible emphasizes repeatedly the "begetting" (procreating as a father) of "sons" and "daughters" (Genesis 5:3–4; Acts 7:29), thus signaling that what is conceived is a human being. The act of conceiving a child is also documented prominently in the Bible, demonstrating the critical importance of conception in the course of the human journey into mortality (Genesis 25:21–24; Job 3:3, 16; Luke 1:36, 39–43).

Psalm 139:13–16

> For thou hast possessed my reins: thou hast covered me in my mother's womb [*while in the womb the author of this psalm is considered a person of worth to God*]. I will praise thee; for I am fearfully and wonderfully made: marvelous are thy works; and that my soul knoweth right well. My substance was not hid from thee, when I was made in secret, and curiously wrought in the lowest parts of the earth. Thine eyes did see my substance, yet being unperfect; and in thy book all my members were written, which in continuance were fashioned, when as yet there was none of them. [*The Lord was able to see the entire person in the womb.*]

Jeremiah 1:4–5

Then the word of the Lord came unto me, saying, Before I formed thee in the belly I knew thee [*God knew Jeremiah even before Jeremiah was conceived*]; and before thou camest forth out of the womb I sanctified thee, and I ordained thee a prophet unto the nations. [*The Lord ministered to Jeremiah, sanctified him, and ordained him a prophet while Jeremiah, a real and living person, lay within his mother's womb.*]

Genesis 5:3–4 (see also Acts 7:29)

And Adam lived an hundred and thirty years, and begat a son in his own likeness, after his image; and called his name Seth: And the days of Adam after he had begotten Seth were eight hundred years: and he begat sons and daughters.

Genesis 25:21–24 (see also Job 3:3, 16)

And Isaac entreated the Lord for his wife, because she was barren: and the Lord was entreated of him, and Rebekah his wife conceived. And the children [*"children"—not merely tissue, not merely a biological potential*] struggled together within her; and she said, If it be so, why am I thus? And she went to enquire of the Lord. And the Lord said unto her, Two nations are in thy womb [*not merely children in her womb, but children and all their descendants—the future lies within the womb, within the unborn person*], and two manner of people shall be separated from thy bowels; and the one people shall be stronger than the other people; and the elder shall serve the younger. And when her days to be delivered were fulfilled, behold, there were twins in her womb [*two lives, two persons were "in her womb"*].

Luke 1:36, 39–43

And, behold, thy cousin Elisabeth, she hath also conceived a son [*a son, not merely a biological potential, was within Elisabeth*] in her bold age: and this is the sixth month with her, who was called barren. . . . And Mary arose in those days, and went into the hill country with haste, into a city of Juda; And entered into the house of Zacharias, and saluted Elisabeth. And it came to pass, that, when Elisabeth heard the salutation of Mary, the babe leaped in her womb [*a "babe," a child, a living person leaped within her womb, able to feel and understand he was in the presence of the savior of the world*]; and Elisabeth was filled with the Holy Ghost: And she spake out with a loud voice, and said, Blessed art thou among women, and blessed is the fruit of thy womb. And whence is this to me, that the mother of my Lord should come to me? [*Mary is here addressed as the mother of Jesus before she has given birth to him, and he is the "Lord," not merely tissue, not merely a biological potential, even as he lies unborn within Mary's womb.*]

MORMON UNDERSTANDING

Official Position of the Church

Following is the official position of The Church of Jesus Christ of Latter-day Saints:

> In today's society, abortion has become a common practice, defended by deceptive arguments. If you face questions about this matter, you can be secure in following the revealed will of the Lord. Latter-day prophets have denounced abortion, referring to the Lord's declaration, "Thou shalt not . . . kill, nor do anything like unto it" (D&C 59:6). Their counsel on the matter is clear: Members of The Church of Jesus Christ of Latter-day Saints must not submit to, perform, encourage, pay for, or arrange for an abortion. If you encourage an abortion in any way, you may be subject to Church discipline.
>
> Church leaders have said that some exceptional circumstances may justify an abortion, such as when pregnancy is the result of incest or rape, when the life or health of the mother is judged by competent medical authority to be in serious jeopardy, or when the fetus is known by competent medical authority to have severe defects that will not allow the baby to survive beyond birth. But even these circumstances do not automatically justify an abortion. Those who face such circumstances should consider abortion only after consulting with their local Church leaders and receiving a confirmation through earnest prayer.
>
> When a child is conceived out of wedlock, the best option is for the mother and father of the child to marry and work toward establishing an eternal family relationship. If a successful marriage is unlikely, they should place the child for adoption, preferably through LDS Family Services.[1]

SAME-GENDER ATTRACTION

BIBLICAL TEACHING

Old Testament

According to the Old Testament, men who have sex together commit an abomination (Leviticus 20:13; 18:22). Under Mosaic law even cross-dressing was defined as sin (Deuteronomy 22:5). The cities of Sodom and Gomorrah were destroyed for fornication and "going after strange flesh" (Jude 1:7).

Leviticus 20:13 (see also Leviticus 18:22)

> If a man also lie with [*have sex with*] mankind, as he lieth with [*have sex with*] a woman, both of them have committed an abomination: they shall surely be put to death; their blood shall be upon them.

Deuteronomy 22:5

> The woman shall not wear that which pertaineth unto a man, neither shall a man put on a woman's garment: for all that do so are abomination unto the Lord thy God. [*Cross dressing, or transgender behavior, is an abomination.*]

Jude 1:7

> Even as Sodom and Gomorrha, and the cities about them in like manner, giving themselves over to fornication, and going after strange flesh, are set forth for an example, suffering the vengeance of eternal fire.

New Testament

Homosexual behavior is clearly defined as serious sin in the New Testament (Romans 1:24–27). The New Testament condemns those who "defile themselves with mankind" (1 Timothy 1:9–10) and compares "abusers of themselves with mankind" with thieves, criminals, drunkards, adulterers, and idol worshipers (1 Corinthians 6:9–13).

Romans 1:24–27

> Wherefore God also gave them up to uncleanness through the lusts of their own hearts, to dishonour their own bodies between themselves: Who changed the truth of God into a lie, and worshipped and served the creature more than the Creator, who is blessed forever. Amen. For this cause God gave them up unto vile affections:

for even their women did change the natural use into that which is against nature: And likewise also the men, leaving the natural use of the woman [*heterosexual sex*], burned in their lust one toward another [*men toward men*]; men with men working that which is unseemly [*engaging in homosexual sex*], and receiving in themselves that recompence of their error which was meet.

1 Timothy 1:9–10

Knowing this, that the law is not made for a righteous man, but for the lawless and disobedient, for the ungodly and for sinners, for unholy and profane, for murderers of fathers and murderers of mothers, for manslayers, For whoremongers, for them that defile themselves with mankind [*engage in homosexual sex*], for menstealers, for liars, for perjured persons, and if there be any other thing that is contrary to sound doctrine.

1 Corinthians 6:9–13

Know ye not that the unrighteous shall not inherit the kingdom of God? Be not deceived: neither fornicators, nor idolaters, nor adulterers, nor effeminate [*men dressing or posturing as women*], nor abusers of themselves with mankind [*engaging in homosexual sex*], Nor thieves, nor covetous, nor drunkards, nor revilers, nor extortioners, shall inherit the kingdom of God. And such were some of you: but ye are washed, but ye are sanctified, but ye are justified in the name of the Lord Jesus, and by the Spirit of our God. All things are lawful unto me, but all things are not expedient: all things are lawful for me, but I will not be brought under the power of any. Meats for the belly, and the belly for meats: but God shall destroy both it and them. Now the body is not for fornication, but for the Lord; and the Lord for the body.

Love

While the Bible is clear about the sin of homosexual sex, it is equally clear about love (Matthew 22:39). Love the sinner, not the sin (Romans 13:9–10).

Matthew 22:39

And the second is like unto it, Thou shalt love thy neighbour as thyself.

Romans 13:9–10

For this, Thou shalt not commit adultery, Thou shalt not kill,

Thou shalt not steal, Thou shalt not bear false witness, Thou shalt not covet; and if there be any other commandment, it is briefly comprehended in this saying, namely, Thou shalt love thy neighbour as thyself. Love worketh no ill to his neighbour: therefore love is the fulfilling of the law.

MORMON UNDERSTANDING

Attraction vs. Action

It is not a sin for a man or a woman to be sexually attracted to someone of the same gender. Likewise, it is not a sin for a man or a woman, married or unmarried, to be sexually attracted to someone of the opposite sex, even if not their spouses. The moral question does not reside in attraction, however strong or inborn or learned; instead, it hovers over the line between attraction and action, including deliberate imagining, as Jesus clearly stated.

The list of human proclivities, particularly sexual ones, is long. In some people, these proclivities are innate; in others they may arise spontaneously and without warning. Sexual yearnings that are innate or arise spontaneously are not sins—even if the attraction is to someone of the same gender. However, it is sinful to cultivate these proclivities, fantasize about them, or otherwise act upon them.

Rationalizations

Moral codes exist precisely because men and women sometimes yearn for what is not in their best interests or the best interests of their spouses, their families, or their community—to say nothing of the commandments of God. Many argue that the mere presence of a yearning, particularly if the yearning is intense, constitutes moral justification to satisfy that yearning. At the extremes of this argument are those who say that men and women have no free will in such matters. They are powerless to resist and would be psychologically damaged if they attempted resistance.

In October 2007, Jeffrey R. Holland, a member of the Quorum of the Twelve, wrote the following to those who struggle with same-gender attraction:

> If your life is in harmony with the commandments, then you are worthy to serve in the Church, enjoy full fellowship with the members, attend the temple, and receive all the blessings of the Savior's Atonement.

You serve yourself poorly when you identify yourself primarily by your sexual feelings. That isn't your only characteristic, so don't give it disproportionate attention. You are first and foremost a son of God, and He loves you. What's more, I love you. My brethren among the General Authorities love you.[2]

Discrimination

The doctrine of moral agency (the power to choose) is precious to Latter-day Saints. People who experience sexual yearnings for others of the same gender have not been stripped of their power to choose. Any assertion that the gift of agency has been withdrawn from those who have this yearning is false and discriminatory. Their trials may be great, but they are children of Heavenly Father. They are not outcasts—they are welcome in The Church of Jesus Christ of Latter-day Saints. They are deeply respected for exercising their God-given power to choose to withstand these yearnings and live happily according to the commandments of God.

Equal Accountability

Faithful Latter-day Saints take the law of chastity very seriously, and they resist efforts to dilute it. Sex outside of marriage is a sin that carries the same weight for all. Those sinning under the influence of homosexual impulses are no less accountable for their actions than those sinning under the influence of heterosexual impulses.

Marriage Between a Man and a Woman

The Church of Jesus Christ of Latter-day Saints considers marriage to be between a man and a woman. Marriage in this form is the foundation of the Creator's plan for the eternal destiny of his children.

The Church usually abstains from taking positions on matters that are being debated in legislatures or litigated in the courts. Once marriage came under attack, however, the Church was compelled to take a stand: The Church of Jesus Christ of Latter-day Saints actively "favors measures that define marriage as the union of a man and a woman and that do not confer legal status on any other sexual relationship."

The First Presidency of The Church of Jesus Christ of Latter-day Saints has issued the following statement:

> We of The Church of Jesus Christ of Latter-day Saints reach out
> with understanding and respect for individuals who are attracted to

those of the same gender. We realize there may be great loneliness in their lives but there must also be recognition of what is right before the Lord.

As a doctrinal principle, based on sacred scripture, we affirm that marriage between a man and a woman is essential to the Creator's plan for the eternal destiny of His children. The powers of procreation are to be exercised only between a man and a woman lawfully wedded as husband and wife.

Any other sexual relations, including those between persons of the same gender, undermine the divinely created institution of the family. The Church accordingly favors measures that define marriage as the union of a man and a woman and that do not confer legal status on any other sexual relationship.[3]

Sexual relationships that are outside of marriage are opposed on the grounds that they seriously threaten the traditional family and the social mores upholding the family; legitimize serious sexual sin; and lead to intolerance, discrimination, and eventually punitive legal action against anyone who openly opposes the sin of homosexual sex or the granting of legal status to sexual relationships other than between a man and a woman.

CAPITAL PUNISHMENT

BIBLICAL TEACHING

Old Testament
"An eye for an eye" is a well-known expression of justice in Mosaic Law (see Exodus 21:23–25; Deuteronomy 19:21; Leviticus 24:20). The Old Testament specifies that a murderer should be put to death (see Exodus 21:14; Numbers 35:30; Exodus 21:12; Numbers 35:16–19).

New Testament
While Christ did not repeal the law calling for murderers to be put to death, he did teach that men should love their enemies and turn the other cheek (see Matthew 5:38–39, 44–45). Paul taught that men should defer to the laws given by those in power (see Romans 13:1–7). Thus, if a lawful judgment is made and a lawful sentence is passed, believers should accept both the judgment and the sentence.

Mormon Understanding

Official Position of the Church

The Church of Jesus Christ of Latter-day Saints released the following statement on May 27, 2003:

> A number of recent press reports regarding capital punishment in Utah have incorrectly implied that The Church of Jesus Christ of Latter-day Saints endorses the state's practice of using firing squads to carry out the death penalty. Following is the Church's position on capital punishment: "The Church of Jesus Christ of Latter-day Saints regards the question of whether and in what circumstances the state should impose capital punishment as a matter to be decided solely by the prescribed processes of civil law. We neither promote nor oppose capital punishment."[4]

Jesus and Capital Punishment

Jesus did not outlaw capital punishment as a form of societal self-defense. He also did not forbid killing in war. Paul in his letter to the Romans acknowledges the legal and moral authority of the civil government to determine when capital punishment is applied.

Justice

The foregoing does not resolve the moral issue of the just application of capital punishment or the method of applying it in individual cases. For example, in "neither promot[ing] nor oppos[ing] capital punishment," the Church does not turn a blind eye to events such as the Holocaust or to cruel and unusual punishment of individuals. Rather, the Church takes the stand that the lawful application of capital punishment, as defined in the civil law of modern civilized nations, is a state function, not a Church function.

Notes

1. *True to the Faith: A Gospel Reference*, 4–5.
2. Jeffrey R. Holland, "Helping Those Who Struggle with Same-Gender Attraction," *Ensign*, Oct. 2007, 42–45.
3. First Presidency, The Church of Jesus Christ of Latter-day Saints, "First Presidency Statement on Same-Gender Marriage," 20 October 2004, http://newsroom.lds.org/ldsnewsroom/eng/news-releases-stories/first-presidency-statement-on-same-gender-marriage.

4. "Capital Punishment in Utah," The Church of Jesus Christ of Latter-day Saints, 27 May 2003, http://newsroom.lds.org/ldsnewsroom/eng/commentary/capital-punishment-in-utah.

❧ 23 ❧

BEYOND THE BIBLE

THE MAGNIFICENT BIBLE

The Bible is the word of God. It is one of the greatest blessings granted to mankind and is the most widely read scripture on the earth today. The Church of Jesus Christ of Latter-day Saints reveres the Bible and encourages everyone to feast upon its pages and apply its teachings to their lives.

THE OLD AND NEW COMBINE

In the centuries that followed the Ascension of Christ, the ancient scripture of the Old Testament was joined with the (then) modern scripture of the New Testament to form a new standard work called the Bible. This uniting of the old with the new was a difficult process. It took hundreds of years to achieve, and it was accompanied by political and religious strife. Many lost their lives in this strife.

The New Testament harmonizes with the Old Testament. Despite this harmony, religious scholars debate inconsistencies, contradictions, authorship, and other theological issues. Sometimes this debate contributes to the salvation of souls; sometimes it does not.

THE ANCIENT AND MODERN COMBINE

Modern scripture is to the Bible what the New Testament is to the Old Testament. The ancient scriptural record of the Bible comes together with modern scriptures to form a new record, which Latter-day Saints call the fulness of the gospel of Jesus Christ. Much like the painful and lengthy process by which the Old Testament was joined with the New Testament to form the Bible, the process of joining the Bible with modern scripture has not been and will not be easy. Much patience, humility, and discernment are required.

It is a difficult process that will take many years to achieve. It has been accompanied by political and religious strife like that which occurred many centuries ago. Many have lost their lives in this pursuit. Divinely inspired religious change does not come easily. There is a price.

The Book of Mormon, Doctrine and Covenants, and Pearl of Great Price harmonize with the Bible. Despite this harmony, religious scholars debate the consistency, contradictions, authorship, and other theological issues—as they did centuries ago. As with the coming together of the Old and New Testaments, achieving the fulness of the gospel in the minds and hearts of all men will require study, prayer, and revelation from the Holy Ghost.

GOD LIVES

God speaks to men in the manner, form, time, and place of his choosing. God spoke through the inspired men who wrote and compiled the New Testament. These men added to the Old Testament; they did not deny it.

God still lives and speaks to his children. He has given mankind modern scriptures in the form of the Book of Mormon, the Doctrine and Covenants, the Pearl of Great Price, and other writings of modern prophets.

Latter-day Saints believe in a living God who is actively involved in the lives of his children. All that God is and all that he wishes to teach his children cannot be encompassed within a single book. The living God speaks, and Latter-day Saints listen.

NEW SCRIPTURE CLARIFIES

New scripture clarifies older scripture. For example, Deuteronomy 24:1 and 3 tells how Moses defined divorce in a certain way. The New Testament tells how Jesus centuries later defined divorce differently, indicating it was acceptable only under the circumstances of fornication. When questioned about the bill of divorcement that Moses defined in the Old Testament, Jesus replied, "Moses because of the hardness of your hearts suffered you to put away your wives:

but from the beginning it was not so" (Matthew 19:8).

In 1 Corinthians 6:19 and Proverbs 20, God's children are warned to respect their physical bodies and refrain from certain substances; however, the Bible provides little in the way of specifics. Section 89 of the Doctrine and Covenants, often referred to as the Word of Wisdom, provides the specifics.

Another example is the unforgivable sin. In 1 John 1:7, we learn that the Atonement of Jesus Christ can cleanse mankind from all sin. However, Matthew 12:31–32 states that blasphemy against the Holy Ghost shall not be forgiven in this world or the next. These two scriptures contradict one another, and "blasphemy against the Holy Ghost" is not defined. Doctrine and Covenants 132:27 defines blasphemy against the Holy Ghost, reconciling the cloudy scriptural paradox left in the Bible:

> The blasphemy against the Holy Ghost, which shall not be forgiven in the world nor out of the world, is in that ye commit murder wherein ye shed innocent blood, and assent unto my death, after ye have received my new and everlasting covenant, saith the Lord God; and he that abideth not this law can in nowise enter into my glory, but shall be damned, saith the Lord.

NEW SCRIPTURE REVEALS

New scripture reveals new doctrines, practices, and principles that were not included in old scripture. This is necessary because man is always being called by God to live a higher law. This call did not end two thousand years ago; it is issued today.

For example, Jesus was quite specific in establishing a higher law when he said the following, as recorded in Matthew 5:38–47:

> Ye have heard that it hath been said, An eye for an eye, and a tooth for a tooth: But I say unto you, That ye resist not evil: but whosoever shall smite thee on thy right cheek, turn to him the other also. And if any man will sue thee at the law, and take away thy coat, let him have thy cloak also. And whosoever shall compel thee to go a mile, go with him twain. Give to him that asketh thee, and from him that would borrow of thee turn not thou away.
>
> Ye have heard that it hath been said, Thou shalt love thy neighbour, and hate thine enemy. But I say unto you, Love your enemies, bless them that curse you, do good to them that hate you, and pray

for them which despitefully use you, and persecute you; That ye may be the children of your Father which is in heaven: for he maketh his sun to rise on the evil and on the good, and sendeth rain on the just and on the unjust. For if ye love them which love you, what reward have ye? do not even the publicans the same? And if ye salute your brethren only, what do you more than others? do not even the publicans so?

New scriptures may also be revealed to introduce new revelation on existing law, doctrine, or principle. An example of new revelation about an old principle can be found in John 13:34 when Jesus taught, "A new commandment I give unto you, That ye also love one another; as I have loved you."

New scriptures may be revealed to give special emphasis or new understanding. The Atonement of Christ is a good example of this. While the word *atonement* (or atone) appears several times in the Old Testament, it appears only once in the New Testament in Romans 5:11. In the Book of Mormon, the word *atonement* (or atone) as relating directly to the mission of Christ appears 37 times. Here is just one such passage where the Book of Mormon prophet Nephi details the critical importance of the Atonement:

> Wherefore, it must needs be an infinite atonement—save it should be an infinite atonement this corruption could not put on incorruption. Wherefore, the first judgment which came upon man must needs have remained to an endless duration. And if so, this flesh must have laid down to rot and to crumble to its mother earth, to rise no more. Wherefore, he has given a law; and where there is no law given there is no punishment; and where there is no punishment there is no condemnation; and where there is no condemnation the mercies of the Holy One of Israel have claim upon them, because of the atonement; for they are delivered by the power of him. For the atonement satisfieth the demands of his justice upon all those who have not the law given to them, that they are delivered from that awful monster, death and hell, and the devil, and the lake of fire and brimstone, which is endless torment; and they are restored to that God who gave them breath, which is the Holy One of Israel. (2 Nephi 9:7, 25–26)

Another Book of Mormon prophet Helaman minced no words when he wrote there is no other means by which a man may be saved:

O remember, remember, my sons, the words which king Benjamin spake unto his people; yea, remember that there is no other way nor means whereby man can be saved, only through the atoning blood of Jesus Christ, who shall come; yea, remember that he cometh to redeem the world. (Helaman 5:9)

Spiritual Amplification

Just as the New Testament provided spiritual amplification of the Old Testament, modern scripture provides spiritual amplification of the Bible.

Paul wrote, "Eye hath not seen, nor ear heard, neither have entered into the heart of man, the things which God hath prepared for them that love him" (1 Corinthians 2:9). Narrowly interpreted, Paul speaks of the afterlife. More broadly interpreted, Paul speaks of all life: lives past, lives present, and lives future—premortal, mortal, and post-mortal. All conditions are situated in the eternities.

God is not dead: He does not leave men to decipher him solely through their decoding of ancient texts. He reveals the truth today as in times past—here a little, there a little. In one instance, the Lord may speak boldly and with painful clarity. In another, he may speak softly, in a still small voice only partially comprehensible by man.

SUGGESTED READING

The Book of Mormon, Another Testament of Jesus Christ. Salt Lake City: The Church of Jesus Christ of Latter-day Saints, 1979.

Burton, Rulon T. *We Believe, Doctrines and Principles of The Church of Jesus Christ of Latter-day Saints*. Salt Lake City: Tabernacle Books, 1994.

The Church of Jesus Christ of Latter-day Saints. (27 May 2003.) "Capital Punishment in Utah." Newsroom, the Official Church Resource for News Media, Opinion Leaders, and the Public, http://newsroom.lds.org/ldsnewsroom/eng/commentary/capital-punishment-in-utah.

The Doctrine and Covenants. Salt Lake City: The Church Jesus Christ of Latter-day Saints, 1979.

First Presidency, The Church of Jesus Christ of Latter-day Saints. (20 October 2004.) "First Presidency Statement on Same-Gender Marriage." Newsroom, the Official Church Resource for News Media, Opinion Leaders, and the Public, http://newsroom.lds.org/ldsnewsroom/eng/news-releases-stories/first-presidency-statement-on-same-gender-marriage.

Gospel Principles. Salt Lake City: Intellectual Reserve, 2009.

Hinckley, Gordon B. "The Father, Son, and Holy Ghost," *Ensign*, Mar. 1998.

———. "A Perfect Brightness of Hope: To New Members of The Church of Jesus Christ of Latter-day Saints." *Ensign*, Oct. 2006.

———. "The Marvelous Foundation of Our Faith," *Ensign*, Nov. 2002.

The Holy Bible, Authorized King James Version. Salt Lake City: The Church of Jesus Christ of Latter-day Saints, 1979.

Holland, Jeffrey R. "Helping Those Who Struggle with Same-Gender Attraction," *Ensign*, Oct. 2007.

Kimball, Spencer W. "When the World Will Be Converted," *Ensign*, Oct. 1974.

Kohlenberger, John R., III, ed. *The Contemporary Parallel New Testament*. New York-Oxford: Oxford University Press, 1997.

The Life and Teachings of Jesus and His Apostles. Salt Lake City: The Church of Jesus Christ of Latter-day Saints, 1979.

McConkie, Bruce R. *Mormon Doctrine*. Salt Lake City: Bookcraft, 1979.

Nelson, Russell M. "Computerized Scriptures Now Available," *Ensign*, Apr. 1988.

The Old Testament Student Manual, Genesis to 2 Samuel. Salt Lake City: The Church of Jesus Christ of Latter-day Saints, 1980.

The Old Testament Student Manual, 1 Kings to Malachi. Salt Lake City: The Church of Jesus Christ of Latter-day Saints, 1981.

Packer, Boyd K. *Preparing to Enter the Holy Temple*. Salt Lake City: The Church of Jesus Christ of Latter-day Saints, 2002.

The Pearl of Great Price. Salt Lake City: The Church of Jesus Christ of Latter-day Saints, 1979.

Shuster, Eric. *Catholic Roots, Mormon Harvest*. Springville, Utah: Cedar Fort, 2009.

Talmage, James E. *Jesus the Christ*. Salt Lake City: Deseret Book Company, 1945.

———. *The House of the Lord*. Salt Lake City: Deseret Book Company, 1968.

Today's Parallel Bible. Grand Rapids, Michigan: Zondervan, 2000.

True to the Faith, A Gospel Reference. Salt Lake City: Intellectual Reserve, 2004.

SCRIPTURE INDEX

ABOUT THE AUTHORS

*E*ric Shuster is the author of *Catholic Roots, Mormon Harvest,* hailed by critics as a uniquely touching conversion story that includes the best side-by-side comparison of Catholic and Mormon doctrine published to date. He is the author of many articles on Mormonism as the founder of the Foundation for Christian Studies (www.studychristianity.org), a nonprofit organization dedicated to the study, teaching, and practice of Christianity in support of essential Christian values and compassionate service across the globe. He is a veteran of the information technology industry, and has held several executive positions in a variety of business disciplines, including CEO of IntelliClear, a global market research and business strategy firm. Mr. Shuster holds an industrial engineering management degree from San Jose State University and an MBA from the University of Phoenix. He and his wife, Marilyn, have three children and reside in Colorado Springs, Colorado.

*C*harles Sale is a freelance writer, editor, and photographer. Mr. Sale began freelance writing during his thirty-year law enforcement career in the Los Angeles Police Department. His writing and editing skills opened doors to an uncommon diversity of special assignments in the LAPD. These included hosting a weekly public-service program for KABC radio, speech writing for the chief of police, and writing or editing innumerable government publications. He was a street cop, investigator, and field supervisor; a curriculum developer and instructor at the Los Angeles Police Academy; a teacher at Glendale College; a proofreader for the *Los Angeles Times*; and an editorial advisor to doctoral candidates at the California Institute of Technology and Jet Propulsion Laboratory in Pasadena. Over the years, Mr. Sale has authored, co-authored, or edited many books and articles, including *Catholic Roots, Mormon Harvest.* He holds a bachelor's degree in English from California State University at Los Angeles. He is the father of five children and the grandfather of seven. He and his wife, Teri, make their home in Colorado Springs, Colorado.